ALL ABOUT SPORTS

Skiing

ALL ABOUT SPORTS

Skiing

KÖNEMANN

CONTENTS

PREFACE

"All About Sports–Skiing" may seem to be yet another of the many skiing manuals that periodically come onto the world markets. However, this is not just another new book; it is an entirely new one, produced after long and careful reflection with the cooperation of many people, all highly qualified in their specific fields. Its most obviously innovative characteristic is its encyclopedic breadth: it ranges from Alpine (downhill) skiing to Telemark, from a survey of the most modern equipment on the market to athletic training, and from the history of skiing to a selection of the most famous ski resorts in the world.

Nowadays, the tendency of most people who frequent ski resorts is to try out different techniques and equipment, and to take note from personal experience of the best trails (pistes).

In recent years various specialized activities have burst onto the snow scene, but always to the fore, to a greater or lesser extent in different parts of the world, has been skiing on trails, commonly defined as "Alpine skiing". In this discipline, from the inception of skiing as a mass sport, technology has always been mindful of a market in constant expansion and year after year has introduced innovative materials and equipment that have had a marked influence on downhill techniques as well. Proof of this became most apparent firstly in competition skiing, and then indirectly in the vast world of recreational skiing, by the way in which more reactive and versatile materials have enabled an ever-increasing number of people without competitive ambitions to reach relatively high standards. Furthermore, whilst in past decades techniques have arisen in and been imposed by a particular school, such as the French or Austrian ones, today the "school"

is the same all over the world. This is mainly because of the interchange of information between those in charge of the various national associations of ski instructors who, by mutual consent, choose to adopt the same teaching methods. So, for example, anyone who begins at a ski-school in France can quite easily continue to learn in Italy or the United States, and vice versa.

The latest radical change in downhill technique was brought about by the introduction of the side-cut, which initially was timidly adopted on the standard slalom skis, then later taken to the extreme of becoming an independent specialty. The experts say that carving will be the technique universally adopted in the next few years, and even in the eyes of non-experts its extraordinary spread on the trails is evident.

Less obvious, although equally important, is the technological evolution in cross-country skiing that is also rapidly expanding because, in particular, of its closer relationship with the natural environment of the mountains. In this case it was the interest of the public which influenced market choices, obliging ski resorts to provide cross-country trails along with the downhill ones in order to satisfy as broad a sector of the public as possible.

The passion felt for nature in the mountains found its full expression later in ski touring and ski mountaineering for which, in addition to technical and physical skills, it is necessary to have a thorough knowledge of the environment. In these activities, too, technology has made considerable progress, but it has been directed towards making the sport less tiring and safer, rather than modifying off-trail skiing techniques.

The really revolutionary progress in the world of snow, however, has been brought about by two specialties which are poles apart: Telemark and snowboarding. Telemark is a return to the past, the rediscovery of the first technique invented to turn on snow, which today has come back in vogue because of its grace and beauty in motion. Snowboarding, which evolved from surfing and skateboarding, has imposed its own styles and methods on the slopes. Today both practices are so widespread as to persuade some businesses to specialize in materials and equipment exclusively for them.

This book, though, is not confined to considering all the above and to analyzing the various disciplines and techniques with the intention of inculcating knowledge in the readership. It informs in a systematic manner, following the teaching method adopted by ski instructors. The evolution happens gradually, from the first contact with the snow to pre-competition skiing techniques, and every experience acquired is transformed into a "level" from which to set off again for subsequent learning stages. Simple and schematic descriptions of the individual movements are accompanied by drawings and photographs highlighting correct and incorrect positions–the latter are easier to recognize in others than in oneself.

For these reasons, "All About Skiing" is a new manual: it is a part of the world of skiing, not just confined to describing it from the outside. A final point however should be made: no manual–not even this one–can replace completely the experience acquired on the slopes with the help of a ski instructor.

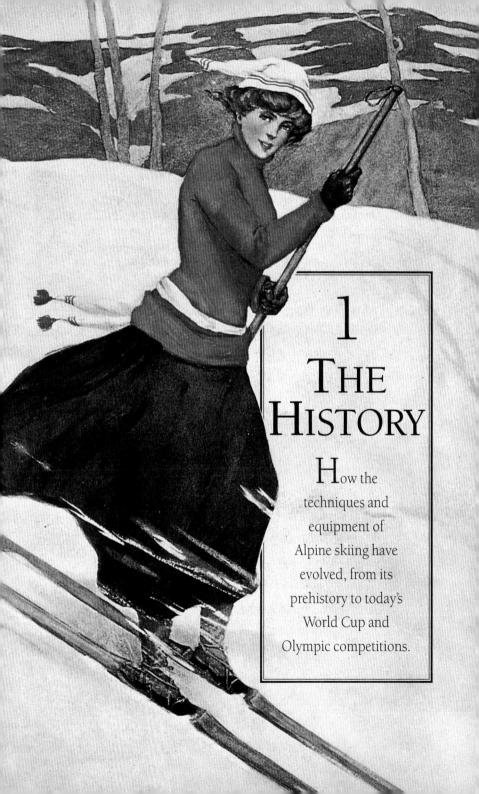

1
THE
HISTORY

How the
techniques and
equipment of
Alpine skiing have
evolved, from its
prehistory to today's
World Cup and
Olympic competitions.

THE PREHISTORY OF SKIING

The use of skis predates even the invention of the wheel. To adapt and survive in places covered by snow and ice, primitive man, a nomad and a hunter, wore on his feet tree twigs woven together (snow shoes) covered with animal skins, in order to increase the weight-bearing surface. On some occasions he made use too of curved lengths of wood in order to walk and also to glide more easily over the snow without sinking in.

However, the origins of real skiing are shrouded in a distant past. Skiing is probably the son of many fathers, born in different and far-apart places, as is the case for other inventions that belong to the history of mankind. The theory of the German, Luther, is the most believable. He maintains that skiing originated among the populations of the Altai Mountains in Mongolia. From here it reached first north America, through the Bering Strait (in the ice age),

and northern Europe, and later central Europe and Asia Minor. The great geographical distances are not a cause for concern: apart from the time available, which could even have been years or centuries, hundreds of kilometers a day could be traveled on skis (the record is 401 km [250 miles] held by the Finn Rantenen). Luther's theory is strengthened by the discovery of similar items of equipment in Manchuria, Siberia, Canada, Iceland, Finland, and Lapland.

The major use and development of skiing as a means of transport over snow,

Above: it is possible that skiing originated in Mongolia and from there spread to the rest of the world.
Top: the Holmenkollen Ski Museet in Oslo, perhaps the most important in the world on the history of skiing.

however, took place in the Scandinavian peninsular, where much important archaeological evidence has been found. In the cave at Rødøy (northern Norway) a rock carving was discovered: it dates back around 7,000 years and depicts a hunter on skis. This is currently held in the ski museum in Oslo (Holmenkollen Ski Museet). Not much more recent (around 4,500 years old) is the Hoting ski. Considered to be the most ancient ski, it was found in Sweden and is presently kept in the ski museum in Stockholm. However, the use of skis in these regions certainly dates back much further. An old Norwegian saga tells of an invasion of those countries 8,000 years before the birth of Christ by a people who came on skis from the north.

Furthermore the derivation of the term "ski" is Nordic: "ski" comes from the Scandinavian word *skid*, which means "covered with skin." In fact, in ancient times the right ski of the Laplanders was short and covered with skin, and was used for pushing, while the longer and narrower left ski was used for sliding.

It is reasonable to believe that the idea of gliding, as opposed to the mere floating over the snow already possible with snow shoes, evolved from this particular long ski that enabled hunting man to approach his prey at greater speed or to flee rapidly from danger.

For written references to skis we must turn to the Greek historian Strabo, who mentions them in his work *Geographica* of 30 B.C.; to Procopius of Caesarea who refers to barbaric people of the north that went about on skis (544 A.D.); and to the Gothic Giordane who in 550 A.D. wrote of a Nordic people regularly using skis.

Left: the rock carving discovered in 1932 on the island of Rødøy, Norway, by Gutorn Gressing, that dates back c. 7,000 years. Above: Lapp hunter on skis (Paris, National Library).

SKIING IN THE MIDDLE AGES

The years around 1000 were full of more or less legendary anecdotes in which skiing provides both the means of transport, and the opportunity for warfare. The populations of the Norwegian Telemark, given the inaccessible nature of the mountains, perfected proper downhill techniques, while in Sweden, Finland, and Russia techniques were developed for advancing over level ground. In Norway, the use of skis was so widespread that a ski contest was already being spoken of in 1050, called the "Saga of King Harald." It seems that in this contest the very able King Harald Hardraade had been defeated by the warrior Heming who was better at descending the "steep run." In Sweden, on the other hand, King Gustavus I of Vasa, together with two of his subjects, in 1520 covered 89 km (56 miles) non-stop on skis in order to drive out the Danish invaders. The legendary feat is commemorated by the famous cross-country marathon known as "Vasa-loppet" that was first held in 1923 and is still contested today.

In subsequent centuries, the progressive civilization of the Nordic peoples almost brought about the disappearance of skis. This was not because they were not being used, but because of the effect of the teachings of Catholicism and, even more so, those of Lutheranism. This latter doctrine, in particular, considered skis diabolical, frivolous instruments, and the peasants of the 16th century that used them were seen as heretics or sorcerers. Only in Lapland is there evidence of a constant use of skis, for the obvious reason of survival. According to Gustav Storm, as early as the 12th and 13th centuries the Laplanders were considered experts at working with wood and attracted clients from Norway and Finland. On the other hand, in central Asia and Siberia where Christianity did not have followers, skis remained firmly on the feet of nomadic tribes known as "savages who lived only by plunder." An extensive use of skis by the Scandinavian peoples was later taken up again mainly for military purposes. In the Renaissance era the Norwegian and Scandinavian armies commonly used skis, so that in 1564, during the war waged against Denmark, the Swedish army was able to make use of as many as 4,000 first-rate skiers.

Below: wolf-hunting on skis (Lapland, c. 1900). Bottom: Japanese hunter on skis of differing lengths (Oslo, National Library).

Chasseur lapon, d'après Jean Skefferus (1675). — Bibl. de l'université d'Oslo. Phot. de la bibliothèque.

18

TWO INTREPID PRIESTS

Despite the association of skis with the peril of sin, it was in fact, around that same time that two prelates contributed to the history of skiing. The first was a Swedish bishop, Olaus Magnus, who, having paid a visit to the regions of the north, left testimony in a book about the history of those peoples. The volume, written in Latin (*Historia de gentibus septentrionalibus*), was first

In 1663, Abbot Francesco Negri of Ravenna, perhaps inspired by Magnus, undertook a journey to Scandinavia and Lapland. A book about this trip–which lasted three years–was published in 1705 at Forlì, entitled *Viaggio settentrionale* ("Northern Journey"). The particular care given to the descriptions by Negri, no doubt prompted by deeply felt affection for those populations and their "strange implements,"

makes the book an especially good document on the history of skiing. The descriptions of the techniques necessary to control the skis are even more precise and thorough than those described by Magnus.

Negri writes that reindeer skins were used on the underneath of the skis in order to make climbing uphill easier, and that once the descent had begun "it is

Left: start of the "Vasaloppet" marathon (1960) that was from 1923 contested in Sweden in memory of King Gustavus I of Vasa.
Right: Abbot Francesco Negri, author of one of the first books to describe skis in Scandinavia (1705).

necessary to make sure the skis are kept parallel." Lastly, in order to turn, it was necessary to "skillfully bend one's line of descent towards one side so forming a curve" aided by "in the hand, a stick with a little wooden wheel hammered onto the end to prevent holing the snow." Negri's descriptions have a unique fascination as people were still skiing in this way at the beginning of the 20th century.

published in Rome in 1555 (first English translation in 1658: *History of the Goths, Swedes and Vandals*). It tells of skis being used for both hunting and recreational activities, with prizes awarded to competition winners. Magnus's book with drawings of skiers and skiing equipment, could be the first manual on skiing.

In the 17th century we have the first evidence of skiing being practiced in the Alps. It seems that a group of Scandinavian soldiers had settled in an area of Carniola (now Slovenia) after the Thirty Years War (1618–48), and thus spread the use of skis among the people there.

THE ORIGINS OF MODERN SKIING

Norway was still the great arena of modern skiing. In the early 19th century, the Norwegians achieved several military victories over the Swedes thanks to a skilful use of skis in battle. This military success encouraged the development of skiing as a sport, and at this stage competitions were being organized which were open to civilians and to military personnel. At that time there was no distinction between downhill and cross-country skiing: the competitions consisted of rather arduous mixed trials that included long stretches of cross-country skiing, downhill races, ski jumping contests, and often also rifle-shooting contests.

One of the most famous competitions was that of Christiania (now the city of Oslo), which took place for the first time in 1767. The winner of the 1874 event was the same Fridtjof Nansen who in 1888 crossed Greenland on skis.

Fridtjof Nansen (top, in an illustration from "Graphic," 1895), in 1888 crossed Greenland on skis. Right: the route followed by the expedition. Below: a moment during the crossing.

In the second half of the 19th century, the Telemark area in Norway was elevated to the birthplace of modern skiing, and Morgedal, a small town of craftsmen who worked with wood, became the capital of skiing. It is here that for the first time the techniques of skiing ceased to be improvised and advanced to a form of science and art, thereby encouraging the sportsman to create personal techniques.

Søndre Norheim (1825–97) was the first of the great skiers whose name has gone down in history as being known beyond the borders of Norway. His technique was much studied and became the bible of the very early ski-schools. Through him was born the legendary technique of Telemark that nowadays has come back into fashion and is much appreciated as an alternative to the traditional technique. Norheim was also the first great ski jumper of whom we have a record. In 1868 he was able to jump over 30 m (90 feet), and then land with the Telemark. In 1885 Norheim

In the photograph, the Christiania Competition of 1894 that was held for the first time in 1767 (from "The Illustrated London News").
Right: the oldest technique of turning on skis is the Telemark, invented by the Norwegian Norheim in the second half of the 19th century.

went to teach his techniques in north America, where together with the Norwegian Hemmestvet brothers he was very successful.

In 1905 another Norwegian arrived in the United States and made his fortune at ski jumping, a discipline much appreciated because it is so spectacular. We are speaking of Karl Hovelsen, who toured America in the troupe of a famous circus of that time: his performance was sensationally successful. Even before its spread in central Europe, skiing from 1854 onwards met with considerable favor in Canada, Nevada, and at the borders of California among the gold-diggers. Among the latter

The main participants in early ski competitions were the military.
Right: a military downhill race near Stockholm (end of the 19th century).
Top: a competition in Michigan (from "The Graphic," 1893).

were some people of Scandinavian origin, who in those circumstances made use of–and helped to spread–skiing, although it remained confined to those areas; reports suggest that until 1900 even postmen used skis to deliver the mail there. However, if Norway can be considered the birthplace of skiing, the Alps were the scene for the technological evolution of equipment and consequently of techniques.

Jumping events, being so spectacular, spread rapidly and were very successful all over the world.
Above: a contest at Duluth, Minnesota (1908). Left: a contest in Norway (1883).

SKIING IN THE ALPS

Skiing arrived in the Alps towards the end of the 19th century and immediately began to spread in an incredible way; the expansion continues today. In no small way this can be ascribed to Nansen's feat, which caught the imagination of the middle classes. His book, *Paa Ski over Gronland* ("Across Greenland on Skis"), had a sensational impact throughout Europe and helped to enhance the reputation of Norwegian ski instructors. The latter naturally adopted the Telemark technique that, however, in time proved inadequate for the Alpine slopes. Unlike Scandinavia, in the Alps the slopes are steep and the snow is often hard and icy. These are the main environmental factors that encouraged the search for more suitable technical solutions.

Some key men were instrumental in the development of skiing in the Alps, and contributed in a decisive way to the evolution of materials and techniques. The

Left: the Austrian Mathias Zdarsky, inventor of the first Alpine ski technique (Lilienfeld, 1896).
Bottom left: a pair of very long skis dating from the end of the 19th century (from "Harper's Weekly," 1891).
Below: a strong boost to the spread of skiing in the Alps was provided by Italian and Austrian Alpine troops during the First World War.

first among these was, without doubt, Mathias Zdarsky, described as "a rough man of the mountains, but also a sensitive artist, who retreated like a hermit to the village of Lilienfeld, not far from Vienna, after having read Nansen's book."

As early as the end of the last century, Zdarsky created a binding that gave greater side stability to the tail (heel), which was of fundamental importance to the control of the skis on hard snow and on steep slopes. Moreover, he was responsible for a reduction in ski length to 180 cm (70 inches). At that time Norwegian skis were as long as 3 m (10 feet).

Zdarsky also carried out comprehensive technical studies, and then devised a new downhill ski technique, which he set out in his book, *Lilienfeld Skiing Technique*, which was published in 1896. Zdarsky specified that "the turn is effected by the rotation of the whole body in the direction of the turn; with the knees half-bent and the weight being evenly distributed on both skis that are in a snowplow-like (wedge-like) position. By using a single pole as a pivot and maintaining a backward position, the skier accomplishes an assisted turn."

The Lilienfeld technique spread rapidly in Europe following on after the Telemark technique, immediately provoking bitter arguments between the supporters of the two different schools. Support for the two techniques was also divided in the Great War of 1914–18, in that the Lilienfeld technique was taught to the Austrian Alpine troops, while the Italian Alpine troops adopted the Telemark.

From the beginning of the 20th century, skiing in the Alps began to be "fashionable."
Below: skiers posing for the camera, postcard, 1900.
Bottom: two posters (Ricordi, 1908; Abel Faivre, 1905) and a postcard, 1918.

GEORGE BILGERI AND THE STEMM-BOGEN

It was George Bilgeri, a colonel in the Austrian army (first a friend, then a rival of Zdarsky), who toned down a little the argument between the two schools. He amalgamated the two techniques (the Telemark and the Lilienfeld) by proposing the alternation of skiing with skis parallel and snowplow skiing: that is, the *stemmbogen* technique. Bilgeri introduced the *stemmbogen* in his manual on the art of skiing in the Alps. This manual confirms how skiing was still considered to be an exalted practice, almost a mystical art, on the one hand; and, on the other, a frivolous activity, a game for the wealthy.

Right: Hannes Schneider (1936).
Below: two bindings from the early 20th century. The heel could be raised, as in today's cross-country skis.

Bilgeri can also be credited with the improvement of bindings that further stabilized the heel (1910). Thanks to the foot being more firmly attached to the ski, Bilgeri could for the first time introduce "stop jumps" executed with considerable weighting and unweighting of the skis which is achieved by the full bending and rapid straightening of the body.

In the 1920s, in order to increase the grip of skis on icy and steep slopes, Bilgeri also made the first attempts at applying edges, although the invention of the proper edge is attributed to Rudolph Lettner.

HANNES SCHNEIDER AND THE ARLBERG SCHOOL

Hannes Schneider began to give ski lessons at St. Anton, near Arlberg in Austria, at just 17 years of age. Thereafter he rapidly accumulated considerable experience that he utilized, in the early 1920s, to codify his method that has gone down in history as the Arlberg technique. In 1924 he even made a film on the subject which goes to show how detailed his study was.

Schneider's technique is based on the principles of keeping the body forward and unweighting the skis at the beginning of the turn together with rotation of the body. Throughout, the body is maintained in a crouching position in order to keep the center of gravity low. The Schneider turn was in fact a kind of *stemmbogen* (snowplow turn with skis kept together at the start and finish). But improvement in technique in those years was due

In the drawing at the top and the photograph to the side, Hannes Schneider's Arlberg technique.
Below: Leo Gasperl in the famous "stop jump" (from "Discesismo," 1955).

essentially to the considerable perfecting of the bindings which fixed the boot more firmly to the ski so as to facilitate the famous stop jumps devised by Bilgeri. Schneider also created the first ski-school organized along modern lines by providing a precise teaching progression and sub-dividing the pupils into graded classes (beginners, intermediate, advanced), a practice still used today.

COMPETITION SKIING

Schneider undoubtedly initiated a new era in the analysis of ski techniques, with the result that in 1932 the study of this subject was included in the curriculum of the University of Innsbruck. Thereafter, however, the development of skiing was increasingly linked to the world of competition, to the downhill contests that were followed and analyzed by ski enthusiasts worldwide. The importance that Alpine skiing as a sport had gained by this time is evident by its official recognition in 1925 by the International Olympic Committee (IOC) of the contests that were held for a week in Chamonix the previous year. Every technique and every ski-school from that time on was inspired by the champion of the moment who sought–and seeks still today–to maximize the effectiveness of his movements in accordance with his equipment, often adopting personal solutions. One such champion was the Austrian Anton Seelos, who in competition used Schneider's technique and increased the rotatory movements of the Arlberg school; he inserted a preparatory counter-rotation before the stretching rotation that marks the beginning of the turn. Seelos's name is also linked to the technical development of skiing because he confirmed the effectiveness of edges. These proved to be indispensable, especially on the icy trails (pistes) which were of concern to skiers at that time, as they allowed descent with the skis perfectly parallel.

Left: Zeno Colò and Leo Gasperl, two important competitors in early international competitions.
Bottom: Leo Gasperl in action with a pupil (from "Discesismo," 1955).
Top center: the first official recognition by the International Olympic Committee was for the contest held in Chamonix in 1924.

THE FRENCH AND THE SWISS SCHOOLS

In 1937 Seelos was called to train the French ski team, and here he met Émile Allais, then member of the Équipe de France (French Team). Allais, by analyzing Seelos's instinctive movements, carried out a thorough codification and defined some principles that subsequently brought about the birth of the French school. These principles were the unweighting of the tails of the skis, effected by an accentuated bending of the knees that transferred the weight forward so as to make a pivot of the toes of the skis, and rotation preceded by Seelos's famous counter-rotation (though less accentuated). Although on the one hand these wide rotatory movements and strong muscular contractions guaranteed a certain efficacy in competition skiing, they did not, on the other hand, prove easy to teach to ordinary ski enthusiasts. However, credit is due to the French for having invented and disseminated in those same years the much-used technique of *dérapage*: side-slipping without turning causes the skier to lose height without particular risk even on very steep or icy slopes. In Switzerland, though, Eugenio Matthias (a doctor who was a ski enthusiast), by

In the photographs below, Leo Gasperl's Italian-style "ruade," based on the technique invented by the Frenchman Émile Allais (in the drawings).

studying the physiology of the movements involved, found that the frequent injuries sustained by skiers as a result of accidents were, above all, due to rotatory movements, which were considered essential to the techniques of that time. He therefore tried to devise a technique that would reduce these risks. Just such an opportunity was presented to him by his meeting with the ski instructor Giovanni Testa who in 1933 ran the ski-school of St. Moritz. Testa was then already using a technique that differed from the others in that it avoided the excessive rotations of the body. Collaboration between the two men led to the introduction of a new technique which clashed with the standard ones and which can be seen as the forerunner of modern techniques. Essentially it was the adoption of a more upright position, with slight bends and stretches in order to shift the weight from one side to the other, thereby avoiding rotations of the whole body. However, despite the fact that almost all ski athletes of the time were using a similar technique to the Swiss one, ordinary skiers were still being taught the rotation of the top half of the body or the Telemark. This was because bindings that fixed the heel firmly were not immediately available everywhere. In any case, the practice of skiing was still considered to be more associated with off-trail tours, often

Below: a pair of skis from the 1930s, finished with a touch of elegance.

in soft snow, where the Telemark and the rotation of the upper half of the body still had ample scope for success.

THE 1930s AND THE 1940s

In the 1930s skiing developed strongly thanks to investment in the mechanization of winter resorts. In this decade, too, skiing at last became an Olympic discipline. The first winter Olympics were held at Garmisch (Germany) in 1936, and the first World Ski Championships took place at Chamonix (France) in 1937.

Up to the early 1940s, competitions were the driving force of technical and technological innovations: slalom and downhill contests took place throughout the Alps; and the "flying kilometer" was introduced, a straight and perfectly level downhill track on which the fastest skier wins. In 1931, Leo Gasperl (Austria) established a speed record at St. Moritz (Switzerland) of 136.6 km/h (85.4 mph) that remained unbeaten until 1947 when Zeno Colò (Italy) set a new record of 159.3 km/h (99.6 mph) on the Piccolo Cervino (Italy). However, competition techniques continued to have little bearing on the skiing

being taught to ski tourists that was founded on the "schools of thought" already mentioned (the Austrian or Arlberg school's Christianias with more or less accentuated rotations of the upper half of the body; the French *ruades*; and the old Norwegian Telemark). At that time there was also considerable public discussion of the subject, with manuals on skiing and teaching methods, plus books written by famous ski instructors or ordinary ski lovers and enthusiasts with specific expertise (engineers, doctors, military personnel). The development of strictly competitive techniques, characterized by the efficacy of positioning and influenced by the improvement in equipment (skis, bindings, boots), however, brought about a slow progressive change in ski techniques up until the great revolution of the 1950s.

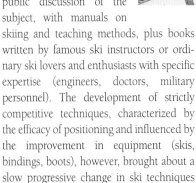

THE DEVELOPMENT OF WINTER TOURISM

From the second half of the 19th century, mountain villages started to be fashionable tourist resorts. For some time mountains had been arousing people's interest and curiosity (as had also the memorable undertakings and conquests of the most famous peaks by mountaineers, especially the English), thus attracting well-educated and well-to-do citizens who stayed in luxury hotels or high-class establishments. And, if in summer guided tours were the favorite pastime, in winter not even noblewomen could resist the exhilarating ski slopes. The presence of this elite brought renown to the resorts; society life typical of the *belle époque* was fostered and the interest of an increasingly large public awakened. Moreover, in the First World War Alpine troops made great use of skis and at the end of the conflict ex-soldier skiers spread this practice in their valleys. In mountaineering, too, that in the meantime had made many converts among city-dwellers, skis were increasingly used instead of snow shoes.

The media, fashion, and advertising have played their part in the spread of skiing.
Left: an advertisement (1929). Top: cover page of "Life" (1927).
Opposite: cover page of "Woman's World" (1929).

WINTER RESORTS COME INTO EXISTENCE

These social and intellectual changes encouraged the setting up and commercialization of winter resorts.

It seems that as early as 1880, near Plumas-Eureka Ski Bowl (California), an enterprising group of miners who were skiers used the mine's transport system (buckets moved by steam engines) to take themselves up to the top of the slopes.

In the 1930s technological progress brought about a spectacular increase in skiing. The installation of cableways, cable cars, and ski lifts which took place in all the most famous mountain resorts of Europe, the United States and Japan, even though very controversial in some cases, triggered an unprecedented increase in tourism. The

construction of ski lifts brought onto the mountains millions of ski tourists who could, in a single day, come down the mountain many times. And so modern winter resorts came into existence, with a variety of facilities associated with skiing so as to satisfy a clientele of differing tastes.

Ski lifts, as well as the spread of competition skiing, gave rise to the identification of a precise way of practicing this sport, that is, "downhill" skiing, which is carried out exclusively on groomed trails. This fact radically changed the characterization of the skier who, having been a lover of tours, became a "consumer of the mountain." The few skiers who remained faithful to traditional concepts preferred to engage in cross-country skiing, or else they were followers of the Telemark technique, thus creating ski mountaineering as a distinct discipline.

However, on the trails (which were beginning to be groomed by mechanical means and no longer by the skiers), the choice of the most effective technique predominated if the objective was competition, or of the most fashionable technique if it was a question of "society" tourism. In

III Olympic Winter Games
Lake Placid, USA
February 4-13, 1932

In the 1930s skiing became a mass sport thanks to the growth of winter resorts, especially in the USA and in the Alps.
Left: a poster of the Winter Olympics at Lake Placid (1932).
Far left: the early seat lifts (chair lifts) at Sun Valley (1936).
Above: ski resort in Switzerland (1930).

any case, the boom in tourist skiing during the 1930s considerably increased businessmen's and manufacturers' interest in developing new and more suitable equipment (skis, bindings, boots, clothing).

Immediately after the Second World War, large resorts specially equipped for skiing were established in the United States. Such resorts, for example Lake Placid (as early as 1932 the site of the third Winter Olympic Games) and Aspen, are now famous all over the world. Special mention should be made of Squaw Valley that was built from nothing in order to host the 1960 Winter Olympic Games. In just four years, trails and infrastructure were constructed; the staging of the games was assigned to Walt Disney. The 1950s and 1960s were the decisive years in the development of ski tourism. Millions of people in Europe, the United States and Japan were skiing, and competitions were arousing the enthusiasm of city-dwellers and mountain valley inhabitants.

In the Alps the strongest growth occurred in the 1960s and 1970s after the people who survived the war had attained a certain economic prosperity and could afford to run a car so making it easier for them to reach the mountain resorts. In those years there was a sharp rise in tourism: huge amounts of capital were invested in order to build new resorts equipped for skiing, sometimes far away from traditionally inhabited centers. Skiing was now a mass sport.

Today there are countless winter resorts all over the world; they are fairly well organized and offer good facilities. Unfortunately, they have also given rise to pollution and environmental problems resulting from, for example, the use of snow-making machines and the construction of grandiose cableways at high altitude.

The modern trend in winter tourism is towards a comprehensive exploitation of the resort, with the construction of "integrated" resorts (straight from your car on to the run), artificial snow making, and night-time illumination of trails (below).

THE NATIONAL SCHOOLS AND INTERSKI

Until 1950, the technical and technological development of skiing was slow, but in the subsequent period there was a real revolution. The new and more effective equipment that then became available, such as high-speed cameras and cine-cameras, made a unique contribution to the scientific analysis of ski techniques.

Within a few years large national schools were created and organized with standardized teaching levels that went beyond the empiricism previously associated with the reputation of some skilful instructors. This proliferation of "experts" gave rise also to the need for a comparison between the various nations (especially the Alpine ones) of their own established national techniques, methodologies and schools. In 1951 Interski was created and it is still today the most important international congress on ski techniques and teaching methods.

From 1951, national schools from all over the world have met annually at Interski in order to compare and discuss teaching techniques.
Left: at Aspen, USA (1968). Below: at Beitostole, Norway (1999).

THE AUSTRIAN REVOLUTION

In 1955, at the Val d'Isère Interski meeting, Austria surprised the ski world by putting forward an entirely innovative technique (and teaching method) known as the *wedel* (French *godille*) in contrast to the, by then, very old technique of body rotation.

The basic movements of the turn no longer started from the top, from the shoulders, going on to progressively involve the lower parts of the body down to the skis. They began instead from the pelvis and the legs. In this way the rotation of the body into the turn, something always considered an unassailable premise, was eliminated. In the revolutionary Austrian technique, the thrust of the turn was caused by a heel push towards the outside, so as to move the ski tails and thereby change the direction of the skis; the heel push was given immediately after a bending–straightening movement of the lower limbs. The Austrian method, devised by Professor Kruckenhauser, came after several years of careful observation of champions during ski competitions, and from the observation of the natural behavior of children at the learning stage. From that time on, almost all the European schools have based their national method on the principles of the *wedel*, and the importance of this technique is confirmed by the fact that many of its principles are still valid today.

Toni Sailer (of Austria) demonstrated the validity of the technique in the world of competition: from 1952 to 1958, he won everything everywhere, including the 1956 Olympics at Cortina d'Ampezzo and the 1958 World Championships at Badgastein. Sailer became a superstar; his technique and his competitive style became the model for all ski contest enthusiasts.

In 1955 Austria put forward a completely innovative downhill technique (wedel), with counter-rotation of the shoulder.
In the drawing the new (left) and the old (right) tecniques compared.
Left: Giovanni Testa in action with the new Austrian technique (wedel).

THE 1960s

In this decade, the work carried out by the various national schools during the previous one, under the influence of the Austrian technique, was endorsed. Both in Europe and America, each school produced its own teaching method that was used to instruct ski tourists in all the winter resorts.

It was also a decade of great innovation in the materials sector in which the technology of ski construction reached truly remarkable levels. Skis were made not only of wood, but also of fiber glass, aluminum, and plastic. The result was a ski that was durable but lighter, softer, easier to maneuver, and required less action to make it turn.

Boots too underwent a fundamental change. In just a few years leather boots tied with laces came to be replaced by plastic boots fastened with metal clips. The resultant greater rigidity made the skier's thrusts and pushes on the skis more effective, and allowed higher side tilt of the leg for better edging. The more rigid and higher boot also secured the heel better in the event of an accident, although over time the increased speed and the twisting movements of the body transferred the risk of shock injury from the heel to the leg.

In the 1960s innovative materials and equipment encouraged the practice of new techniques (top: the "short-radius" turn). Above: double-boot boots. Left: a section of a ski with wooden core (hickory and ash), cover of plastic material, and carré caché edges.

Downhill technique in competitions had to adapt to technological development. Materials and equipment were of primary importance to a champion's performance. As proof that they were (and are still today) the driving force behind

and was one who had great sensitivity in his feet and legs. But the gap between the skiing taught by the schools and that practiced by ski athletes was still truly enormous. In teaching, the side push of the tails after unweighting still predominated. In athletic competition, "steering," or rather the total elimination of sliding, was already being talked about. The most influential supporters of this theory were the Frenchmen Jouber and Vuarnet.

technical evolution, one need only remember that while differences between athletes' times in the 1950 Olympic contests were several seconds, by the end of the 1960s they were reduced to just a few tenths of a second. The new materials and equipment enabled high performances to be attained generally, not just by a few undisputed champions.

The most influential representative of high-level competitive sport in the 1960s was probably the Frenchman Jean-Claude Killy, a superb champion, several times winner of the Olympics, and a proponent of a great school. Once again the technique involved many movements that were considered necessary in order to make the skis change direction; the athletes maintained a certain distance from the slalom posts, carrying out rather rounded and sliding turns. The champion was an agile and quick-off-the-mark athlete, capable of repeating model techniques to perfection,

The Frenchman Jean-Claude Killy (below) and the Austrian Toni Sailer (top) were the most influential representatives of the competitive sport in the 1960s.

THE 1970s

In the next decade the techniques of the schools began to draw closer to those of competition: the technological means available (especially the cine-camera) provided an opportunity to precisely analyze body movement in contests and to codify them in order to identify fundamental principles. The basic movements of great champions fueled the techniques of the national schools and thus served as an example to recreational skiers.

One undisputed champion who inspired the techniques of those years was the Italian Gustav Thoeni. He provided a new interpretation of competition skiing. His action differed from that of other athletes: he combined dynamic movement with precision. Thoeni was the object of comprehensive motion analyses carried out with high-speed cine-cameras.

The attention of researchers and technicians focused on the codification of the athlete's movements in the various stages of a turn. Everything was analyzed, even the movements of the hand and the head. The fundamental movements extrapolated from Thoeni's technique were the following: 1–bending, 2–stretching, 3–angulation, 4–anticipation. Bending involved the lower parts of the body (hips-knees-heels); stretching was the opposite movement to bending; angulation was understood as a position: to be precise, the angle existing between the axis of the legs and that of the upper half of the body which is helpful in attaining edge hold; anticipation was the projection of the pelvis towards the front-inside of the subsequent turn, which allowed edge change. For many years these four principles dictated the rules of the teaching of skiing.

By analyzing the action of Thoeni it was possible to see how the ski athletes of that time were obliged to perform many bending–stretching movements. These movements, by creating accelerations in favor of, or against, the force of gravity, allowed the weighting or unweighting of the skis. Unweighting, carried out in the first stage of a turn, helped to direct the skis towards the new turn. Weighting, carried out in the second stage of a turn, produced a greater twisting of the ski and a greater setting of the edge in order to maintain the intended course. The edge hold resulted from the projecting rotation movement of the hip towards the inside of the turn.

However, this technical development was, of necessity, linked to the technological development of the ski and the boots. One should bear in mind, in particular, the great contribution of fiber glass and plastic materials. These materials, combined with wood in the manufacture of the ski, considerably changed the mechanical characteristics of the equipment–especially the flexible response after twisting which in jargon is called the "reactivity" of the ski. Athletes were able to utilize as best they could this reactivity, with rapid bending-- stretching movements and changing the edges. The characteristics of the flexibility and the rapid flexible response of the ski

were fundamental. In the more technical disciplines (that is in the slalom and the giant slalom) speeds then were not great and the distance between the gates was almost half what it is today. Everything took place on irregular terrain and on rather soft snow, the kind of conditions that encouraged the rapid deterioration of the competition trail. The perfect athlete was an agile skier, who exploited to the full his sensitivity and his ability to rapidly adapt to the terrain.

The Italian Gustav Thoeni (opposite page at St. Moritz in 1974) put forward a new and different interpretation of competition skiing; his technique was analyzed at length, even using high speed cameras in order to codify his movements.

FROM THE END OF THE 1970s TO THE 1980s

Towards the end of the 1970s another great champion marked an important stage in the development of techniques. This was the Swede Ingemar Stenmark whose technique was very different from that of Thoeni.

The different way of steering the skis was obvious. Thoeni was in the habit of following quite a direct line towards the gate, proceeding to turn with agility by performing the famous push step (a sort of skating turn). Stenmark, on the other hand, used only occasionally the push step;

Below: in current slalom contests ski athletes pass very close to the plastic sprung post; in the past the rigid post obliged skiers to keep their trajectories at a certain distance and therefore to increase the distance they covered.

indeed he used to make sure that the skis hardly ever diverged, but rather that they followed parallel paths.

To ski like Stenmark, or rather as if on two tracks, became the goal for competition skiers. Stenmark's superiority was in his ability to perform rounded turns and to slide less than other skiers, so coming quickly out of each turn. To achieve that, he exploited to the full a specific characteristic of the ski, the side-cut. Stenmark provides yet another example of how ski athletes' techniques are conditioned by the equipment available to them.

THE DOMINATION OF TECHNOLOGY

In the 1980s the attention given to equipment was even more intense. For example, not only were qualities contributing to the smooth-running of skis evaluated, but also the shape of the ski (side-cut), anti-vibration characteristics, and the coupling of the

bindings. In the world of competition, Derbyflex plates between the boot and the ski were adopted, on to which the binding was fixed. The plates were designed to lessen the vibrations transmitted from the ski to the body of the skier. However, it was discovered that the plate allowed the ski to distort beneath the boot, the area of the ski that normally remained straight because of the boot's rigidity. This means that a ski with a plate forms a smaller arc than a ski without it, and draws a trajectory with a shorter radius, or rather makes a tighter turn. On the other hand, a ski with a plate is heavier and more rigid, therefore suitable only for ski athletes who can develop higher levels of force.

Technology influences downhill techniques nowadays even more than it did in the past. Bottom: modern downhill equipment and the first anti-vibration plate (Derbyflex).

A spiraling evolution had commenced: in the space of a few years a ski action that was agile and quick became one that was less dynamic and more governed by force. The competition skier became more and more a complete athlete, well endowed physically and trained to bear increasingly strong force loads.

THE EARLY 1990s

During the 1990s competition techniques underwent such sudden and radical changes that only a few champions were able to absorb them, which they did by adapting to the new demands of the equipment.

One of these champions was the Austrian Marc Girardelli, who in the space of a few years rapidly adapted first to the advent of the sprung slalom post (that replaced the rigid wooden one), then to the plates. In the slalom, the plastic post that was flexible at the base enabled ski athletes to follow trajectories never previously attempted. With the fixed post the skier's whole body had to pass outside it, but with the sprung post the athlete could pass on the inside by knocking down the post with one arm. Girardelli, whose technical training had been with the rigid post, tried several ways of knocking the new post down by using both the inner and the outer arm, until he decided definitively in favor of the latter. This trend was also adopted by other ski athletes, given that bending the body towards the inside of the turn made it possible. But Girardelli accomplished the most important technical change by adapting to the introduction of plates and risers. These two components enabled the skier to bend the body even more and develop greater indices of force.

THE ERA OF FORCE

At this point an inevitable adaptation of techniques to new equipment had been set in motion, and in the first half of the 1990s the growth rate of this phenomenon was extraordinary. The preparation of competi-

Top: the Austrian Hermann Mayer; opposite: the Italian Kristian Ghedina, two symbolic representatives of the combination of power and technical ability.

tion trails also further influenced the change that was under way. Artificial snow was increasingly used, which, with its fine crystalline structure and the subsequent preparation work, made the trail very compact and smooth. This surface was so hard that it forced (and still forces) ski athletes to accurately use well-prepared skis with very sharp edges and a wide angle of incidence, and with plates and risers that enable inclinations to be increased.

The conclusion arrived at was that the ski determined whether some difficult stretches of trail could be negotiated successfully. Increasingly, the ski was chosen in relation to its geometrical characteristics as well as for smooth running and flexibility. To sum up, skis with ever more side-cut were adopted which favored the carrying out of more rounded, slide-free turns.

Two competition skiers who more than any others succeeded in synthesizing the concepts of technicality with those of force and power were without doubt Alberto Tomba and Hermann Mayer. They symbolize the modern ski athlete, in whom force and power must be judiciously integrated with agility and acrobatic talents.

THE ADVENT OF CARVING

The last great innovation in the world of skiing is called "carving." This is the precise action of moving without sliding, as if a line were being drawn in the snow. The ski proceeds along a line determined by its tip and traveled along by the whole edge, as if it were leaning into a curved track. In order to do this it is necessary to have skis with considerable side-cut, or rather with a considerable difference in

width between the tip, the center, and the tail. A ski with a lot of side-cut is called a carving ski. The traditional ski also has side-cut, but much less than the carving ski; as a result, the cut turns performed with traditional skis are much wider than those performed with carving skis. On the other hand, sliding turns are better controlled with traditional skis. Of course the ski greatly affects techniques, in that the movements feasible with skis that have a lot of side-cut differ from the movements that can be performed with more traditional skis.

Carving is the latest technological and technical development in skiing. Below: a carver engaged in a turn; you can see the obvious track left in the snow.

COMPETITIONS IN MODERN TIMES

The Englishman Arnold Lunn was the putative father of Alpine ski competitions. In 1911 he organized the first downhill racing contest at Crans Montana (Switzerland): the "Roberts of Kandahar Cup." He can be credited too with the first slalom contest that took place in 1922 at Murren (Switzerland). The competitor had to descend a course marked out by flags and so was obliged to carry out all the kinds of turn known at that time. Lunn intended the contest to reproduce the same conditions as open terrain where the skier had to descend a slope between trees and rocks.

In 1928 the first Alberg-Kandahar event was held at Murren. This competition put together the downhill and the slalom contest, and was created out of an exchange of ideas between Arnold Lunn and Hannes Schneider. It was a combined competition and the placings were drawn up on the basis of the total time taken to complete the two races. The downhill trail was not groomed, it was only marked by fir branches; the slalom trail was groomed and marked by flags.

The Italian athlete Deborah Compagnoni participating in a World Cup contest (1999).

In 1930 the congress of the Fédération Internationale de Ski (FIS: the International Ski Federation, created in 1924) at Oslo recognized downhill and slalom as competition disciplines: these would be subject to Lunn's rules.

In 1931 the first FIS competition was held at Murren, with a downhill race. In 1936 the first Winter Olympics were organized with the inclusion of Alpine ski contests. In 1937 the first World Championships took place at Chamonix (France). In 1950 at the Aspen (Colorado) World Championships, a new Alpine discipline, the giant slalom, was included.

In 1966 the World Cup was introduced. This comprised a series of contests (downhill, slalom, giant slalom) arising from Serge Lang's good intuition; there is a rankings list for each discipline and one which includes them all.

In 1981 a new Alpine ski contest got under way, the super giant, that in 1982 was introduced also into the World Cup and in 1987 into the World Championships at Crans Montana. Today the competitions in which skiers compete are downhill, slalom, giant slalom, super giant and combined event. The combined event consists of slalom and downhill and came from the World Championships at Schladming (Austria) in 1982.

KEY STAGES IN THE HISTORY OF SKIING

5000 B.C.	Reputed date of a rock carving portraying a hunter on skis (Rødøy, Norway)
30 B.C.	The Greek historian Strabo (63 B.C. – 20 A.D.) writes about skiing in his work *Geographica*
544 A.D.	The Byzantine historian Procopius of Caesarea describes Nordic populations on skis
	Giordane, Latin historian of Gothic origin, writes of a Nordic people utilizing skis
1520	King Gustavus Vasa travels 89 km (56 miles) non-stop. In 1923, the legendary "Vasa-loppet" is contested in memory of the event
1555	In *Historia de gentibus septentrionalibus* by Olaus Magnus, the first detailed description is found of peoples who make use of skis
1705	*Viaggio settentrionale* ("Northern Journey") by Francesco Negri contains the first technical description of ski movements
1767	First ski contest at Christiania (jumping and cross-country)
1888	Fridtjof Nansen crosses Greenland on skis
1895–7	Søndre Norheim introduces the Telemark technique
1896	Mathias Zdarsky invents the Lilienfeld technique
1897	Wilhelm Paulcke, with other mountaineers, crosses the Bernese Oberland, the first great undertaking on skis in the Alps
1900	The first Ski Clubs are created
c. 1910	George Bilgeri codifies the *stemm-bogen* technique
1911	First downhill contest
1914–18	Use of skis by Alpine troops
c. 1920	Introduction of edges
c. 1920	Introduction of the Arlberg technique, codified by Hannes Schneider
1922	First slalom competition
1924	The Fédération Internationale de Ski (FIS; International Ski Federation) is founded
1924	The first film on ski techniques is made
	Schneider establishes the first modern ski-school
1925	Recognition by the International Olympic Committee (IOC) of the first "Winter Olympic Games"
1928	First Alberg-Kandahar event
c. 1930	Anton Seelos invents the French technique
1930	The FIS recognizes downhill and slalom as competition races
1936	First Winter Olympics at Garmisch (Germany)
1937	First World Championship at Chamonix (France)
1946	The Head company manufactures the first skis with metal components
1950	First giant slalom contest
1951	First Interski congress
1950s	The Austrian technique is created
1960s	The first skis and ski boots in fiber glass and plastic materials
1966	Introduction of the World Cup
1960s	The French school is established
1982	First super-giant contest in the World Cup
mid-1990s	Advent of carving

2
ALPINE SKIING

From the first steps on the snow to the most advanced techniques with traditional and carving skis. Analysis of the competition disciplines: slalom, giant slalom, downhill.

INTRODUCTION

At one time, each state, each region in which there was an officially recognized ski-school adopted its own technique. Consequently, each national ski-school used its own methodology, dictated by its specific culture and traditions. Only from 1955 did national techniques gradually begin to fall in line with each other, so converging towards a single form of training.

Today, in short, there is no longer much difference between the American school and the Swiss school, between the Norwegian school and the Japanese school. Moreover, carving, the most recent development, has further contributed to the process of unification between the national techniques.

On the other hand, what is still very different is the method of teaching: this reflects also the organizational and cultural level of the official institutions that within a nation deal with ski techniques and methodology.

THE NOVICE SKIER

First of all let us make clear that this first section is devoted to those people who have never had any experience on skis–that is, beginners. However, some of the advice that we shall give may prove useful also to those who have been skiing for a long time but pay little attention to certain details. Let us see then what organizational and technical stages a beginner must follow in order to tackle skiing safely and with the certainty of learning with enjoyment.

A beginning skier must have access to an easy and wide nursery slope and, even better, the help of an instructor.

Choose your resort
The first thing to do is to find out if, in the resort which you intend to choose, there is a nursery slope which is easy and supervised by qualified ski instructors.

The ski-school
It is just as advisable to find out also if there is a proper ski-school. If this is the case, we advise those starting to ski to have one-to-one lessons with the ski instructor rather than with a group, or with not more than another two people at the same technical level (that is, beginners). If the first lesson is

one-to-one it may last just an hour, and a second lesson can take place the following day. If lessons are taken in groups of two or three people with an instructor, it is preferable that the first lesson lasts for at least two hours. The remaining hours of the day should be spent repeating the exercises that have been learnt with the instructor.

The equipment
Finally, it is necessary to find out whether the school provides equipment (skis, boots, poles) or if a hire service is available near the trails (pistes) or ski-school. In fact for those who are new to the sport, it is fine to hire skis; indeed it is the best thing to do before deciding upon what will be an expensive purchase. After the first four or five lessons one can think about buying the equipment most suited to one's own needs. For those of you who prefer to purchase the equipment before learning to ski, it is advisable to put yourself in the hands of experts and of competent and reputable retailers, as the

most expensive equipment is not always the most suitable to the requirements and abilities of a beginner.

This advice applies also to boots. If purchasing boots remember to buy them for the exact size of the foot (not bigger!), making sure they are of good quality and not "competition" boots. It is better not to skimp on boots; save money instead by buying cheaper skis that, in any case, it is advisable to change after two or three years of use (see chapter on "Equipment").

In the choice of equipment, skis are certainly important, but boots are even more important. Initially, at least, boots should meet the technical requirements but also be comfortable.

Clothing

For a skier the approach to the ski runs starts from … the bedroom! In other words, when one starts to put on the correct clothing it must above all take account of the outside temperature, but also of the probable fatigue experienced during the first day on skis. Clothing therefore will have to be "multi-layer," so that a garment can be easily discarded should movement be intense and the temperature mild, and can be swiftly put back on at the end of a period of activity or during rest times. Furthermore, you will not be caught out by any rapid climatic changes that are particularly frequent in the winter period. If during ski activity you become hot, you can of course take off your anorak; remember, however, to put it back on as soon as the exercises are over. Choose a place, near the trail, where you can leave the things that you may want to temporarily offload (anorak, hat, gloves, etc), or – better still – entrust them to a person who is with you.

From inside to outside the ideal clothing is the following:

- short-sleeved T-shirt in breathable material
- long-sleeved high-neck jersey (better with a zip at the neck) in cotton or light fleece
- long cotton underwear (long-johns) if you suffer a lot from the cold
- knee-length socks in cotton, wool or a mixture of fibers (one pair of socks only, not two, and not in coarse wool)
- heavy woolen sweater

- anorak and ski pants or salopettes (waterproof dungarees): the "two-piece" (jacket plus trousers) is preferable to the one-piece ski suit
- use five-finger gloves, not mittens that cover all the fingers together, because they allow more freedom of movement (and it is not true that they do not keep the hands as warm)
- head-gear is very important: the head loses up to 30% of body heat. Therefore, if it is cold put on a woolen, fleece or, if necessary, a furry hat
- ski goggles / sun-glasses: sunlight and the intense reflection of the snow can cause eye problems, sometimes serious ones if people are particularly sensitive or if the sun is very strong. The wind is another nuisance. It is as well, therefore, to equip yourself with ski goggles that will protect the eyes from ultra-violet (UV) rays and fit well on the face (front and side protection). Should there be poor visibility, ski goggles or sun-glasses with clear lenses are of considerable help
- in the sun, protective creams are of use to everyone (except in rare cases of people with particularly tough skin) and indis-

pensable for children and the fair-skinned. Do not be deceived by the cold or the breeze: in the mountains the sun burns and the skin is prone to dehydration. This is usually appreciated too late, when in the evening one tries to remedy burning with an after-sun cream that does not cure but gives only temporary relief.

Ski boots

The boots must not be cold when put on; this should be done in a warm environment. First of all, you should open the upper part of the boot by raising the tongue and holding back the two upper edges. Once the foot is inserted, it is a good idea to tap the heel on the ground so as to fit it firmly into the inner boot. Then get the tongue to adhere to the shin bone and close the two plastic edges of the shin guard. At this stage, starting from the instep, the clips can be fastened. Lastly, should the boot have them, the forefoot and shin bone clips are fastened.

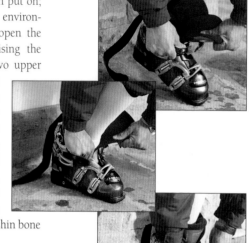

*Right: the correct way to put on boots:
open wide the shell and raise the tongue;
slip in the foot; fasten the clips starting
from the instep.*

WHAT IS SNOW?

Snow is formed in the atmosphere, in conditions of humidity and low temperature, when microscopic water droplets crystallize around very small nuclei formed of ice and atmospheric dust particles. When this starter crystal becomes heavy it falls towards the ground, becoming increasingly large because of the additional humidity and because it combines with other crystals, so forming a "snowflake." But the shape of these crystals varies according to the temperature: from 0 to –5 °C irregular little needles appear; from –15 to –20 °C, however, star-shaped discs are formed (see figure).

How to carry skis

Skis should be carried on the shoulders with the tips facing forwards and downwards. The part of the ski in front of the binding rests on the shoulder and the skis are held in place with a single hand: the weight of the arm will be sufficient to keep the skis evenly balanced. When you are walking close to other people lower the tips of the skis a little so that the tails are up; then you will not run the risk of hitting someone. In lines (queues) at ski lifts or at the ski-pass ticket office, or in any particularly crowded place, off-load the skis from the shoulder and hold them upright in front of you. All other ways of carrying skis are, in general, more tiring and awkward, or at least risk causing inconvenience to others.

Skis, if carried badly, can hamper movement and harm other people.

49

On the slopes

With a ski instructor

It is of fundamental importance to approach the sport of skiing correctly, and the safest way of doing so is to have a ski instructor. As we shall see, especially in the first stages of learning, choosing the right place for tackling the first descents and for learning the first movements is essential. A wrong choice, in this respect, can lead to incorrect as well as tiring movements or, worse still, cause accidents. The guidance and teaching provided by a ski instructor removes all worries and cares with regard to the methods to be used for the first movements, and avoids incorrect basic approaches that will affect subsequent learning. Our advice therefore is to rely on an experienced instructor, at least in the early stages: advice on basic techniques and conduct is certainly worth the modest initial expense.

Without a ski instructor

If you wish to get on the slopes without the guidance of a ski instructor, take things calmly and patiently. Choose a trail with groomed snow and avoid fresh snow. Above all, do not rush to use a ski lift: this is a step to be taken later. Even before attempting to ski, get accustomed to the snow and to a simple slope by walking in ski boots. Then leave the skis in a safe place where they will not cause inconven-

ience (not on the ground), grasp the poles and, remaining on the edge of the trail, walk for a few minutes uphill, downhill, and diagonally. If possible try also to get the boots to slide along a gentle slope by pushing yourself with the poles. Having done this, fasten the skis to the feet. Choose an absolutely level area, far away from other skiers. Arrange the skis perfectly parallel on the ground. Check that the soles of the boots are clean and are free of snow or ice, then slip them into the bindings.

Before inserting the boots into the ski bindings, it is necessary to thoroughly clean off snow from the soles (opposite). Then (below) the tip of the boot is slipped under the toe-piece of the binding, the heel is placed in position and locked with a firm downward push.
Right: the correct way to hold the poles: slip the hand through the bottom of the wrist strap and then grasp the grip of the ski pole

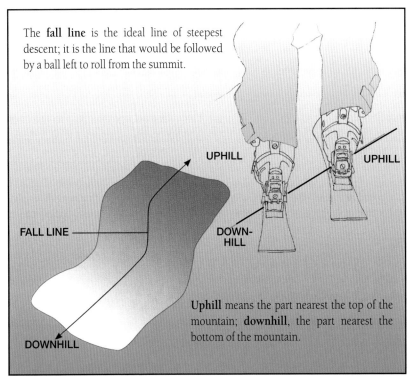

The **fall line** is the ideal line of steepest descent; it is the line that would be followed by a ball left to roll from the summit.

UPHILL

UPHILL

FALL LINE

DOWN-
HILL

DOWNHILL

Uphill means the part nearest the top of the mountain; **downhill**, the part nearest the bottom of the mountain.

First movements

Staying on the spot, make several movements to get accustomed to the skis: raise one leg, then the other, bend your knees and come straight up again with the support of the poles. Then take some small steps forward, first lifting the skis then sliding them alternately (1). Also carry out small side steps, both by lifting the ski and by making it slide (2). Finally, keeping the skis parallel, try pushing yourself with the poles for short stretches. The level trail will guarantee a stop after sliding just a few meters (yards) (3).

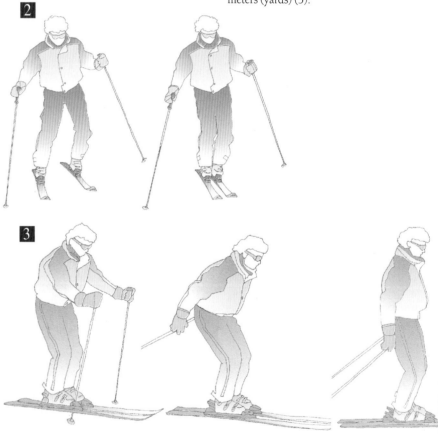

Changing direction

From a stationary position, perform small steps spacing out the skis and bringing them together again like a pair of compasses. The movement is achieved by opening out one ski at the point and moving the other one towards it until the desired direction is reached. Similarly, the tail can be opened out and the other ski drawn towards it. In the first situation, the poles rest behind the tails; in the second, in front of the tips.

Doing the snowplow (wedge) standing still

If the harsh braking with a stick is excluded, the snowplow is the oldest technique known to control speed. It is effective for stopping or for slowing down after having started to glide, and it will be particularly helpful on sloping terrain. The basic snowplow position is attained by making the ski tails slide sideways so as to open them and by keeping the tips relatively close. To facilitate the movement the first few times, it is better to space out one tail at a time. The snowplow at this stage serves to "try out the position," or rather as an approach to the complete snowplow movement that will be performed in future during a descent.

Avoid bringing the knees together and crossing the ski tips.

53

Methods of ascent

If the slope is only slight, it is sufficient just to push yourself along with the ski poles keeping the skis parallel. When this isn't enough, it is advisable to try skating. With an even steeper slope the methods of ascent to adopt are side-stepping and herringbone (see also the chapter on "Cross-country skiing").

Herringbone

You walk forwards, uphill, with the ski tips wide apart: while the ski tips should be kept far apart, the ski tails must be kept close together without crossing. The weight of the body falls on the inner edges of the skis.

Take care not to cross the backs of the skis.

Side-stepping

Step and keep the skis transversally (crosswise) across the fall line; the ski is moved sideways uphill by edging it into the snow, the downhill ski is then moved up, and so on. It is of fundamental importance that the skis remain edged and at right angles to the slope, otherwise you will slide downhill.

1. Moving mat
2. Rope tow
3. Surface lift (drag-lift)
4. Two-seater seat lift (chair lift)
5. Four-seater high-speed detachable seat lift
6. Gondola or cabin lift
7. Cable car

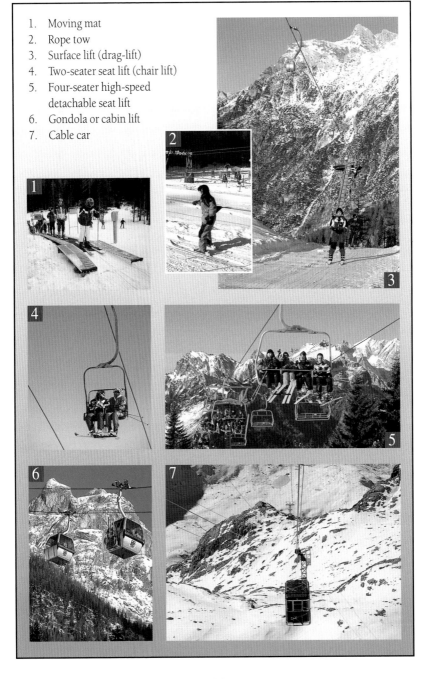

The basics

In skiing, as in every sport, there are "basics," that is, those positions or movements considered as the starting base for subsequent movements that are more difficult. Alpine skiing is based on the skier gliding in unison with the skis in a direction that goes from uphill to downhill brought about by the force of gravity.

Skiing, therefore, is not based on a propelling force effected by human beings, as happens in many other sports activities (for example, all the disciplines in which man must run or pedal). The skier (save in exceptional circumstances and in particular in cross-country [Nordic] skiing) does not have to push his own body forward. It is the force of gravity that causes the skis to move, while the skier has to carefully control his direction. The skier acts in effect to constantly control his motion.

The basic position

The basic ski position must be as similar as possible to that of a person when he is standing up, with the sole difference of keeping the leg joints (heels, knees, hips) slightly bent in order to be ready to control loss of balance caused by any unexpected sliding.

In this position, the basic concept of equilibrium must be observed: that is to say, the center of gravity must fall within the support base. "Support base," in this case, means that which is formed by feet and not the wider one created by the skis. The skis in fact increase the surface area of the support base, but if the center of gravity falls outside the support base of the feet this does not guarantee good body control.

To recognize the correct position, that is, one which is evenly balanced on the support base of the feet and not on that of the skis, it is necessary only to check that the weight of the body rests totally on the soles of the feet. This state

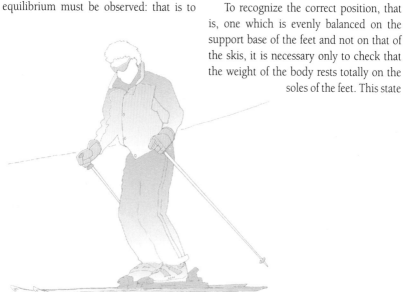

allows the skier to maintain equilibrium with a few essential muscular contractions.

Left: basic position with skis flat.

When the weight of the body rests on the calves or on the shin bone (these are the front and back support points on the ski boot) it means that the wider support base of the skis (not the smaller one of the feet) is being exploited; the precious condition of body alignment has been lost. In such a situation it is probably necessary to intensely contract a lot of muscles in order to maintain balance, though often the skis do not respond to the commands.

For the sake of convenience we distinguish two basic positions:
• basic position with skis flat
• basic position with skis edged.

The first basic position is carried out on flat terrain or while one descends the fall line. The second is carried out when the skis traverse the fall line.

Right: basic position with skis edged.

Controlling sliding

Sliding must take place principally in the longitudinal direction to the ski, that is to say, forwards. Also there is a slip in the sideways direction that is an integral part of a turn and of speed control.

Longitudinal glide downhill (or descending along the fall line)

• Description

For beginners, descending along the fall line is the first proper exercise that arouses a strong feeling of traveling downhill. The exercise should be carried out on a short (20–50 m; 60–150 feet) stretch of gently sloping trail that ends on the level or even better in a counter slope. Alternatively, on a not entirely suitable slope, the presence of a ski instructor provides the help necessary for stopping. The objective is to maintain balance, or rather the correct support on the feet, during the whole descent.

• Positioning

After climbing uphill (see p. 54) the skis must be rearranged in a parallel position with the tips facing downhill. In order to achieve this, the ski poles are placed downhill, on the same line as and about a meter (yard) apart from the skis, so as to act as a buffer. Then you proceed as for the direction change from a stationary position until reaching the start position.

• Technique

Lean the body slightly forwards: this movement will guarantee control of the slight subsequent acceleration. Remove the support of the ski poles by pointing them backwards. Keep the body relaxed with the weight over the whole soles of the feet. Let yourself slide forward without fear: the level or slightly uphill terrain will act as a brake.

Before putting the skis parallel, move the body slightly forward.

Side-sliding (preparation for side-slipping, or dérapage)

• Description

This is an extremely important basic maneuver, which is an essential part of the turn. It entails sliding not forwards but sideways, with the ski edge sweeping, or "stroking," the snow. It is not difficult to do, but you must use skis that are suitable for the exercise (neither too shaped, nor too long) and your boots must be tightly fitted (your foot should not be able to move at all inside the boot).

It should be done on the type of slope previously described, where the snow is compacted and of a consistent quality. You should avoid trying it on very soft snow

(such as just after a snowfall) or on icy snow. Nor should it be attempted on undulating ground.

• Positioning

Adopt the position described in the "side-step" (p. 54), with your skis at right angles to the fall line, and slightly edged on the mountain or uphill side. Make sure that your body is correctly positioned, as described in the basic position (p. 56). Keep your muscles as relaxed as possible, and make sure that you are standing with your weight firmly balanced on your feet.

• Technique

Your skis must be edged, as described in the basic position for the side-step. Lean on the uphill, or mountain ski, and let the valley ski slide out sideways roughly 20–30 cm (8–12 inches), at the end of which you again edge it. Then slide your mountain ski down to join it. Carry on with this series of "sideways sliding steps," repeating the movement at least half a dozen times. When you reach level ground, make a 180° turn (p. 53) so that you are facing the opposite way, side-step up the slope again, and again carry out half a dozen sliding steps, now pointing the other way. As you get more practice, you will be able to get your skis to slide parallel and in unison, without using steps. It is important that your skis always remain at right angles to the slope: the tips should not descend further than the tails and vice versa. In the former case you would end up sliding forwards, and in the latter you would start to slide backwards.

While you are side-slipping, be careful to keep your skis always parallel, without ever opening out the tips or the tails.

Traversing

• Description

Traversing involves moving across the fall line. You should adopt the position described for the side-step ascent, with one ski slightly higher up the slope than the other (p. 54). This is another extremely important basic position for keeping your balance when you are in a lopsided position, as will often be the case in future.

• Positioning

In the basic position for the side-step ascent, all you need to do is keep your skis slightly edged, while keeping your muscles as relaxed as possible.

• Technique

Lift your poles from the snow, and with a small push forward, let yourself glide, while keeping your center of gravity and your ski edging under careful control. This will mean that your skis will move in a slightly curved trajectory, until the forward impetus comes to a stop.

• Variation

A good way of stopping the traverse is to open out the tail of the downhill ski slightly, in a movement that could be seen as a preparation for the snowplow.

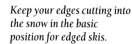

Keep your edges cutting into the snow in the basic position for edged skis.

ARMS HELD OUT
IN FRONT AND
SLIGHTLY WIDE
OF THE BODY

TORSO
LEANING
SLIGHTLY
FORWARDS

KNEES AND
ANKLES
SLIGHTLY BENT

SKIS CONSTANTLY EDGED

BASIC POSITION

Controlling your speed

The traverse and the sideways slide are the basic movements used to control speed, and are defined as learning stages, in that they make it possible to move on to the next stages. This does not mean that it is impossible for anyone. to reach a more advanced level without having passed through the stages that are suggested here, but to do so would certainly be much more difficult and tiring.

Once you have tried out all the different types of sliding, it is a good idea to master a basic method of speed control and stopping. Speed control is done with the snowplow.

Descending along the fall line in the snowplow

• Description

This is one of the most important techniques for a beginner who wants to be sufficiently in control of his actions right from the first day. It is one of the techniques that has been in use since the beginning of the 20th century, and is just as effective today. However, it is a technique that you will only use temporarily, and will abandon as soon as you are able to control parallel skis. But although it is only a stage to be passed through, it represents an important breakthrough for beginners, since it enables them to have control of their skis, leading to safer skiing, and this in turn means greater self-confidence and more enjoyment.

To make the snowplow, set your skis on the slope with the tips close together and the tails apart. In this way your skis will advance in, so to speak, a mixed manner,

moving both sideways and forwards, and creating friction on the snow. The ideal terrain to try it is the same as that used for the *Schuss* (or longitudinal glide), a short slope ending in level ground or a counter-slope.

• Positioning

Having ascended a gentle slope, set your skis with their tips pointing downhill, and with their inside edges gripping the snow. Before doing this, you should plant your poles towards the valley, straight ahead of you and about a meter (yard) from the skis, so as to hold yourself steady. Then proceed as for the change of direction, until you reach the start position.

• Technique

With your skis set wide apart in a snowplow, shift the weight of your body slightly forward. Then remove your poles from the snow, and hold them behind you. Keep your body relaxed, with your weight distributed evenly on both feet. Let yourself slide forward, trying not to increase the edge grip too much. You can brake by pushing out the

tails further (in a symmetrical manner) and at the same time making sure that you maintain your edging on the snow.

Traversing snowplow

• Description
This is without doubt a useful exercise for beginners, even if its use is limited to a very few occasions, since you will almost immediately be moving

on to parallel ski control. In any case it is a learning stage for the real snowplow turn, and guarantees your being able to get your balance when in a lopsided position.

• Positioning
Starting from the side-step ascent position (p. 54) adopt the basic position at a diagonal. Then make a snowplow with your tails only a little apart.

• Technique
Raise your poles and give yourself a push to start moving, keeping your center of gravity and your edging carefully under control. It is best not to open out the downhill ski too far, and to keep your weight mostly on the uphill ski. Keep your torso turned towards the tips of your skis.

Starting from the basic position with edged skis, adopt the snowplow position by slightly opening out the tail of the downhill ski.

The snowplow (wedge) turn

• Description

The basic snowplow is the essential basis for controlling skis safely, and the snowplow turn is the mother of all future turns, and has always been a staple of ski-schools all over the world. Nowadays the snowplow turn is only a halfway point, but all the same it is an important starting point for correct skiing.

Of all the many snowplow turns, only the two simplest will be described here, which are differentiated by their starting positions:

• from the fall line
• from the diagonal

Starting from the fall line

After descending a few meters (yards) in a snowplow down the fall line, swing your left or your right foot round slightly to point your skis to the right or to the left respectively. This movement should be simultaneous with shifting your weight onto whichever foot is on the outside of the turn, by slightly increasing the edging on that ski: left if the turn is to the right and right if it is to the left.

Starting from the traverse

After descending a few meters (yards) in a diagonal snowplow (p. 64), point your ski tips downhill by turning your body slightly. The turn may then be completed as just described in the snowplow turn starting from the fall line, or you may simply do a snowplow stop.

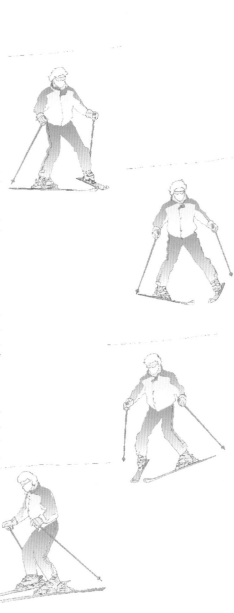

Points to note

Snowplow turns can also be accomplished by twisting the whole body in the required direction. This method is helped by skis which are short and shaped. Although this method will serve its purpose (change of direction) when you are going faster or are skiing on steeper slopes, it can turn out to be very inefficient, generating a swing in the body mass that goes out of control. In other words, you will end up "corkscrewing," turning further than you wanted to.

SNOWPLOW TURN

HEAD, SHOULDERS, AND
TORSO FOLLOW THE
DIRECTION OF THE SKI TIPS

KNEES AND ANKLES
SLIGHTLY BENT

POLES POINTING
BEHIND

SKI TIPS CLOSE
TOGETHER, WITHOUT
CROSSING

BODY WEIGHT
DISTRIBUTED EVENLY
ON BOTH FEET

TAILS KEPT WIDE APART
ARMS WIDE OF BODY

THE INTERMEDIATE SKIER
Introduction
The intermediate skier is someone who has already got over the first technical hurdles, and so can no longer be considered a beginner. The level of achievement he has reached enables him to tackle runs of medium difficulty, but he tends to go at a very limited speed. He tends not to use the snowplow or wedge any more except in particularly difficult situations, and he has no problems in controlling parallel skis, although his style and coordination are variable.

The slope
The choice of slope is of fundamental importance if you are not to land yourself in dangerous situations. It is a good idea for an intermediate skier, if not acquainted with the runs to be attempted, to get hold of a detailed map of the ski resort, on which are marked the difficulty ratings of the runs and any refreshment areas, so as to be able to make a preliminary plan for the day.

Another important task is to check equipment.

Before putting on the skis check the settings of the bindings and if necessary make the required adjustment using the tools (screwdriver, pliers) that are almost always available at the bottom or at the top of the ski lifts.

Before starting to ski it is also important to allow yourself a few minutes' warm-up to help your muscles.

The first time that you use a pair of skis, you must check the settings of the bindings, adjusting them if necessary with a screwdriver.

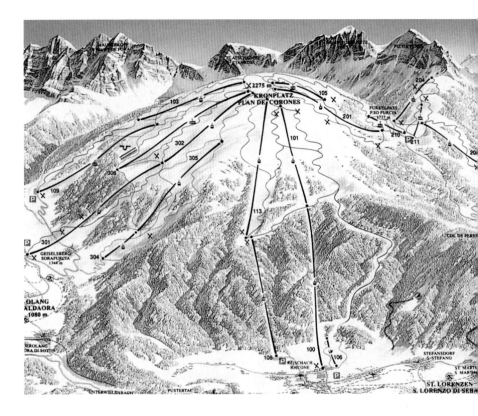

The basics

Even an intermediate skier must rely on certain fundamental techniques to improve his skills and to ensure that he has good ski control. As has already been said, the basic principle for the skier is to control his movements and the various dynamic situations that the slope presents. For the intermediate skier, "basics" means aiming for total control of parallel skis on any type of slope.

Therefore we can consider the following procedures to be fundamental:
• body alignment
• side-slipping (*dérapage*)
• steering (carving)

Map of a ski resort: the difficulty levels of the runs are marked in different colors, shown on the boards positioned at the start of each run.

• the Christie stop
• parallel turn
Other types of movement described by ski-schools of various countries are an elaboration of these basic principles.

71

Body alignment

As we have already seen with the beginner (p. 56), alignment is important because it is the essential starting point for good balance. At this stage the only difference is that the intermediate skier has to control alignment at a higher speed. Apart from this, the body alignment goals at this level are exactly the same as those already described.

Controlling side-slipping (*dérapage*)

• Description

Side-slipping is an exercise which even the most expert skier should never give up. It involves allowing parallel skis to slip sideways down the slope without any obvious shift in body balance. It is generally used on fairly steep runs where the surface is smooth, and entails alternating a few seconds of slipping with a few seconds of increased edging.

• Positioning

Set your skis parallel and at right angles to the slope, with the edges biting into the snow (p. 61). Turn your torso and face towards the tip of your downhill ski.

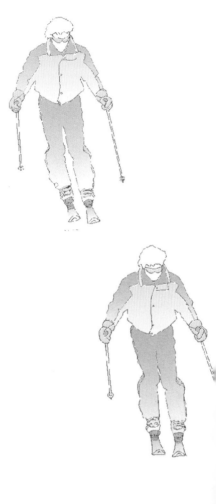

• Technique

Decrease the amount of edging by slightly tilting your ankles and knees towards the valley. In this way the running surface of your skis will flatten out on the snow and your skis will slip sideways, although it is unlikely that they will do so parallel and in unison. In order to avoid the tips going lower than the tails, it is necessary to keep your torso slightly turned towards the valley, and to avoid rotating the rest of the body either to the left or to the right.

To halt the side-slip you must once again increase the grip of your ski edges on the snow by tilting your ankles and knees towards the mountain. Repeat this movement six to eight times and then practice it facing the other way.

72

When side-slipping, all you need to do is adjust the amount of edging to slow down your descent.

Steering

• Description

Steering is a very specific type of ski control. It is a type of gliding movement in which the skis are tilted onto their edges and move forwards in a perfect line, with their edges cutting into the snow, and with minimal sliding. Choose a fairly easy run that is not too steep. When the tracks made by the skis are very narrow, like a mark left by two knives, steering, or carving, is at its maximum and is described as a "cut." This particular type of ski control will be looked at in more detail in the section on expert skiers.

• Positioning

Set the skis parallel and at right angles to the slope, with their internal edge cutting in (see basic position with edged skis). Use your knees and ankles to keep the edges cutting sharply in. Keep your torso facing the tips of the skis.

• Technique

Pushing off sharply with the ski poles, slide a few meters (yards) forward, while keeping your body in the same stance as at the start. The skis will follow a curved trajectory and will thus turn back towards the mountain, so bringing movement to a halt.

Later on, the angle at which you set off will vary; no longer traversing the slope, but with the tips turned increasingly downhill, until you are starting with your skis set on the fall line, with their edges cutting in (first on one side and then on the other).

• Variation

An interesting variation is to alternate without stopping between sliding (*dérapage*) and carving with your skis moving slowly forwards. The aim of this is to perform both types of slide correctly, as well as to keep control of balance and alignment during transition from one to the other.

Facing page: when steering is well performed the ski tracks will be clearly visible in the snow. In the drawings below different starting angles are shown.

The Christie stop
• Description
This is the classic parallel ski stop, the one which is sometimes seen done in a rather cocky manner by moderately skilled skiers at the bottom of the trails, and it bears a close resemblance to the Christie stop in ice-skating.

A skier who can perform the Christie stop no longer uses the snowplow, and has fairly good control of parallel skis.

This maneuver can in theory be carried out on all types of terrain, but you have to be careful on gentle slopes with very soft snow, where it is possible to get stuck, and on steep icy slopes (where it is possible to lose your edge grip and to fall inwards).

The effectiveness of a Christie stop also depends very much on the quality of your equipment and on how sharp your edges are. Skis that do not bend and sharper edges will obviously guarantee a better result even on hard or icy snow.

• Positioning
The Christie stop can be carried out after a series of turns of any type, or at the end of a piece of straight downhill descent.

• Technique
For the first few times, at least until you have acquired the necessary mastery of your skis and are well able to evaluate the snow conditions, the Christie stop should only be attempted in a wide open space, far from other people, since it can need much more space to perform than you anticipate. So it is better to try it out several times in a safe area before carrying out stops somewhere where you might risk a collision.

The aim is to release your skis on the fall line, to turn them to the left or to the right, then to let the weight of your body

76

down onto them again. You start with a knee bend, following which you straighten up fairly quickly; at this point you point your ski tips in the required direction (right or left: the choice must be made previously), letting your heels slip in the opposite direction. Then you bend your whole body again slightly, taking care to keep your torso turned downhill.

Warning
When you point your skis to the left or to the right, your body must not follow your ski tips, but must swivel in the opposite direction; this is to avoid your skis turning more than the required amount, which would make the curve too tight.

Last stage of a Christie stop: the torso is turned towards the valley and not in the direction of the skis.

The parallel turn

• Description

The parallel turn represents an important milestone for the intermediate skier. It is usually performed with the skis slightly apart (20–30 cm; 8–12 inches), and so not with skis in total unison. Setting your feet a little distance apart guarantees better balance to begin with. The whole maneuver relies upon the skier's ability to have precise control over sliding and carving, drawing both skills together for the perfect final result. It should be performed initially on easy or fairly easy runs, and on snow that is compacted and not icy, after which you may progress (but only after you have had quite a bit of practice) to steeper runs.

• Positioning

Start with a diagonal glide not far off the fall line. It will be of great use if before this and on an easy piece of ground you practice bending and straightening your whole body during a slide, in training for the turn itself.

YES

NO

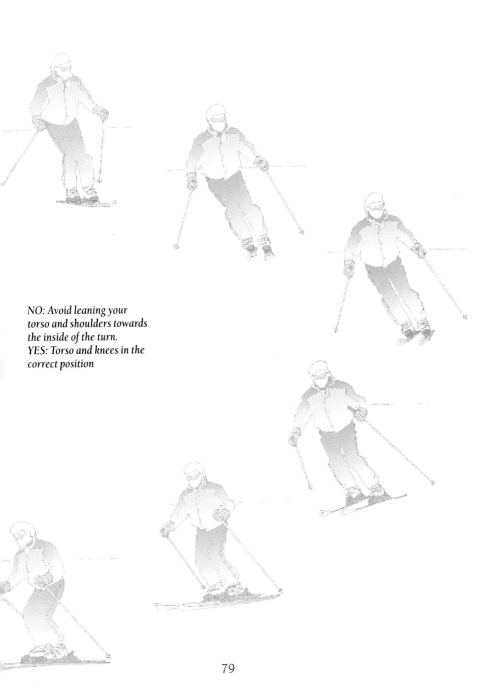

NO: *Avoid leaning your torso and shoulders towards the inside of the turn.*
YES: *Torso and knees in the correct position*

• Technique

The way it is performed is heavily influenced by the type of ski used (see the chapter on "Equipment").

The classic technique can be described as follows: a knee-bend, a straightening up as the skis are pointed downhill, and then–once the halfway point of the turn

has been passed–another knee-bend until the end of the turn.

The more shaped the ski is (the narrower its central section as compared with its tip and tail), the closer the trajectory will be to a semi-circle. With skis of this type the degree of carving is greater and sliding is less likely to be involved.

If the skis are only minimally shaped (skis of a traditional type) the trajectory will be more of an oval shape, and there will be more sliding.

Points to note

Bending and straightening up movements will also vary according to the type of ski used. The more shaped and the more flexible the skis are, and the shorter, the less pronounced the movement will be. Conversely, the less shaped and the less flexible the skis are, and the greater their length, the quicker and the more pronounced will be the movement required.

NO: Avoid leaning into the turn and losing your edge grip.
NO: Avoid tilting your pelvis backwards.

PARALLEL SKI TURN

SHOULDERS IN LINE WITH HIPS

TORSO IN LINE WITH THE TIP OF THE OUTSIDE SKI

HIPS, KNEES, AND ANKLES BENT

FEET SLIGHTLY APART, IN LINE WITH HIPS

THE EXPERT SKIER
Introduction

An expert skier means someone who has been skiing for several years (4–6 years), who has spent quite a bit of time on the slopes during the winter season (more than two weeks in a season), and who ideally has some experience of off-trail and summer skiing. This will, of course, vary greatly from person to person: someone young and athletic can, in the space of two or three years, become a

good skier; on the other hand someone who is getting on in years and is less athletic, and who only spends a few days a year skiing, might never become an expert skier.

Expert skiers can be divided into many categories, which in essence depend upon the differences in their characters and in their level of fitness, rather than on their experience. Some favor wide turns at a constant speed, and love well-groomed trails, with smooth terrain on which they can get the best speed out of their equipment.

Others find tight turns, performed at a more moderate speed, more appealing. Yet another group love steep icy slopes, where they can constantly put their own skills to the test, or trails with bumps (mogul fields), or off-trail skiing.

Even for expert skiers, leaving aside their personal preferences, there are certain "basics" upon which all the more specific skills depend.

The slope

The choice of which terrain to use must obviously be made according to the characteristics of the individual as described above. You are encouraged to assess carefully the condition of the various runs, especially after changes in weather conditions, such as heavy snowfalls, a steep drop in temperature or, conversely, a period of fairly warm weather. When in doubt it is advisable to consult the local information services or the ski-schools.

Besides this, the importance of checking equipment cannot be overstressed (sharpening the edges, settings of the bindings, boot fastenings, adequate clothing), nor can the important period of warm-up before you tackle the first runs.

The basics

With all his experience, an expert skier has already acquired certain "universal" basics, skills that are useful to all skiers. Some of the ones dealt with are: body alignment or control of the center of gravity (p. 56), side-slipping (p. 61), and carving (p. 92). These three maneuvers, with the variations described, can be considered as the basis even for advanced skiers, who must also, however, be able to rely on certain fundamental skills, appropriate only to the expert level.

The following basics will be dealt with straightaway:
• sequence of wide-radius turns
• sequence of short-radius turns (*wedel*)
• carving turns

Right: key stage of a wide-radius turn. Note how the legs lean for good edging.

Sequence of wide-radius turns

• Description

Turns that are described as "wide radius" turns do not in fact have any set measurement for their curvature, but they may be approximately identified as having a radius of between 20 and 40 m (60–120 feet). In any case the turns do not all have the same radius, but rather a variation of radii, since the trajectory described is not at all a perfect semi-circle. In general, however, all turns performed without side-slipping with a traditional ski, making use of the light shaping of the ski, may be called wide-radius turns. Therefore the radius of these turns is principally affected by the extent to which the ski is shaped (the greater the shaping, the smaller the radius).

The term "traditional" is used to describe the skis that are currently in use in the mass tourism market, and so does not include carving skis.

• Technique

First of all the skier must reach a certain level of speed on a medium-steep slope.

The first element in the sequence of movements is a preparatory phase, in which the skis are not yet turning but the body is getting ready to carry out the next movements. During this phase the knees are slightly bent and the torso leans slightly forward; in addition the inside ski pole is placed forward (the right pole if the turn is to the right and vice versa), without being planted.

The second phase gives the approach to the turn. Proceed as follows: plant the pole and edge your skis while straightening your body. The edged skis will automatically "enter" into a turn.

In the third phase the body bends again slightly, while edging is increased; the torso remains turned towards the tip of the outside or downhill ski. This phase constitutes the link with the next turn. The knee bend of the third phase will thus serve as preparation (or it could be called the first phase) for the new turn.

Points to note

If performing a succession of wide-radius turns causes you to build up excessive speed, such speeding can be controlled in two ways: 1) by making tighter turns; 2) by using controlled side-slipping or sliding.

NO: Avoid leaning back
too much.
NO: Avoid over-weighting
the inside ski, causing the
outside ski to open out.

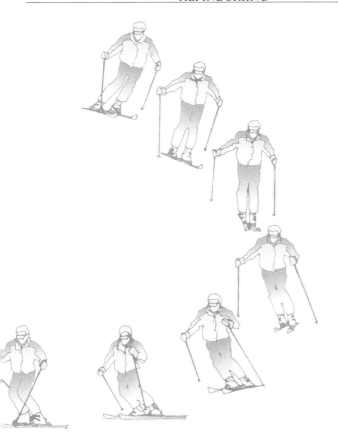

Sequence of short-radius turns (wedel)
• Description
Just as with the previous maneuver, short-radius radius turns have no stipulated amount of curvature either.

It is generally agreed, however, that they are approximately half the size of wide radius turns (10–20 m [30–60 feet]). Wide-radius turns may be performed either on medium-difficulty slopes or on steep slopes. The basic idea is that the shorter the radius, the more the turn is slid. It is worth pointing out that the skis do not follow a neatly cut, or carved, trajectory (which can happen on the other hand in wide-radius turns), but need careful slide control, which is achieved by restrained swiveling of the lower leg. If one were to attempt to quantify this, it could be said that wide-radius turns are 90–100%

carving, while tight turns are made up of 90–100% controlled sliding.
• Technique
Following a small downhill spurt to build up a bit of speed, you begin the sequence by bending your knees and body and holding the pole ready on the turn side. Next, in the phase of straightening up and planting the pole, you straighten up much more energetically than you would in a wide-radius turn, to make it easier to point the skis in the required direction (the start of the turn). This occurs as a result of swiveling the lower legs, while the torso and arms remain turned towards the valley.

Finally you bend your knees while increasing the edging. This movement, coupled with holding the new pole at the ready, also constitutes the first phase of the next turn.

NO: Avoid getting ready for the turn by over-bending and sticking your hips out behind you.
YES: Planting the pole gives rhythm, energy, and confidence to the sequence of movements.

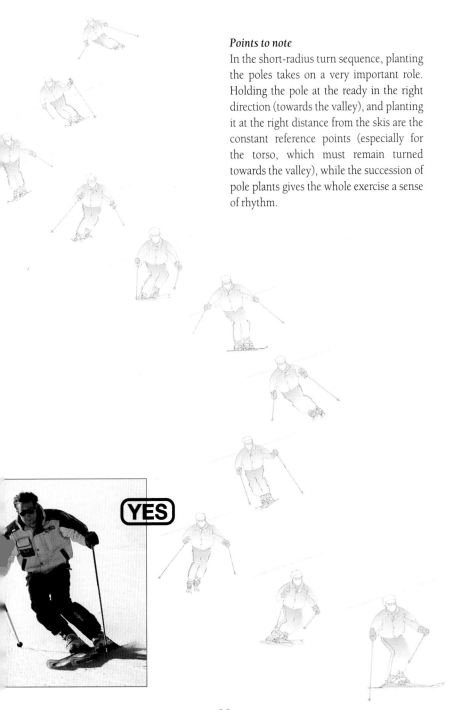

Points to note
In the short-radius turn sequence, planting the poles takes on a very important role. Holding the pole at the ready in the right direction (towards the valley), and planting it at the right distance from the skis are the constant reference points (especially for the torso, which must remain turned towards the valley), while the succession of pole plants gives the whole exercise a sense of rhythm.

YES

SHORT-RADIUS TURNS

LEGS LEANING TO
ENSURE EDGE GRIP

FEET WEIGHTED ACCORDING TO
THE CENTRIFUGAL FORCES

HEAD TILTED TO KEEP
OPTICAL HORIZON
STEADY

ARMS EXTENDED
WIDE FOR NATURAL
BALANCE

TORSO SLIGHTLY
LEANING AND FACING
THE POINT OF THE
OUTSIDE SKI

Sequence of carved turns

Carved turns are the most recent arrivals on the skiing scene. They can only be performed with specially designed carving skis, which are very shaped. Nowadays ski-schools in all the different countries include this type of turn in their repertory, either as a technical achievement in itself, or as a preparatory step for the next stage of learning. They are turns that need physical exertion and excellent balance, but choosing the right ski for the purpose can make the maneuver easier for anyone. –

The carved turn must be performed with the maximum amount of steering, in other words with the edges constantly "cutting"; the skis never slide, and they produce clean, neat lines, drawn by the shaping of the skis, as well as by the skier's ability to tilt the skis and his own body.

This maneuver is derived from the action of competitors in World Cup races, who were the first to execute trajectories like perfect cuts in their efforts to make their movements as quick and effective as possible without losing speed. Today top-level competitors use skis that are much more shaped than in the past, both in slalom and giant slalom. Carving skis for

In the wide carved turn the body leans hard towards the inside of the turn until it is brushing the snow.

amateurs are even more shaped than the competition skis used by professional athletes.

Carved turns can be carried out on any slope, from easy slopes to the very steepest, provided that the snow is of uniform quality and of a good consistency. One characteristic that sets these turns apart from other types is that their trajectory is very close to the arc of a circle. In fact, carved turns are called "round" turns, precisely because they not only make the skier change direction, but carry on to complete their trajectory till they bring the skier to the point of swinging uphill into the mountain. Good carvers are capable of accomplishing a full 360° turn.

Fun carving turns can only be performed with suitable fun carving skis.

Wide turns

• Description

The wide carved turn is the queen of all carved turns, the most harmonious, the sweetest and at the same time the most aggressive. As far as the dynamics are concerned, it is the closest imitation of the giant slalom turns of competition skiers, in that its size, and the energy and the sensations involved are the same.

For anyone who is new to this technique, it is better to try it out first on easy or medium slopes.

• Positioning

The first thing to do is to check that there is enough space to perform turns of this sort. Carved turns need more space than normal turns; so as a general rule you should make sure that the width in particular is sufficient (20–30 m [60–90 feet] minimum).

• Technique

Allow the skis to run for a few meters (yards) down the fall line and then, with a slight tilting of your knees and pelvis, shift the skis onto their inside edge. The skis will immediately start to turn and you will need to lean your whole body over more to combat the centrifugal force. It should be done in such a way that the body lean starts from the bottom and not from the top: in other words the lead should be in the order knees-pelvis-torso, and not vice versa.

The turn continues until the moment when you feel yourself being "pulled" towards the next turn. At this point simply change edges, as well as the way that your body is leaning, so as to start a new turn.

Points to note

The precise moment just described (in other words where one turn ends and another one begins) is difficult to pinpoint. It depends on many factors: speed, design characteristics of the skis, and the arc on which the turn has started. It is up to the skier (in this case to the carver) to recognize the moment when he should no longer combat the centrifugal force (in order to carry on in the turn he is engaged on) but use it in order to start the new turn easily. If you miss this moment you will

then be obliged to make more pronounced body movements to be able to effect the next turn.

In the wide carved turn body movements are usually reduced to the minimum, in that there is no need to drive the skis with constant shifts in body weight. At most it may be necessary to use your joints to absorb some of the gravitational force which is naturally increased in a turn. The skier's action could be compared to the action of a car's shock absorbers on a bend. In this way the skier prepares himself for the start of the turn with his legs straight, to then bend them slowly as the turn progresses, thus absorbing its flattening effect.

Carved turns can make the whole body lean in a striking manner. Leaning in this way could induce the skier to put his hand on the slope in order to correct his own balance or simply to increase the excitement by trying to touch the snow. But it is important to avoid doing these turns with the sole aim of touching the snow with your hand. Such an action would mean excessive unweighting of the skis, which would notably increase the trajectory of the arc (in other words the skis would start to go in a straight line). Besides this, there is a risk of hand or shoulder injury, especially on soft snow where the hand would sink, causing a lot of friction. To avoid injury and to make it possible to set your hand down for balance, special hand guards can be worn.

NO: Avoid leaning from the shoulders; you risk losing control of your outside ski.
NO: Do not try to touch the snow with your hand at all.
YES: Body leaning correctly, with the lean starting from the feet.

Narrow turns

• Description

These turns are very different from traditional ones and can only be performed with carving skis. Their radius can also be very small (6–8 m [20–25 feet]), but they need to be performed quickly, by someone who is experienced and physically fit. Until a few years ago these turns were the prerogative of carvers; now, thanks to specialized skis, they can be performed even by slalom competitors (i.e. those involved in slalom).

All turns are performed with maximum carving, and therefore you must concentrate on getting the maximum response from your skis. It is better to try out this type of exercise for the first time on easy or medium slopes.

• Positioning

Narrow carved turns need much less lateral space than wide ones, but you should remember that the last turn (the one that you will use to stop) will be wider and will traverse the trail. So before

In the short-radius carved turn, the skis are fully edged, while the arms behave in the turn as they would if you were running.

finishing the maneuver with a wide turn, you should check that no other skier is on a collision path.

• Technique

Slide a few meters (yards) down the fall line (till you reach a speed less than that used for the wide carved turns). Then, with a firm tilt of the knees and the pelvis, edge the skis on the inside of the turn to be performed. The skis will immediately enter into the turn. You then instantly abandon this turn and change edges, thus initiating the next turn. Whether or not you use the poles is optional, but a good active rhythm, dynamic and highly punctuated, can be achieved without poles.

Points to note

You should not perform a series of narrow carved turns on steep slopes; this would be to risk building up excessive and uncontrollable speed. The starting speed should also be moderate to avoid unpleasant repercussions. To perform the first few turns you will probably also need to make your leg bending and straightening quite pronounced (especially if the start speed is reduced), in order to turn the skis quickly and get into the desired rhythm.

360° turns

• Description

This is the great novelty in carving, the turn that more than any other sets this technique apart from traditional methods. Until very recently this type of turn was the prerogative of snowboarders, who were the first to start the trend of pure carved turns (i.e. the "sliced" turn, or the turn with maximum carving).

It is not an easy maneuver. On the contrary, to perform a 360° turn with continuous pure carving, you need suitable terrain, technical expertise, balance, experience, and the right skis. To perform a 360° turn with traditional skis would be inconceivable, in that you would need to be going at breakneck speed and have an enormous amount of clear trail available. With carving skis it is possible to perform a 360° turn with a radius of about 15 m (45 feet) (or even 5–7 m [15–20 feet] with very short, shaped skis).

• Positioning

Even more than with carved turns, in which the movements of skiers are atypical and unusual (moving sideways and towards the mountain), the 360° turn needs particular care so that the carver's path does not cross that of other skiers. It is therefore advisable to make sure that there is enough space to carry out the full circle, and that no other skier is about to enter the zone you have chosen to perform it in.

In addition the choice of slope is also of fundamental importance; you need a medium-steep slope at the end of a steeper descent.

• Technique

Allow your skis to run for a few meters (yards) down the fall line (until you have built up a speed similar to the speed used for wide carved turns), and then edge your skis with a subtle tilting of knees and pelvis.

The entry into the turn must be progressive, not sudden, and carved up till

the moment when the ski tips are turned again uphill, towards the mountain. This is where experience comes in.

By leaning back very slightly (this will anyway follow on from your body's position in relation to the slope) shift your weight a bit more onto the tails, keeping the skis well edged.

Further twisting the tails round will complete the spiral turn.

The aim of course is to describe a path that is more like a circle than a spiral.

The method described is the simplest way of achieving a 360° turn.

Points to note

The type of snow is the deciding factor in this maneuver; the ideal type of snow is cold and well compacted. In some conditions, especially a new fall of snow or snow that is beginning to deteriorate at the end of the season (i.e. snow on which a sure, safe grip cannot be guaranteed), it is almost impossible to perform a 360° turn.

Central stage of the 360° turn.

Hand support

It sometimes happens in carved turns that the slant of the body is so extreme that it becomes necessary to touch the ground with a hand in order to re-establish balance. In this case the hand should be set down lightly in front of you on the inside of the turn and allowed to slide over the surface of the snow.

This action, which in theory was only ever to have been a simple mechanical prop, has instead been responsible for creating an exciting link between the carver and the slope. Skiers have discovered the pleasure of caressing the snow with their hand during a turn, as the climax of a movement that is as risky as it is enjoyable.

Some skiers, right from the start of the turn, set off (wrongly!) with the intention of bringing their hand down to ground level to touch the snow, forgetting the other movements that are necessary if the turn is to succeed properly. If it is not done in the right way, putting your hand down on the ground can in some cases turn out to be very risky. Your hand may well in fact become buried in the snow, at the risk of injury not only to your hand, but also to

your knee and shoulder. Carving hand guards serve the purpose of allowing your hand to glide better over the snow, while at the same time guaranteeing a minimum touch down so that balance can be maintained. These hand guards, available in different shapes, are only for use on ground of uniform quality with well-compacted snow, and their use on wet snow and unknown terrain should be avoided.

Below and left: examples of how hand guards are used to touch down on the snow in ultra-carved turns.

BUT SKIING HAS ALWAYS BEEN CARVING!

The technique of carving was born with the introduction of skis that were highly shaped, although carving has always been a characteristic of skis, ever since Nansen's time (at the end of the 19th century). It has always been known that shaping is the essential quality that makes a ski turn, but only in recent years have trails become wide and smooth enough for skiers to take a real advantage of this factor.

The first carving competitions took place in 1995 in the United States, on a course of eight turns designated by colored trail markers, but the followers of this sport were few. It was in Europe that the fashion for carving really took off, above all thanks to a handful of people who had faith in the technical qualities of the ultra-shaped ski, and in its use in teaching. The front runners were the Swiss, who made carving their technical forte, and used it as a publicity stunt; this had a very noticeable influence on all the ski-schools of the Alpine nations. In 1996 the CIA was founded (Carving International Association), which saw a number of Swiss, Italian, French, and Austrian experts involved in organizing a series of competitions leading to a final overall placing. It was an outstanding success; the competitions, which took place in the most famous Alpine resorts, were attended by thousands of enthusiasts.

CARVED TURNS

HEAD TILTED SO THAT
THE WHOLE BODY IS
NOT LEANING OVER

ARMS MOVING SO AS
TO REMAIN AS A PIVOT
FOR THE TURN

HAND SOMETIMES SET DOWN
TO IMPROVE BALANCE ON
THE SKI EDGES

LEGS SLANTED TO ENSURE MAXIMUM COUNTERACTION OF CENTRIFUGAL FORCES

BOOTS IN MAXIMUM POSSIBLE CONTACT WITH SNOW

EXCEPTIONAL CIRCUMSTANCES

Introduction

Occasionally, even in the most renowned resorts, you will find stretches of trails where the snow and ground conditions are a departure from the norm, so that technique must be adapted to suit the situation. You are most likely to encounter the following:
• bumps (moguls)
• very steep gradients
• ice

Bumps or moguls

For some people a slope with bumps can be the most pleasurable experience in skiing, for others the most unpleasant, according to individual tastes and skills. Some of the large skiing resorts set aside one run as a bump area, for the delight of bump fans (and also–it may as well be said–to save on the use of trail machines).

Methods for getting over bumps are as varied as the shapes of the bumps themselves, and the skill used in tackling them is an expression of the skier's imaginative use of technique.

Nevertheless, the two main methods may be summarized as follows:
• Getting over the bump by turning the skis on its lip, or summit. For this the legs are bent in order to absorb all the strain; the upper body controls

Above right: performing a turn on a bump; the change in direction takes place on the lip of the bump. Below right: going over bumps by following the fall line.

balance by remaining turned towards
the valley and leaning slightly forward;
the ski pole is held ready for planting.
• Getting over the bump by skiing over
into the hollow. Your legs must be
straightened to keep your skis in contact
with the snow as they enter the hollow;
the upper body controls balance by
remaining turned towards the valley and
straightening up slightly; the pole is held
ready for planting.

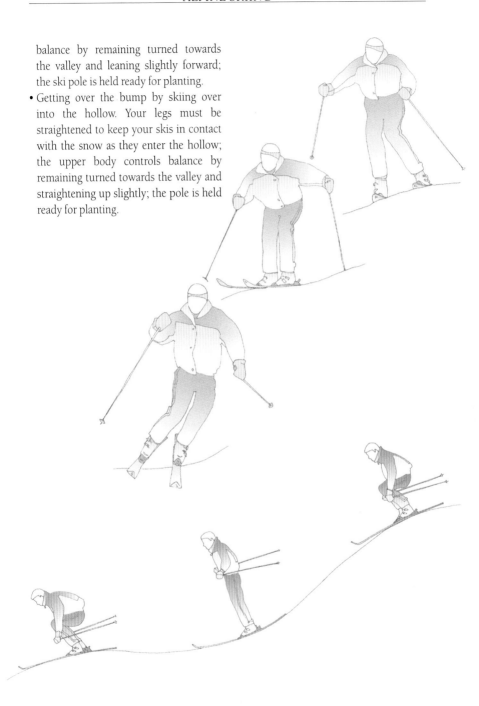

Skiing on steep gradients

Skiing on steep slopes is an experience highly prized by expert skiers, who are often hunting for trails with very steep drops.

Without going into the subject of skiing in extreme conditions, the skiability of a steep slope is heavily affected by the quality of the snow. The best conditions are when the snow is very cold and well compacted, so that it is possible to get a safe grip with expert economical use of edging and weighting. However, these ideal conditions are rarely encountered, usually only in the very early morning in the coldest months of the year, in January or February. More often, in fact, the surface of a very steep slope will turn out to be icy or covered in bumps (moguls). In addition to this, there will often be an alternation of bumps and ice patches only a few meters (yards) apart, turning the trail into a veritable assault course.

All that will be given here are a few hints as to the general technique to be adopted on steep slopes; for how to deal with icy slopes or bumps, you should refer to the relevant sections.

On steep slopes short-radius turns are the most frequently used, because of the

necessity of keeping a constant check on speed. These turns should be performed in the traditional manner, namely with side-slipping on the turns rather than carving, since carving requires broader movements to unweight the skis and turn them quickly. Short-radius carved turns can in any case only be performed when the surface is smooth and uniform, and are generally only used by expert skiers, though even they find that the greatest problem is often loss of balance, i.e. shifting the body's weight too far back. This is a very common occurrence, caused by the continual acceleration and braking that is entailed on steep slopes.

As a rule, therefore, your body should be leaning slightly forward before launching into a series of narrow turns on a steep slope.

For less expert skiers, finding oneself at the top of a very steep drop can seem a terrifying prospect. The important thing is not to panic, and to reject the idea of taking off your skis. Do not forget that this is exactly what skiing equipment is designed for: to aid controlled descent, as opposed to boots and hands or, even worse, your backside.

Bearing this in mind, then, and by keeping your weight on your feet (weighting the downhill ski slightly more) you can go down without making a single turn, by simply using side-slipping (*dérapage*). If the worst comes to the worst, you can simply side-step down. When the

Skiing down very steep slopes requires excellent balance and very strong legs.

slope becomes a little less steep or is nearly at an end, and you feel a little more secure, turn your skis to the fall line with a firm movement.

If, however, you have completely lost your nerve, do not be embarrassed to continue side-slipping till you reach the bottom of the slope.

Skiing on ice

Ice on the trails occurs predominantly when the weather is warmer, in the spring, when the snow gets melted by the sun during the day, while sub-zero temperatures at night cause it to freeze again. In these sorts of weather conditions ice patches can appear on the trail, especially on south-facing slopes which are exposed to the sun's rays for longer during the day. The same thing can occur even during the day on steep south-east facing slopes, where the snow first melts and then freezes with the early afternoon shadows.

In addition to this, the sliding turns of skiers play their part in sweeping aside the covering of snow, causing large ice patches to appear everywhere.

Ice on the trails rarely covers a very extensive area. It is usually found in patches, limited to about 5–20 m (15–60 feet) in size. In any case, the most important thing when it comes to ice patches is the state of your skis; if the edges are not sharp even a very capable skier can do very little. At most, an expert skier can skillfully disguise the fact that his skis have lost their grip, but if his edges are not sharp he will never be able to rely on getting a good hold. The edges must in fact cut into the ice, and if they do not anyone will end up slithering uncontrollably downhill.

Having made it clear that the condition of the skis is the most important factor, the best method of crossing a patch of ice is to anticipate it. The moment you spot one you should make sure that you begin your turn before you reach it; in this way by the time you get to it your skis will already be edged enough to ensure a good grip.

If you are only crossing the ice patch in one direction, all you need to do is make sure that your skis are well edged before crossing it.

It is trickier if you do not notice the ice patch in advance and it catches you by surprise in the middle of a turn, causing you to slide. In this situation you should see if increased edging is sufficient to give you the grip that you need. If this is not

Above: coming upon a patch of ice without warning demands very quick reactions from the whole body in order to maintain balance.

enough to stop you slipping, then you must bring your legs up and center your weight again while you try to regain edge grip. It may be necessary to quickly change direction. Clearly all this has to take place in a matter of seconds, with perfect balance maintained throughout.

THE COMPETITION SKIER
Introduction

A competition skier is a true athlete, someone who devotes himself to the sport on a daily basis, either as a professional or as an amateur.

A competition skier normally begins training in late spring or early summer by working on his overall fitness and then refines his technique in late summer and autumn. Winter is entirely devoted to competitions.

As has already been pointed out in the section on the history of skiing, competition skiing has always been the driving factor in the development of new techniques and technology. The champion skiers have set the example for ski-schools, young competitors and recreational skiers, and in some cases have even brought certain ski resorts to worldwide fame.

Alpine competition skiing comprises four specialized areas: slalom, giant slalom, super-giant, and downhill racing. A fifth specialized area is combination skiing, which entails adding up the points gained in slalom and in downhill skiing at the same event. There is no one competitive technique that can be considered the best for all the areas of competition. As a general rule it could be said that the most important idea is to complete the whole run with as little braking as possible.

"Competition" skiers are not only great champions but also amateurs who participate in local events.

Slalom

The slalom course is marked out by single poles, colored alternately blue and red, and set 8–15 m (25–45 feet) apart by the course plotter. Participants weave through these poles at high speed. This makes the action very exciting to watch. For many years now sprung poles have been used, which give way when hit by the competitors, but remain fixed in the spot where they have been planted. In the normal turn of a good skier the skis will follow a trajectory outside the pole, while the body, leaning over to combat the centrifugal force, passes inside the line of the pole. The skiers actually strike the poles and need to wear special helmets, hand guards, and shin guards to avoid injuries. Slalom competitions take place in two heats, and the competition time of each competitor is obtained by adding together the time of both attempts. The competition course includes "horizontal" and "vertical" gates, and it is the combination of these that creates the so-called "figures."

The technique used in slalom

The main technique of slalom is to make a rapid series of turns while braking as little as possible. This rapid series of turns forces the skier to change edges very quickly, while still keeping his balance and not slowing the speed of his progress at all. Given that space allowed for each turn is very small, the latter results in a combination of sliding and carving. The recent introduction of very shaped skis, however, is changing even slalom turns into round carved turns.

The skier's movements, besides being very quick, must also be reduced to the essential: his feet and legs must shift very quickly to locate the angle needed to create the turn, while his torso and arms must remain in an almost fixed position to provide pivotal inertia. Besides this, his arms must always be held out in front, so that he can strike the poles with his hands. Exaggerated leg bending and straightening are not involved; rather, the skier has to decide at each turn which movements will

be most effective in changing edge. Sometimes the skier has time, between one pole and the next, to straighten up slightly, which allows him to switch edging and so to initiate the next turn; at other times his legs remain bent and he has to use his feet under his body to steer the skis into the turn.

Giant slalom

The giant slalom course is marked by gates that are made of two poles linked by a cloth. The gates are colored alternately blue and red, and set at a distance of between 15 and about 25–30 m (45 and 75–90 feet) apart, at the discretion of the course plotter.

Because of the speed at which he progresses (which can be as much as 80 km/h [50 mph]), the skier's actions must be highly dynamic and concentrated, using all his balance and strength. In giant slalom the gates are again made of sprung poles, which bend as the skier passes (if he strikes them) and remain firmly anchored in place.

The fact that they are allowed to strike the pole has meant that even in giant slalom skiers tend to execute turns ever closer to the gates, which is advantageous for their speed.

Despite the fact that the poles are flexible, striking them can be violent and dangerous, especially for young competitors, who wear specially protected clothing.

The technique used in giant slalom

The main technique of giant slalom is to perform a dynamic and intense series of turns while braking as little as possible. Edge changing involves broader movements than are used in ordinary slalom, with more pronounced and obvious bending and straightening, but the exact nature of these movements depends entirely on the peculiarities of each individual course and slope. Courses which are sharply angled and very steep slopes require more pronounced movements; the skier straightens his body for the whole of the first part of the turn, and bends his legs for the second half. On courses with less sharp turns and on flatter runs, on the other hand, you will often see the skiers almost motionless in an aerodynamic posture in their efforts to obtain the maximum glide from their skis. During the curve it is essential for the skier to be able to control his center of gravity as huge centrifugal forces come into play. In more recent years the use of shaped skis has brought about a marked increase in the restraining forces; the skiers have to be able to withstand extreme loads (more than three times their body weight) owing to the fact that shaped skis increase the amount of carving and reduce sliding.

Supergiant

Supergiant is the most recent introduction to the competition scene. It began in 1986, in an attempt to create an event that would draw the crowds and make televised viewing more interesting. The supergiant course is a cross between the giant slalom and downhill racing. The gates are two poles linked by a cloth, are alternately blue and red, and the distance between them is never normally less than 30 m (90 feet).

The technique used in supergiant racing
The main technique needed for supergiant is the ability to build up high speeds on a course that requires wide but sharp turns.

The skiers who are emerging in this discipline are among the strongest and bravest ever seen. They have both technical ability and sheer strength, and are cool headed and decisive at the most demanding and risky moments. It is no coincidence that the best supergiant skiers are also the top competitors in giant slalom and in downhill racing. The way that the skis are steered is the same as in giant slalom, although some modern supergiant courses look more like downhill courses.

Downhill racing

Downhill racing is the oldest sport in Alpine skiing. It has always provided a display of courage and skill coupled with high gliding speeds. A downhill course is largely given its character by the location, in that the track follows the twists and undulations of the trail.

On the track numerous gates are set up, signaling the course boundaries, and in some instances limiting speed. The gates are made of red plastic poles linked by a red or orange cloth; these cloths are larger than those used in giant slalom. The distance between the gates depends entirely on the conformation of the slope. Occasionally, when visibility is poor, small red flags are placed on the left side of the track and green ones on the right.

The technique used in downhill racing

There are few guidelines for downhill racing, but the competitive element is high. The aim is to complete the course at great speed, braking as little as possible. The average speed in a race is around 100 km/h (60 mph), with speeds of over 140 km/h (90 mph) at some points. In these circumstances variations in the gradient of the trail become an enormous

obstacle to be overcome, using the highest skill and concentration. The downhill skier must possess one fundamental ability: he must remain calm and decisive, regardless of the speed at which he is careering down the slope, and the risk of resultant injury.

In a downhill race certainly the most exciting displays of skill are seen in the jumps caused by the sudden changes in gradient. The skier approaches the jump by drawing his legs right up to his body to minimize the dragging effect of the air. If the skier "opens" his body, he is likely to be thrown off balance backwards, and to land on the tails of his skis, risking a fall or knee injury.

Equally exciting to watch are turns performed at high speed, in which the skier tries to locate the ideal trajectory where there will be the minimum friction produced by the snow on his skis or the air on his body. In the less demanding turns the skier is able to maintain the so-called "egg" position, which means that the legs are tucked up as tightly as possible under the body, so as to be as aerodynamic as possible. The modern downhill skier is usually an excellent all-round athlete, who is also able to tackle supergiant and giant slalom courses successfully.

3
OFF-TRAIL SKIING

The various types of snow that you will encounter off trail (off piste). The ideal approach, advice for beginners, and common faults.

Groomed versus ungroomed snow

Right from the start the word "trail" has been used to mean a place where the snow has been deliberately "plowed" to make it easier to ski through and to improve downhill skiing (i.e. "piste"). Plowed snow on the trails has made the job much easier for millions of beginners, allowing downhill and cross-country skiing to become sports for the masses.

In today's ski resorts the snow is constantly groomed by the trail machines. As a result, off-trail skiing is on the whole a more difficult exercise, in that unplowed snow, in which the skis tend to sink, makes it much more tiring to change direction.

So be wary of anyone who suggests to you that off-trail skiing is fun and utterly easy. It is easy, for someone who has quite a bit of experience of the various techniques, so as to ensure their own safety, and for anyone who has done sufficient step-by-step training for these conditions. On the other hand it is difficult for those who approach it in a haphazard manner, taking a gamble on something that they have never tried before, when they quite likely have very little skill or experience of skiing in general. It is equally difficult for those who have learnt to ski using very shaped skis, performing only round, carved turns; in unprepared snow it is more a question of making adjustments in edging not just for the type of turn desired but also for the type of snow encountered.

Off-trail the snow is not "groomed" by the trail machines, which means that the condition of the snow varies more, and the right techniques must be used.

The skier and off-trail areas

At the beginning of the 20th century those who wanted to learn to ski had to do so on unprepared snow, or at any rate on snow that was only roughly groomed by the skis of the skiers themselves. Nowadays anyone who wants to learn to ski has nursery slopes available where the incline is very slight and the snow is very smooth. The next step for developing skiers is to try out progressively more demanding runs, until, having attained a high level of skill, they are able to tackle the most difficult runs. After spending a few years trying out the resorts with the best and the most famous runs, it is very probable that these skiers, now expert, will decide to test their abilities off trail. If they then find this a satisfying experience, they may become such off-trail enthusiasts that they travel the world (funds permitting) in search of resorts that offer organized off-trail skiing, accompanied by skiing instructors. They may eventually wish to try out some of the great skiing sensations and the extreme gradients that can only be reached by helicopter (Canada, the Alps, and the Caucasus are famous for their heliski itineraries). Some may even take up ski-mountaineering, which takes the passion for snow beyond straightforward downhill skiing, involving the mountaineering skier in a much closer rapport with the mountain. Off-trail areas that lie right beside the trails are the most popular; they are

naturally much easier to get to with ski lifts and it is easy to get back onto the trails from them. These areas can provide gentle, open off-trail skiing, but sometimes they can also hide very dangerous traps. Rocks and ravines are often found where the trails have been dug out of a forbidding and rocky mountainside, while pits, stones, and roots hidden by the snow are the pitfalls of wooded areas. Unless accompanied by an expert guide, you should on no

With experience you will learn to evaluate the state of the snow, based on weather conditions and how much sun it is exposed to; you can then pick your route with foreknowledge of possible problems.

account venture off-trail on summer glaciers. However, off-trail areas beside runs that go through gentle grazing land at medium altitude are less risky.

All this is not intended to scare off the reader, nor to approach this wonderful branch of skiing in a contradictory way. All that is intended is to make it very clear that the skier who intends to try out off-trail skiing must be acquainted with the area where he intends to try it. All too often in recent years we have witnessed tragically serious accidents when skiers have ventured outside the trails. Partly responsible for this are the media, and those film producers who, simply in order to find convincing ways of selling their products, have not hesitated to entice people with spectacular images of skiers in fresh snow, inviting skiers to experience the "adrenaline rush," the "no limits" scenario, as if it were a banal video game. This is how free-riding started up, a pretty risky type of off-trail skiing only within the reach of a small minority, who have well and truly caught the skiing bug, captivated by its spectacular, eye-catching nature. It is unwise to try to persuade others to ski off trail, unless they are at the same time well-informed as to what is possible, and as to the limitations imposed by the mountain itself; otherwise off-trail skiing ceases to be the fun and safe sport that it should be.

None of this takes away the buzz of off-trail skiing which you will certainly experience; your feeling of exhilaration lifts you sky high, as your body is immersed in powdery snow and floats as if hanging between the mountain and the horizon, as your ski disappears for a moment under the white blanket and reappears as if by magic after a breath-taking moment.

Carving skis and snowboards are also suitable for off-trail use.

Different types of snow and methods for dealing with them

Ungroomed snow is much affected by changes in the weather, which determine the consistency of the snow covering. The greatest alterations are caused by shifts in temperature, which can sometimes change the snow from dry and powdery to wet and heavy in a matter of hours. But the position of the run in relation to the angle of the sun's rays can also bring about marked changes in the course of a day. So it is easy to deduce that the best and the most consistent snow is snow that has been kept very cold at a constant temperature, though there are also occasions when, even in the spring, the snow becomes a pleasant surface to ski on as soon as it is warmed by the sun's rays.

As a general rule, the best off-trail snow is found at high altitudes, where the cold is more intense, and where humidity levels and air pressure are lower. Snow-covered mountain slopes facing north and north-east are those which have the best quality of snow covering, in that the sun's rays in the daytime reach them only at an oblique angle and for very few hours (in some cases not at all). Slopes facing south and south-west, on the other hand, because of their exposure to the sun, are almost never suitable for off-trail skiing, and in some cases can present the risk of snow becoming dislodged (avalanches).

Besides temperature, humidity, air pressure, and sunlight, wind also affects the snow covering. Either during or just after a fall of snow the wind can pile up the snow in leeward areas and sweep clear the windward slopes. The different types of snow and the subtle shifts in technique required for each are described on the following pages.

From top to bottom: wet snow, wind-blown snow, and damp snow.

Powder snow

Powder snow is often also called soft, and it is the most enjoyable of all to ski on. It is produced by snowfalls in temperatures of a few degrees below freezing, and it is made up of fine crystals, either single or sticking together in small groups, which have not yet become compacted. A certain amount of air remains trapped between these crystals which makes the covering of snow very light. To give you an idea of its consistency, if you scoop some up in your hand, you

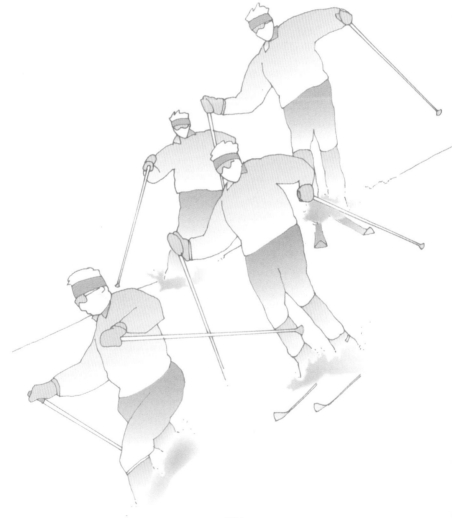

cannot make it into a snowball! This particular characteristic, of being light and insubstantial, means that it has no weight at all under skis; both your skis and your legs inevitably sink, but resurface easily with the smallest backward tilt of your feet.

Skiing on (or rather, "in") this type of snow, equates to a skiing experience of harmonious fluidity; there must be no sudden movement, while the pressure of the skis must be smooth and constant.

As far as technique is concerned, you must take care to keep your weight carefully centered, and not shift your feet too much; you must not lean on the back of your boots too much, or attempt to turn using only the tails of your skis. Leaning slightly backwards can help the ski tips to float up, but a constant leaning back position is not right for this situation.

To change direction all that is needed is to bend and straighten in a barely perceptible manner, gentle as the turn itself, without ever turning your skis too much. This last concept (one that holds good for all types of untouched snow) needs to be made quite clear: turns should never be too tight, which means that the curve should finish before you reach a point where your skis are at right angles to the fall line, at which point you risk tumbling downhill all the while that the skis are still completing their turn. Another piece of useful advice is to keep your skis tightly together, so that your weight is more evenly distributed over both skis. On the runs turns are frequently performed by putting all the weight on the outside ski.

On unprepared snow, however, if the outside ski is weighted more it sinks further than the inside one. The outside ski would then, as it sinks, turn sharply, and passing under your body would send you tumbling on the downhill side. It is therefore better to weight your skis equally and to hold them as close together as possible.

Finally the poles: if the snow is very soft, so that your body sinks markedly, your arms should be held higher, with the pole ready for planting. The pole plant will not of course feel the same, or be as effective, as on the trail, but it will help to unweight your skis at the beginning of the turn, and will serve as a reference for your torso, which should keep as still as possible and remain facing downhill.

Damp snow

When the temperature during and after a snowfall is close to zero, the snow covering that forms is more solid and compact. The snow crystals tend to lump together, and at the same time there is less air in between the crystals. To give you an idea of the consistency of this snow, if you scoop it up in your hand it is easy to squash it into a snowball. Skiing on this type of snow feels heavier (and in fact the density of this snow is greater) and more tiring, owing to the fact that when the skis sink in it requires a more pronounced movement (compared to in powder snow) to bring them to the surface again. This does not mean that this sort of snow is difficult; it is, in fact, one of the best types of off-trail snow! The movements made are a bit firmer, but fluidity and continuity of movement are still essential, with slow bending and straightening, and all sudden shifts of weight are to be avoided.

The rule of keeping your weight evenly distributed on both skis still holds good for this type of snow; the skis must never be too far apart. Although, in general, your body will sink less compared to in powder snow, you are much more likely to be affected by the problem of one ski sinking deeper than the other. This is because the thicker consistency of the snow increases the responsiveness of the ski that is more weighted (probably the outside one),

causing the turn to finish in a swift and often unexpected manner, which sends the skier flying in a downhill direction. So, in this type of snow also, you should avoid allowing your skis to point straight across the fall line, and give preference to turns with wider trajectories.

Pole planting can be very useful; however, it is essential to refrain from rotational movements of your upper body.

Occasionally, when the skis begin to sink too deeply, it can be very effective to bring your feet up, while keeping your torso steady to maintain the center of gravity.

Crusty snow

If the weather is fine and sunny for a few days following a snowfall, the increased warmth and the effect of the sun's rays cause the top layers of snow to begin to melt. This top layer becomes high in water content, which freezes again during the lower night-time temperatures. The result is that a few days after the snowfall the top layer becomes hard and crusty. How thick this crust is depends totally upon the extent of the daytime warming, i.e. to what depth the surface snow has been melting in the day and re-freezing at night. On average, however, a few centimeters (1–2 inches) are enough to produce typically crusty snow, which can be very deceptive and difficult to ski on.

The main problem is that it is not possible to determine at exactly what moment the crust of snow will give way under the weight of the skis. The smallest shifts in weight can cause it to give way, and this can occur at the start, middle, or end of a turn. As an approximate rule it is always from the middle of the turn onwards that the crust breaks, owing to the increasing load on the skis. But this is not to say that the crust is of uniform thickness, and this makes it all the more difficult to predict when it will give way.

You therefore need a high degree of sensitivity to recognize even the slightest subsiding of the surface under your skis, relying on all your on-trail and off-trail experience. The moment the crust begins to subside, you must be ready to reduce the load on your skis, by bending your legs a little or even by swiftly pulling your feet right up to absorb the weight. Being able to swiftly redistribute weight in changeable conditions is normally only possible for very advanced skiers, and the truth of it is that even the best of skiers find that they cannot get out of crusty snow unscathed.

At any rate it is clear that lighter and more sensitive skiers, whose style is less aggressive, are better able to manage this type of surface.

Again, in snow of this type, everyone should follow the rule of distributing their weight evenly on both skis, and avoid giving preference to either one.

Ski poles, besides providing rhythm and helping to lighten your body, can be very useful at moments when you risk losing your balance.

Wind-blown snow

Amazing patterns are created, shifting snow plays around with the contours of the mountain, and small rocks and hollows become collaborators in a natural artistic project, when the wind carries away the soft, fresh snow as it falls. This is how snow accumulates in all the wind-protected areas, to varying degrees of depth and lateral spread, while in areas exposed to the wind all that is left is the old layer of snow, the previously formed blanket, polished and swept clean until it becomes ice.

Off-trail areas then become a continual alternation between ice (or hard snow) and soft deep snow, all in undulating, sinuous mounds which are reminiscent of the sea when it freezes unexpectedly during a storm. The surface is amazing to look at but also very deceptive, since in the space of a few meters (yards) your skis can sink, bringing you to a halt, or slip on ice and shoot out to the side.

It is impossible to draw up a strict code of rules for skiing on such varied terrain; once again it is the skier's ability that controls the situation. In such conditions experience plays a vital role, and the most important skill, in wind-blown snow, is to be able to recognize areas where the snow may well be crusty or soft, and to prepare yourself in time to deal with them.

With the former (hard, crusty snow) you must be prepared to control a sudden acceleration of your skis; if you manage this well, this will be in a forward direction rather than sideways. This is done simply by keeping your weight carefully centered; try to avoid pushing your feet forwards, and hold your torso and pelvis in a slightly forward position.

With the latter (soft snow) you must be ready to deal with your skis possibly braking very suddenly, as they sink deeper into the snow: make sure that your weight is well centered in anticipation of this sudden slowing down by tilting your torso and pelvis back slightly.

In both cases your arms should be held wide from the body in a slightly forward position to improve balance, with your ski poles held ready to help you if need be.

Wet snow

Wet snow means snow that falls in the mildest months of the season, and that is subject to very marked changes in composition, owing to the daytime rises in temperature that naturally occur in springtime. Most of all wet snow means snow that is melting, and is as a result full of small water particles, which give it very high density.

Wet snow is therefore very heavy and subsides easily underfoot, and its particles tend to slip around among themselves, as well as on the compacted layers below (this means the previous snow covering, which is often icy, or the ground itself). Wet snow is the least suitable for off-trail ventures, since there is a high risk of the upper layer slipping, and thus of snowslides.

As far as technique is concerned, this type of snow requires a greater effort on the part of the skier than other types, because, in the event of the skis sinking, the action required to bring the tips back up is much more tiring. Besides this, wet snow does not allow easy sliding, and so a final problem that should be mentioned is very slow progress and a lack of momentum.

Overall, wet snow, because of the associated risks, is not considered suitable for off-trail skiing.

Some advice for beginners

Certain characteristics of off-trail skiing have now been described. You might at this point easily be led to believe that off-trail skiing is only within the capabilities of top-level skiers. Even among experts it is true that there is a widespread belief that you cannot ski off trail unless you are a more than competent skier.

In reality, even less expert skiers can be suitably prepared for virgin snow, so long as they observe a careful progression towards increasingly difficult techniques and terrain.

The following are the main requirements for an easy approach:

- a gentle slope beside a trail, that is easily accessible
- new (fresh and untouched) snow, that is not too deep, i.e. maximum 10–15 cm (4–6 inches)
- cold, powdery snow, that you will find in the morning after a snowfall; you should avoid the heavy, wet snow that is typical in the spring periods

The first venture off trail for either adults or children is a formative experience. The latter are often accompanied by their ski instructor so that they can practice in different situations, and build up their understanding of different movements. Off-trail is without doubt one of the most beautiful and enjoyable settings for skiing, where the variety of conditions encountered encourages learning and sets your imagination free.

· An inexperienced skier can start on short untouched stretches beside the trail, on gently sloping ground. However, it must be pointed out that skis go slower in fresh snow than on the trails, and very flat slopes are therefore unsuitable.

Ungroomed snow beside the trail is the ideal place to try out off-trail skiing for the first time.

Here is a list of useful exercises for familiarizing yourself with unprepared snow:

- practice walking with your skis at a slight diagonal slant
- make small changes of direction by lifting one ski and turning its tip out
- starting from the trail, slide at low speed, at a diagonal, into the untouched snow; next alter the angle that you cross it by pointing your skis more downhill

- on a gentle slope, point your skis decisively downhill, by lifting up the tip of first one ski and then the other
- on a gentle slope, aim downhill and ski for a bit with your skis very close together, and then for a bit with your skis slightly more apart (but never with legs wide apart)
- on a gentle slope, head downhill and practice bending and straightening up; next practice shifting your center of gravity backwards and forwards
- on a gentle slope, head downhill and plant your poles alternately; next, do this coupled with bending and straightening: hold the poles at the ready as you bend, and plant them as you straighten up
- on a medium-steep slope, practice gentle, slow parallel turns, while trying to keep your torso facing the valley.

These few brief hints are no substitute for a good ski instructor, who will not forget the psychological angle as he guides his pupils through the process of learning.

YES: To gain confidence in fresh snow, start by gliding off the trail onto the ungroomed snow without changing direction at all.
YES: Then attempt the start of a turn, but be ready to correct your balance at any moment.
NO: If the weight of your body is all on one leg, one ski will sink in further than the other and you will risk losing control of your skis.

Off-trail skis

Off-trail equipment need be no different from that used on the trail. However, there are some skis that are better suited than others to untouched snow. The most versatile are all-round or free-ride skis, or even high-performance skis, but not competition skis. All the skis just mentioned are on average 5–10 cm (2–4 inches) shorter than the skis used by recreational skiers a decade ago, and have more flexible tips and heavier tails. You should avoid using skis that are too long or rigid, like those used in competitions, and skis that are very heavy or fitted with plates or risers. Even carving skis, which are very shaped, short, and fitted with plates, are likely to be more of a hindrance than a help. In fact, although they have very wide blades at the tip, which in theory are suitable for "floating" in

Off-trail skis should not be too long, and only minimally shaped; they should be wider at the waist than skis ordinarily used for downhill trail skiing.

fresh snow, they are fairly narrow in the middle under your feet (at their "waist") and they are weighted down by the plates; all this means that they tend to sink. Besides this, in untouched snow excessive shaping is unnecessary, in that you do not need to try and carve turns as you do on the trail; furthermore excessive shaping can create problems on variable terrain, such as wind-driven snow, or even mixed terrain where the ground is not level.

Then there are specifically designed powder snow skis. These so-called "fat" skis are short and very wide and ensure optimum flotation, but they are less suitable for hard surfaces.

You should pay particular attention to the bindings, which must be of a very high quality. The strain on them when they are forced open in fresh snow is less intense, but much more varied than the strain put on them on the trail. The bindings must be guaranteed to open in all directions, including diagonally and uphill.

Lastly, you are advised to make sure that your skis are well waxed; trail snow allows skis to glide, or run, easily even without wax, but fresh snow, especially when it is cold or damp, has a braking effect, rendering your movements less efficient.

Common faults

Skiing on ungroomed snow often makes people over-anxious, which in turn affects the quality of their skiing. The biggest worry arises from the conviction that the skis will be difficult to turn, while in fact all that it requires is the very same movements as those already put into practice on the trail.

Here is a list of common faults:

• Leaning too far back: fearing that the tips of the skis will sink in too deep, skiers tend to adopt an exaggerated leaning back stance. It is true that slightly leaning back can sometimes prevent the tips from sinking in (when, for example, you are moving from a patch of hard snow to a patch of soft or damp snow), but

Right: feeling unsure of the crusty surface can make you tense your muscles too much, which will tire you out quickly. Below: body leaning back too much, and thrown off balance on the inside of the turn.

134

Above: being in too much of a hurry to turn often unbalances the body and results in a fall. Right: the skis are too far apart and difficult to control.

constant leaning back is never necessary and can make you tense your muscles too much, which in turn can make it more difficult to maneuver your skis.

• Muscular tension: apprehension during the first few attempts at off-trail skiing usually makes people tense their bodies all over, which is certainly not conducive to control and coordination of movement, which should instead be fluid and gradual.

• Being in a hurry to turn: this too is the result of a state of anxiety, arising from the fear that it will not be possible to turn the skis. This leads to twisting the whole body, in an attempt to turn the skis by force. As you might expect, the skis do not turn, or do so eventually after strenuous twisting movements that are dangerous for knees and ankles.

• Too tight turns: When skiing on the trail, especially on steep or icy sections, you get used to performing complete turns, with your skis turning so much that they end up going straight across the fall line (perpendicular to it). On untouched snow it is better to perform more open turns, without ever letting your skis point at right angles to the fall line; this will prevent your skis getting stuck at the end of the turn, which may make you fall.

4
SNOW-
BOARDING

A new craze, derived from surfing.
Which equipment to get for your chosen
style. Basic and advanced techniques.

INTRODUCTION

Snowboarding first made its appearance in the United States at the end of the 1960s. It was a few surfing enthusiasts who started it, tired of freezing to death in the ocean waves in the winter; rather than remain idle they decided to try to surf on fresh snow. To begin with they used their actual surfboards, but they soon realized that these had many limitations in snow, and so they began to investigate new designs and production technology. This led to the birth of the first small businesses that developed the new materials; next to appear were steel rims on the side of the boards, wooden cores, and the new shapes and colors that were typical of these years.

It was at this time too that the first snowboarding legends sprung up and the first great snowboarders made a name for themselves, champions such as Terry Kidwell, Tom Sims, Jake Burton, and José Fernandez. However, it wasn't until the mid-1980s that snowboarding really took off, in a way that was to make it one of the most popular and widely practiced winter sports for the young.

Snowboarding can be described as a fusion of many other sports: surfing gave it elegance and fluidity of movement, and the idea of hunting out "waves" of fresh snow to surf; it inherited its exaggerated hand movements, the jumps and the half-pipe from skateboarding; and skiing provided technical precision, carving, and a healthy respect for the mountain. As time passed this new sport developed its own identity, a whole new world, and a whole new lifestyle. The snowboarding world even has its own exclusive jargon and way of dressing.

The young find it a particularly appealing sport, and in order to try it out many find themselves up in the mountains for the first time in their lives. The secret of its success lies in the fact that it is relatively easy to learn, and that skills are quickly acquired; it generally only takes a few hours of tuition and practice to be able to snowboard, or "ride," down an easy slope before trying more ambitious maneuvers.

Left: snowboarding combines friendship, sport, and respect for the environment.

DIFFERENT TECHNIQUES

Having first assimilated various characteristics of the sports from which it originated, snowboarding has since split into different branches, largely thanks to the many competitions that have been organized. At the end of the 1980s, for example, people even took part in competitions over bumps (moguls), which had typically been a part of freestyle skiing, or in banked slalom races (slalom on virgin snow), which were the equivalent of riding a long wave in surfing.

Today there are basically three main snowboarding styles:
• freestyle
• free-riding
• Alpine

Freestyle is the one most favored by the young, and also the most dangerous. A freestyler performs huge jumps, and uses the half pipe, which is a run dug out of the snow in the shape of a half-cylinder. Soft bindings are used for the half pipe, and aerial leaps are made first to the right and then to the left, crossing from side to side and making maximum use of the lips of the cylinder.

Then there is free-riding, the latest craze to emerge, which favors open spaces, with fresh snow and wide, empty trails (pistes). Free-riders are prepared to trudge all the way up the mountainside, to find a totally untouched, virgin slope to descend. Soft or "step-in" bindings are used.

Finally, there are the Alpine snowboarders, or Alpiners, who search for trails of compressed snow where their boards can cut in, such as giant slalom runs, where they perform daredevil feats. Hard bindings are used.

Each of these branches of snowboarding requires specialized equipment; there is a huge variety on the market, which can be very bewildering for a novice.

Below left: freestyle; below right: free-riding.
Bottom: Alpiners.

EQUIPMENT
Boards

All snowboards belong to one of three main groups: Alpine, free-riding, or freestyle. They are differentiated by their shape and the amount of flex, and when choosing one, consideration must be given to technical specifications, the branch of snowboarding to be practiced, and the character of the person who will use it. Each board is designed with one specific activity in mind, and one type of "rider," and so you need to have a very clear idea of what you want before you buy. Alpine boards are longer and narrower, with short tails and a very long cutting edge, and they are used in slalom and giant slalom competitions, and fast, carved races on the trails.

Free-riding boards are fairly long (though less than Alpine ones), wide, and they have a fair bit of flex; they are the boards recommended for turns and fresh snow.

Lastly, freestyle boards, which are the shortest and widest, and fairly rigid; these are used for jumps and acrobatics in the pipe and in snowboard parks.

It is also important to take into consideration the length of your feet when choosing a board, in that if the board is too narrow for your feet they will stick out over the edge and get in the way of turns. So, long feet, wide board. They are generally constructed in one of two ways, those with wooden cores and those with composite cores. The former are easily the most common, and guarantee better performance, but building them is a much more painstaking and therefore costly affair, while the latter are generally called "injected," since their core is made by an injection of polyurethane, packed at high density inside the mould.

Bindings

Bindings come either hard, to be used on Alpine boards, or soft, for the other two

Below left: rigid boots for Alpine boards; below right: soft boots for free-riding. Facing page: soft boots for freestyle.

types. Hard ones are used with rigid boots (like boots for downhill skiing), and are either made of metal, or metal and plastic. The soft ones are used with special boots, called in fact soft boots, which are rather like après-ski boots, but are totally waterproof and reinforced, and are mostly made of plastic.

Boots

Snowboard boots are of different types according to the type of board. Soft boots are made of leather and special plastic, and should be tightly fitted, especially around the ankle. Boots of different levels of rigidity are available on the market; the hardest are intended for use in free-riding, or extreme freestyle; the softest are for ordinary freestyle.

"Step-in" is an entirely different type of shoe binding. This involves a clip, or mechanism, that opens and shuts automatically, and it is very comfortable for holiday or free-riding use.

Top left: the three types of board, distinguished by their length, but most of all by their degree of shaping, which determines the radius of the turns that can be performed. From left: freeriding, freestyle, and Alpine. Top right: different types of binding; above: hard; below: soft and step-in.

CLOTHING

The clothing worn by snowboarders has made trails very spectacular to look at, with eye-catching colors and loose-fitting garments, which would be inconceivable in downhill skiing. This is because the snowboarders' movements mean that clothing must not be constricting, must be comfortable and totally waterproof.

Snowboarders often sit or kneel in the snow, and, when they are "riding" through fresh snow, they are continually enveloped in a white cloud. So it is easy to see why the materials used must be above all thoroughly waterproof.

Jackets and trousers are usually not too padded (duvet style); it is better to have only medium padding in the jacket and to wear more layers of jumpers and fleeces, since snowboarders are very active and get very hot. When it is warmer it is better to take off one of the inside layers and to keep the jacket on as protection against the wet snow. Jackets are loose and generously cut, partly because this is the fashion, but mostly to allow arms and legs the necessary freedom of movement. It also means that riders are more elegant to watch in action. Over the years gloves have evolved to have reinforcement and protection for the wrist and fingers, which are very open to injury in snowboarding.

A good wooly hat completes the snowboarding image.

Even after their day's exertions on the trails ("après-snowboard"!), young riders can easily be spotted because of their particular style of dressing, which they also share with skaters, surfers, and windsurfers, all sports that are in some way connected.

Above and opposite: riders are set apart from ordinary skiers by their very distinctive style of dressing.

STARTING OFF

One of the factors that has contributed most to the popularity of snowboarding is that it is undoubtedly easier to learn; gliding on the board is really very easy. At an elementary level especially, after a minimum of basic training, including taking a few tumbles, you will calmly be able to descend slopes that are not too steep in total control and without any problem. This does not mean that after a couple of hours you are ready for a very demanding slope, only that you will get instant pleasure from your board.

To begin snowboarding all you need is to be in reasonable shape, and not afraid of taking a few tumbles (they very rarely result in injury anyway) or of getting soaked by the snow. You do not need to know how to ski, but it certainly does help.

Before describing some simple exercises for learning, you will need to understand a few basic concepts connected to this sport. Luckily enough for English speakers, snowboarding was born in America and all the technical jargon is in English, and is never translated into other languages (this would reduce its trendy appeal), so you will not have any problems understanding the jargon wherever you choose to practice the sport.

Below left: a regular snowboarder.
Below right: a goofy.

SNOWBOARDING TERMINOLOGY

4 x 4	standard fixings
aerial	a jump, when you might "get big air"
Alpiner	someone who uses an Alpine board
Alpine	branch of snowboarding similar to downhill skiing
banked slalom	competition run through fresh snow
boarder cross	type of race with various obstacles and jumps, with four people competing at a time
flex	amount of give, or flexibility, in the board
free-riding	anything that can be seen as freedom of movement (fresh snow, turns etc.)
free-rider	someone who goes free-riding
freestyle	branch of snowboarding that includes jumps, parks, and the half pipe
freestyler	someone who does freestyle
goofy	someone who has their right foot forward
half pipe	trail dug out of the snow in the shape of a half cylinder, used for jumps
jump	a snow jump, also type of trampoline (professional jump)
park	trail where obstacles and jumps are set up, for practicing technique
shaping radius	radius of the circumference that coincides with the curve on the side of the board: the shorter the radius is, the more shaped the board
rider	a snowboarder
reaction	how well the board recovers after a really testing maneuver
regular	someone who has their left foot forward
set back	how far back the stance is in relation to the central point of the cutting edge
stance	the position adopted on the board by the rider
step in	type of automatic binding used for soft boots

Basic stance

Once you have grasped how to stand on the board, you are ready to head for the snow, making sure that you select a nice piece of wide, level ground, free of obstacles and people. Then you can strap on your board.

How to strap on the board varies according to the type of board used, but in any case you should always attach your front, or forward, foot first.

On level ground you need to carry out a period of "acclimatization"; you need to find your balance, by jumping in different ways, and raising and lowering your body. The stance that you eventually adopt should be as natural as possible, not too tiring to hold for a length of time. Your weight should be distributed on both feet (just slightly more on the forward foot), your arms should be held wide, and your torso and your face should be facing the direction that you would be moving in. This is the basic stance. If you don't get this

Right: whatever type of binding and style you choose, you must always attach your front foot first. Below: to edge your board you have to flex your ankles and knees until you raise the downhill edge off the snow. Left: toe-edged board; right: heel-edged board.

YES: Torso and legs
correctly positioned in the
toe-edged stance.
NO: Torso leaning too far
forward over knees (above).
NO: Snowboarder in too
upright a stance, leaning
back slightly, and twisting
his pelvis (below).

right now, it will have a damaging effect on everything that you learn.

The thing that determines the position of the various parts of the body is how the bindings are angled on the board. On an Alpine board the bindings are angled in the direction that you will be advancing, which means that the rest of the body will face this way too.

On a freestyle board, where the bindings are less angled, your body will be side-ways facing, and only your head will be turned to face the direction that you are traveling.

Your body should be "engaged," which means that you should be relaxed but at the same time always in a state of readiness.

You must at all costs avoid a tense, rigid stance, or, conversely, an overly relaxed one.

The first movements

The next step is to learn how to move on level ground, with only your forward foot strapped into the binding, using a pushing technique. This will enable you to get out of difficulties in places where you don't feel confident. Your weight should be mostly on your forward foot, while you push yourself along with your rear foot as if you were on a skateboard. Use your arms to keep your balance. It is quite normal at first to fall over often; getting up again is certainly easier if there is a friend there to help you, but relying on this is a bad habit: you will have to learn to get up using your own efforts, and so you may as well learn to do so as soon as possible.

Front and back–toe-side and heel-side

One key concept to get used to straight away is the difference between your front (toe-side) and your back (heel-side). Clearly toe-side means facing forwards, and heel-side means behind you, but there's more to it than that.

To begin with, let's say that the toe edge of the board is the edge where your toes are, and the heel edge of the board is the edge where your heels are. From this it follows that if you find yourself on a slope with the toe-side of the board "edged" (cutting into the snow on the uphill side),

To push off, plant the rear foot on the ground level with the forward foot. Then put your rear foot on the board and work on your balance (if you didn't push hard enough the first time, try again). Stretching your arms out in front of you will help you to glide further.

148

you are toe edged, and in this case you can perform a toe-side slide or a toe-side diagonal. If, however, you start a turn from this position that crosses the fall line, this will be a heel-side turn, in that you will have your back to the turn, and you will be heel edged. The concept of toe-side and heel-side thus refers to the movement that you are carrying out, and is always changing. In a toe-side diagonal, for example, the uphill (or mountain) edge is the toe edge, and the downhill (or valley) edge is the heel edge. In snowboarding you always use the uphill edge, especially at beginner's level, otherwise falls can be disastrous.

NO: Pushing too hard with the rear foot and opening arms too wide (top).
NO: Head and shoulders too hunched, body not correctly "engaged" (center).
YES: Torso, arms, and legs correctly positioned.

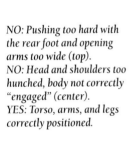

Sliding down the fall line

One of the first moves to practice is slipping straight down the fall line.

Toe slip

The toe slip is always the one to tackle first, because it is easier to find the delicate balance on your ankles; but be careful, as you will not be able to see where you are going. Once you have checked that there are no obstacles, off you go. Keep your torso upright, your arms wide, and your

YES

YES: Head turned uphill, arms wide open for balance. By flattening the board you will decrease the amount of edging, and will start slipping.
NO: Shoulders not in line with the board, which means that there is no longer a steady edge grip; heels will slip downhill.

NO

knees bent. You should be able to feel the board's movements when you move your ankles: by flexing and unflexing you lessen or increase the degree of edging and control your speed. Your face must remain turned to the mountain; never try to turn downhill, or you are likely to trigger a turn.

Heel slip

In the heel slip you no longer have the problem of not seeing where you are going, but the problem of "feeling" the degree of edging; it is more difficult to keep your balance when standing on the heel edge, but with a little practice you will succeed.

YES: Using arms and delicate ankle movements to balance, and trying not to shift weight too much either onto the tip or onto the tail of the board.
NO: Shifting the weight of the hips too much onto the forward foot, causing the tail to lose its grip.

Diagonal slide

When you have mastered the previous exercise, you can try out the diagonal slide, or traverse.

Toe-side diagonal slide

Start with a toe-side fall-line slip, and then, in a decisive but smooth movement, without any sudden movements, turn your head and shoulders towards the tip of the board, i.e. in the direction that you wish to go, while keeping your weight on both feet,

YES: Torso and head correctly positioned, with only slightly more weight on the forward foot. The forward foot is weighted down, and the head and torso are turned in the direction that the board is going.
NO: Do not try to fling your arms too wide, or you will trigger a turn.

YES

NO

NO

without leaning back, and your arms well spread to maintain balance.

Heel-side diagonal slide

In the heel-side slide be careful not to swivel your shoulders too far round, or to put too much weight on your forward foot.

To find out whether you have done this properly, check that you have left a track behind you that is 40–50 cm (16–20 inches) wide, running diagonally across the fall line.

YES

NO: Torso too hunched, and shoulders too much in line with the board.
YES: There is slightly more weight on the forward foot, and face and torso are turned in the direction that the board is pointing.

The elementary turn

Finally comes the turn, which will be the elementary turn to start with. First the toe-side turn, so you must start off on the heel-side diagonal slide.

Elementary toe-side turn

When you feel confident in your position, turn your head, shoulders, and torso in the direction that you wish to turn; this combination of movements, which needs to be dynamic and graceful, may be called the rotational swing, and can be found in all snowboard maneuvers, at whatever level you are, or type of board you are using. It should become automatic, and is the way that you steer your board and control where you go. This rotational swing starts off a chain movement that is transmitted down through your pelvis and legs until it reaches the board, which will then start to change direction.

In the toe-side turn you will need to use your abdominal muscles, your back muscles, and the muscles in your buttocks and legs for this rotational swing to work properly, while always remaining "engaged."

This is the point when you must change edges, so as to abide by the rule of always keeping your mountain edge in contact with the snow. In an elementary turn the change takes place just as you point down the fall line, since you are still going at a fairly low speed; when your speed increases the change will need to take place a little earlier, owing to the different forces that will be at work.

NO: Rotational swing overdone, which puts balance out.
YES: Correct stance, with the right rotational swing.

Start the turn from a diagonal toe-side slide by making the rotational swing, allowing your legs to follow the movement. Note how the board flattens in the middle of the turn, and the edging is changed, before going on to complete the curve.

Elementary heel-side turn

The heel-side turn is the same as the toe-side one, but in reverse. You start off from a toe-side diagonal slide and turn your head and torso in the direction of the turn. This way, however, the rotational swing works better because your body's joints will work with you in the heel-side turn. In the toe-side turn you have to remain "engaged" and use your muscles (abdominal, back, buttocks and legs) to make the rotational swing work better.

You change edging when you are pointing straight down the fall line.

Start the rotational swing from the heel-side diagonal slide position, keeping your body upright and letting your legs follow the movement. Halfway through the turn start to change edging; by carrying on your swing into the turn you control your direction.

NO: Rotational swing overdone (picture to the right).
YES: Arms and torso correctly positioned, in readiness for the turn.
NO: Be careful not to lower your heels too much in the last stage of the turn (below).

Basic turn

A slightly more complex turn, a step up from the elementary, is the basic turn. In this turn you need to lower and raise your body, and it is carried out at greater speed.

Bending and straightening movements are characteristic of high-energy, superior-level snowboarding; you will already have gained a much better grasp of technique, and can put this to use in the wide-radius carved turn. Movements are spread out evenly throughout the whole turn, making it effective and elegant, and lovely to watch. This visual harmony is in fact another reason why snowboarding has become so popular.

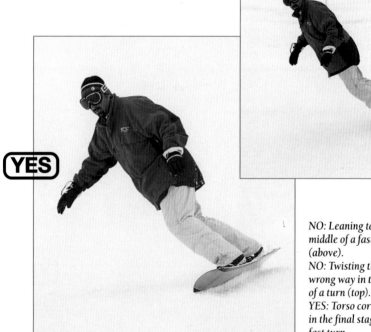

NO: Leaning too much in the middle of a fast turn (above).
NO: Twisting the body the wrong way in the final stage of a turn (top).
YES: Torso correctly angled in the final stage of a fairly fast turn.

Bend at the ankles and knees to lower the center of gravity, without lessening your edge grip. Then straighten up while swinging round towards the front inside of the turn. Halfway through the turn change edges, while keeping your rotational swing going. Finally, with your heel-side now edged, begin to bend in order to counteract the forces at work.

Basic heel-side turn
From a toe-side diagonal slide prepare yourself by bending ankles, knees, and hips, and then immediately straighten up, making the rotational swing at the same time. To be effective these two movements must be simultaneous. About halfway through the turn you bend again, which will allow you to control the board as it comes out of the curve.

NO: Pelvis too far forward, and shoulders too much in line with the board in the last stage of the turn (top).
YES: Weight evenly distributed on both feet.
NO: Forward leg too stiff; the torso leans right forward to compensate for the backward shift of the center of gravity (below).

161

FACE TURNED IN THE
DIRECTION OF THE
TURN

ARMS HELD
SLIGHTLY
FORWARD AND
WIDE OF THE BODY

TORSO UPRIGHT
AND SLIGHTLY
AHEAD

KNEES AND ANKLES
BENT

BASIC TOE-SIDE TURN

FACE TURNED IN
THE DIRECTION
OF THE TURN

TORSO
UPRIGHT AND
SLIGHTLY
AHEAD

ARMS HELD
SLIGHTLY WIDE
OF THE BODY

KNEES AND
ANKLES BENT

BASIC HEEL-SIDE TURN

Carved turn

This maneuver will follow on naturally when you have perfected the basic turn. In it all movements are carried out with maximum efficiency, so that your overall performance requires minimum effort and is elegant to watch. The ideal place for it is a wide, medium-steep slope, where there are no obstacles or other people. You need to think about your movements in terms of time, not just space (bending, leaning, and so on). What you are finally aiming at is to complete the whole turn with your board well edged, without ever losing contact with the snow, and without any sliding.

Toe-side carved turn

For the toe-side carved turn you start off with a heel-side diagonal slide, which you keep going until you have built up a good speed. Prepare yourself for the turn by bending your legs; as you straighten up again your action should be coupled with the rotational swing. You can now start to lean your body towards the inside of the turn. Immediately after this you change edges from heel to toe. When you are going at high speed this can be done earlier, while still in the diagonal slide you started with, since the forces at work will be sufficient to keep you balanced even at the start of the trajectory.

As you switch edges you should start to close the turn. At this point the most commonly made mistake is being in too much of a hurry.

You do not need to bend your legs again immediately to get to the end of the sequence of movements, when there is in fact still over half the turn to complete. The forces that are at work in a turn performed at high speed are at their greatest during

YES: Board perfectly edged; pelvis, torso and head in the correct position.
NO: Torso leaning inwards too much, and pelvis too high.

the last quarter of the curve, and it is during this stage that you need to counteract them.

At this stage you must still be able to bend down and take control of events. If you are already in a squatting position halfway through the turn, you are not leaving yourself any margin for recovery in case of anything going wrong in the critical stage of the curve.

Heel-side carved turn

For the heel-side carved turn you start from a fast, carved, toe-side diagonal slide.

Bend your legs, followed by simultaneously straightening up and making the rotational swing. Immediately afterwards comes the edge change from toe to heel edge. The moment this is complete you must begin to close the turn, but without hurrying.

Once again, in this turn, the forces at work at high speed are greatest during the last quarter of the curve, and this is when you need to be able to counteract them. So yet again, you must leave yourself a certain margin for error, which means not using up the final knee-bend too early in the turn.

YES: Correct stance in the final stage of the turn: body poised and turned in the direction of the movement. NO: Pelvis too far forward, resulting in loss of pressure on the tail of the board, and in loss of carving.

167

NO PERCEPTIBLE
CHANGE IN
TORSO"PELVIS TILT
THROUGHOUT THE TURN

SHOULDERS AND
TORSO SLIGHTLY
AHEAD OF THE
REST OF THE BODY

KNEES ALWAYS
ACTIVE

CARVED TOE-SIDE TURN

FACE TURNED IN THE
DIRECTION OF THE
MOVEMENT

SHOULDERS
SLIGHTLY
FORWARD

BODY BUNCHED UP TO
COMPENSATE FOR THE FORCES
AT WORK IN THE FINAL STAGE OF
THE TURN

CARVED HEEL-SIDE TURN

5
TELEMARK

Revival of an early skiing technique.
Equipment and gear.

Early Telemark

As we saw in the chapter on the history of skiing, Telemark is universally recognized as the earliest skiing technique. It was officially born in 1868, after Norwegian champion Søndre Norheim won a ski jumping competition. After a flight of 33 m (100 feet), he landed and stopped using the so-called "angel" technique. Norheim astonished everyone by the elegance and style of his movements, which were later to form the basis of Telemark. Still today, jumps are judged partly on the technical ability the skiers display in their Telemark landings. On the cusp of the 19th and 20th centuries, skiers everywhere learned the Telemark technique. It remained in vogue until ousted by the Austrian downhill/

parallel skiing technique. But keen downhill skiers still preferred the Telemark technique well into the 1930s. After then, however, it was pretty much forgotten until its revival the 1970s.

Modern Telemark

Telemark was re-born in the early 1970s at Crested Bute, Colorado. A group of keen skiers decided to use old skis with bindings and accessories identical to those available in the early 20th century. Curiosity about Telemark spread rapidly to other US ski resorts. This was also encouraged by the landscape of north America with its huge mountains and gentle valleys that make ideal "free-heel" skiing terrain. "Free-heel skiing" is the self-explanatory term that many accomplished skiers use to describe Telemark. The discipline then spread mainly in areas with suitable slopes and quantities of snowfall, above all in the United States and Norway, where downhill skiing often goes hand in hand with ski touring. In other areas traditionally connected with skiing (such as the Alps), Telemark has not really taken off, although it is practiced there by a specialist group of keen skiers and experts who are always ready to explore new and different techniques.

All the trailblazers of modern Telemark are American. The best known is Paul Parker, already a legendary figure for keen Telemarkers. Parker was the first to bring the modern renaissance of Telemark to world attention. This happened at the 1983 Interski meet at Sesto Pusteria in Italy where he made perfectly balanced downhill runs over an extremely rough trail that even the best downhill skiers were finding tough going. (Just a reminder that Interski

is the annual get-together of ski instructors from around the world.)

Generally Telemark is taken up by fairly advanced skiers in search of new thrills. Otherwise it is practiced by keen skiers, who are interested in the whole ski culture and want to experience the historical roots of the sport for themselves. It does not really matter what type of skiing they normally prefer, be it cross-country, downhill or anything else. What matters is the motivation that spurs them on to learn a new technique. They can bring their own experience to all aspects of Telemark that are similar to the techniques they already know. In fact, Telemark employs natural stances that are typical of the "gliding step," with one leg in front of the other. To look at, it often seems similar to cross-country skiing. On the other hand, the fact that the skier runs downhill, edges his or her skis and rotates his or her body are all

akin to downhill skiing. This is why Telemark is rated as the eclectic synthesis of several disciplines, a view reinforced by its elegant stances and the natural feel of some of its movements.

Nowadays, there are two distinct technical trends in Telemark. One is firmly connected to the traditional style that came out of the Nordic countries. The other involves a more innovative style, derived from downhill skiing.

Telemark, the first skiing technique ever invented, has enjoyed a revival in recent years. Enthusiasts of "free-heel" skiing shun the groomed runs in favor of woods and open slopes.

NORDIC STYLE

In the Nordic style of Telemark (of which the Norwegians are absolute masters) movements are decisive and not very dynamic, almost like a succession of static postures. Skiers use long, straight skis, similar to traditional downhill skis. This means that they must make very decisive movements to effect a turn. At the same time, the skier maintains a prolonged kneeling stance or genuflection from beginning to end of the turn, but has to compensate for this by means of an exaggerated torso stance (in other words, leaning out of the turn).

Below: off-trail provides the ideal terrain for the Nordic style of Telemark skiing. YES: The classic Nordic position.

Movements in the classic "knee-bend" turn. One leg lags behind while the weight remains distributed on both feet.

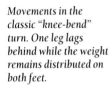

DOWNHILL (ALPINE) STYLE

The downhill style of Telemark is a development of the Norwegian style, mainly promoted by the Swiss and Italians. Overall, it is more fluid and dynamic with movements and postures closer to downhill skiing and snowboarding. The skier uses shorter, slightly waisted skis that require a minimum of movement to engage a turn. The skier starts the turn by gently bending his knees. The turns themselves are rounder, more controlled and less erratic. The body is consequently more compact and turns in the same direction as the turn, almost eliminating the need for any torso compensation.

In short, the downhill Telemark style is more for on- than off-trail skiing, which is where the Nordic style really comes into its own, not least because it is off trail that traditional or touring skis perform best.

Below: typical downhill stance. Comparison between (bottom left) downhill style and (bottom right) Nordic style.

The drawings on this page show the way the skier shifts the kneeling stance from his right leg to his left.

EQUIPMENT

Skis

As we've already seen, there are different kinds of Telemark skis. These can be roughly divided into three types.

• Touring. These are light and have metal edges; they are barely waisted and tend to be fairly long, very similar to cross-country skis.

• Downhill. These are wider and have more sidecut, similar to on-trail Alpine skis.

• Telecarving. These are like modern sidecut skis and are by far the shortest of the three. They are also fitted with booster plates beneath the bindings, like hypercarving skis.

The characteristics of the touring skis put them close to cross-country skis, whereas the downhill and telecarving skis conform to the classic downhill requirements for a ski: flexibility, elasticity and little longitudinal torsion.

Boots

Just as in downhill skiing, the boots play a fundamental part in delivering good technique and pleasure.

Slide the toe of the boot into the binding toe piece. Then rest your weight on the heel and engage the binding heel piece.

If the boots are too big, for instance, then they will hinder the way your movements are transmitted to your skis. It is important, therefore, that the boots fit your feet perfectly.

Telemark boots come either in leather with laced fastenings or in plastic with buckle fastenings.

The leather ones look very much like the old-fashioned ski boots that were used right up to the 1960s. They are fairly low cut and tend to go out of shape with wear, sometimes getting quite soft too. They need a lot of looking after but are particularly dear to the hearts of the aficionados of old-style, traditional Telemark.

The plastic boots with liners or inner boots are, on the other hand, far more like downhill boots. They are higher cut and come with buckles for micro-adjustment. Some also come with a cuff release or walk adjuster, a device that enables you to adjust the boot cuff. When the cuff is fully locked, the boot is more rigid and better suited to downhill skiing. When the cuff is freed, the ankle can move more. This is better for touring (in other words they allow you to walk more easily when your skis are still on your feet).

When skiing on trail, the boots need lateral rigidity in order to get the skis to edge properly.

In all cases, Telemark boots need flexible soles that enable the foot to be easily flexed when bending.

Above: correct position of skis during turn.
Left: your weight must be spread over both feet.

FORWARD ARM
PREPARING
THE POLE

LEG FORWARD AND BENT,
CONTROLLING THE
DIRECTION OF THE TURN

SKIS EDGED

ALPINE TELEMARK

TORSO TURNED
IN THE DIRECTION
OF THE SKI TIPS

REAR LEG
WEIGHTED AND
WELL BENT

FOOT BENT AND
HEEL RAISED

6
SKI MOUNTAIN-
EERING

The gradual shift from on-trail (on-piste)
skiing to ski touring and ski mountaineering.
Equipment, gear and techniques. Skiing
safely and avalanche dangers.

INTRODUCTION

Ski mountaineering is akin to mountain climbing. It is mainly done in winter and spring when skis are used to climb up and ski down mountains, gullies, and snow-covered valleys without ever going anywhere near a lift or groomed trails (pistes).

Mountaineering skiers operate in a purely Alpine environment. It is normal to cover terrain of widely varying profile, to climb mountains, to find panoramic views and to cross glaciers.

Far away from the trails and lifts, there is no doubt that the mountains in winter exert their own fascination. They reward you with extraordinary views and sensations. But they also conceal enormous dangers that all too often turn fantastic treks into tragic adventures.

Ski mountaineering is not, therefore, for everyone. It takes an expert skier, able to tackle the most difficult slopes without undue effort, a skier who loves and respects nature, one who has properly prepared for the trip and knows the mountain inside out. But the skier who possesses all these qualities can look forward to the rewards of the wonderful sensations the sport has to offer.

Ski touring and ski mountaineering are the most complete form of skiing in the mountains. Provided you have perfected your technique and have plenty of experience, you can reach any place in the most varied of regions.

SKI TOURING

Ski touring, on the other hand, is within most people's reach. It can be described as the soft version of ski mountaineering. But it too requires proper training and knowledge of the mountain. It is, in fact, inspired by the same love of nature and desire to escape the crowds, but does not call for the enormous degree of prowess required by ski mountaineering.

Ski touring is seen as a means to go trekking over the snow without using marked trails or tracks. It tends to stick to terrain with a similar profile that can be traversed fairly easily. It does not require mountaineering skills as it does not tackle rock and ice. It is the natural progression from cross-country skiing and can be done wherever the mountains are not particularly steep or dangerous. Ski touring is best practiced in areas with wide valleys and gentle slopes.

Nevertheless ski touring does call for specialist equipment and techniques. These are half-way between those of cross-country skiing and ski mountaineering. The gear must be light enough to enable the skier to remain agile over long stretches, rough terrain and steep off-trail slopes in a wide variety of snow conditions.

Skiing off trail, even if it is just to cross a valley or to get from one village to another, is a fascinating way of rediscovering what it was once like to ski. We forget that skis were, in fact, invented as a means of transport over snow at a time when man had no other means of getting around.

Because ski touring covers a variety of disciplines, has no competitive aspect and is completely free of the dictates of fashion, it gives those who practice it a glimpse of what skiing used to be like. It is an extraordinarily satisfying form of skiing, one that combines elements of Telemark, cross-country, downhill and ski mountaineering.

SKI MOUNTAINEERING

On the whole, people start ski mountaineering only when they have reached both physical and skiing maturity. Ski mountaineers tend to be adults who have grown tired of skiing the ordinary groomed runs and the hordes of people you always find there. They are looking for a more complete and satisfying relationship with the mountains.

Ski mountaineers must, therefore, be highly experienced in all basic skiing techniques; they must be able to ski the steepest and iciest slopes without a hitch. They have to be able to cope with sudden changes in snow conditions (from ice to powder snow) as well as tackling uneven ground. But above all they need to be passionate about mountains, they need to yearn to taste the emotions nature offers at these high altitudes. If they do not possess all these qualities, they will not have sufficient motivation to overcome the fatigue, the sacrifices and the inherent risks that go with the terrain. Finally, ski mountaineers must also be familiar with mountains in the summertime, have experience of high-altitude trekking, and know the basics of rock climbing.

Here is a short run-down of the qualities a ski mountaineer must possess:
• Mastery of skiing techniques
Off-trail downhill techniques are different to on-trail ones, although the underlying idea is the same. The art of balance and automatic reflexes learned on trails are an essential ingredient for starting off trail.

NO: This skier's stance on the trail shows that his technique is not sufficiently advanced to tackle the difficulties of ski touring/mountaineering. YES: Good technique on the trail is the basic prerequisite needed before tackling the full range of snow conditions found off trail.

Good skiers will have little difficulty in adapting their way of skiing to fit the type of terrain they encounter.

• Physical fitness

When you are ski mountaineering you have to climb up before you can ski down. It is therefore essential to be at the peak of aerobic fitness and have sufficient stamina before undertaking an outing. The minimum training period is four weeks, with three training sessions per week.

• Knowledge of the mountain

If you do not know the mountain where you are planning to go ski mountaineering, then you should take time to go on a few guided summer climbs, get to know the mountain and its rules.

• Sufficient spirit and motivation

You need to really want to get away from the trails and to have time to enjoy the space and images that the mountain has to offer.

This does not mean that ski mountaineering is a sport reserved for an elite few. Indeed even intermediate skiers with little knowledge of the mountain can get a

Above: your first ski touring/mountaineering treks should be done in a group led by an experienced guide.

taste of it provided they are accompanied by an expert. Otherwise a sudden change in weather or any other unexpected event can turn what seems like a basic little trek on the map into an arduous struggle.

Even young skiers can start ski mountaineering, provided their technique is good enough and, above all, that they really care about the mountain. In this case, apart from the obvious proviso of being accompanied by an expert adult, the most important thing is to choose the route carefully, paying special attention to length and climb.

As a rough guide, children between nine and 12 years should not be faced with more than two to three hours of climbing, and even then this should be interspersed with at least three or four rests and sufficient amounts to eat and drink.

Equipment

As always with skiing, the choice of equipment is of paramount importance. Since the conditions of ski mountaineering are so different from those of other types of skiing (well off the groomed runs and often far away from ski resorts) it is essential that the choice of gear be made with far greater care. Much of the usual on-trail equipment is not suitable, whereas certain items of specific equipment are indispensable.

Skis

In theory a fairly short pair of downhill skis should be all right. But if you need to buy new skis anyway, then it is well worth considering skis specifically designed for ski touring or mountaineering. Apart from being shorter, their weight and flexibility is also different. By and large, all major ski manufacturers make models specifically designed for ski touring or mountaineering and there is a wide range to choose from. The first thing you will notice about them is a hole in the tip and tail. This is so that, if the need arises, they can be lashed together to use as an emergency gurney or sled. This feature is something that probably 90% of skiers do not have and have never missed.

There are only two main factors to take into consideration for this type of ski:

• Ones that are very soft and short are suited to powder snow, a condition dreamt of by all ski tourers/mountaineers but not very often found in the Alps, where you are more likely to encounter hard or old snow (*Firn*). In these conditions, a more rigid ski will grip better.

• Exaggerated sidecuts, like those on carving skis, have also been tried for ski touring/mountaineering. In these conditions, how-ever, their serious limitations immediately became apparent. The ski scarcely grips either when climbing uphill or when skiing downhill. Above all it does not provide any grip on steep traverses, and is less maneuverable on soft snow and in tight turns. It is advisable, therefore, to choose a ski that is only slightly waisted.

Bindings

The bindings used in this sport are very specific. They have to allow the boot to move. When climbing uphill, the heel lifts out while the toe acts as a hinge. When going downhill, on the other hand, the heel is locked. There is a fairly wide range of suitable bindings on the market. You can choose from metal bindings – which are robust but rather heavy – to lighter, step-in bindings that are particularly useful and comfortable in difficult conditions. There are even ultra lightweight bindings designed for use with specific boots. They all feature booster plates

that enable your leg to sit at a more comfort-able angle when walking up steep slopes. These plates also allow enough room for the *Harscheisen* (metal spikes, like crampons) that are needed to give additional grip when climbing icy snow or crossing steep slopes. Finally, touring/mountaineering bindings use the old-style safety straps. At the edge of a crevasse you could not trust the kind of ski brakes used on downhill skis to stop the ski disappearing over the edge.

Right: bindings fitted with crampons for ascents over icy slopes. Above: short skis, suited to fresh snow, with a hole in the tip so they can be used as an emergency sled. Left: safety straps replace the ski brakes that are found on trail skis.

Boots

This type of boot is far lighter than its on-trail cousin. The outer shell is plastic and has "Vibram" profiled soles. There is a detachable inner lining in extremely soft material, again with a lightweight rubber sole so that the linings themselves can double up for use inside the mountain huts. The shell is usually designed so that the upper part is flexible, freeing the skier to walk or even climb in them if necessary. Compared to a downhill boot, all these features mean that the touring/mountaineering boot is less rigid and supporting when skiing downhill. Some models are more comfortable for climbing and others more effective when skiing downhill. This is because, for the moment at least, there is no ideal solution. Any choice you make is therefore a compromise, which will be dictated by your personal preferences, and the type of use you envisage getting from your boots. Walkers who like to tackle a number of mixed routes tend to opt for a boot more suited to climbing, whereas people who really get a thrill out of steep downhill runs and are perhaps even thinking of wearing the same boots for on-trail skiing will tend to plump for the more downhill-orientated models.

Poles

The poles ordinarily used in on-trail skiing are perfectly all right, provided they have fairly wide baskets (which are often interchangeable). You can, however, buy special touring/mountaineering poles. These are telescopically extendable and are unquestionably more comfortable since you can adjust their length to suit the changing conditions. Modern telescopic poles no longer jam like the old ones used to. They are, however, less robust than ordinary poles while definitely being far more expensive.

Poles must be variable in length in order to adapt to a variety of conditions, especially during the ascent.

Skins

You cannot do without skins when climbing uphill on skis. Nowadays they are made from synthetic materials (happily, the term "skin" is a hang-over from the days when sealskins were used for this purpose). One side of the skin is smooth. You spread this with adhesive and stick it to the bottom of your skis. The other side has stiff hairs on it, all facing the same direction, which prevent the skis from sliding back during the ascent.

Nearly all modern skins are also fitted with tip and tail hooks, which ensure they fit the skis better and also makes it easier to take the skins off. The adhesive (which is sold separately) has to be re-applied at the start of each season.

Below: skins are tightly stretched over the skis, starting from the tip. The skins are then waxed to stop snow building up on them. Bottom: ski tip hook.

Clothing

The same multi-layered clothing is worn for ski touring/mountaineering as for winter mountain climbing: snow pants (best with a bib) or salopettes, padded jacket and underneath layers of clothing. Very often when you are climbing uphill and the sun is shining, all you need is a T-shirt. But when you are skiing downhill, or at the first sight of a cloud, you may well need to put your down jacket back on again. Apart from one pair of heavy-duty gloves, another pair of lightweight ones (in cotton or polyester) proves useful during ascents. Even though you may think a headband looks more chic, make sure you've got a woolly hat in your rucksack. Finally, it is far better to wear a pair of lightweight UV-resistant sunglasses than goggles, which are frankly useless when skiing downhill.

Rucksacks

No ski tourer/mountaineer can do without a rucksack. You can take a summer mountain model and add the ski-carrier side straps that all good manufacturers offer as optional extras. However, there are a number of rucksacks on the market specifically designed for ski touring/mountaineering (which can double up for summer mountain use).

Opposite: clothing, gear and, above all, the weight of the rucksack mean that a completely different stance is needed for downhill ski mountaineering compared to trail skiing.

SAFETY

One specific and absolutely indispensable piece of kit is an avalanche beacon. This is a small transceiver that emits a radio signal facilitating the search for and hopefully rescue of a person caught under an avalanche. Each member of a ski touring/mountaineering party should not only have an avalanche beacon, but should also know how it works.

They should also have an avalanche shovel and an avalanche probe to use when searching for people buried under an avalanche. Together with their avalanche radio beacons, these are the basic ingredients of the emergency kit.

Another useful safety device in avalanche territory is an airbag. This is a specially designed, self-inflating balloon that the skier can trigger in order to create a "float" should an avalanche hit.

Still with regard to safety, it is a good idea to carry a cell phone. Now that coverage in mountainous areas is so much better than it once was, the cell phone is about to be promoted from a useful accessory to indispensable safety device.

A GPS (Global Positioning System) is becoming one of the devices most frequently used on ski touring and ski mountaineering treks of any length. This electronic instrument uses data from satellites in earth orbit to pinpoint your exact geographic position.

Ropes, ice ax, crampons and short gaiters are also indispensable if you are crossing glaciers or tackling slopes that involve climbing.

Finally, you cannot go out without a compass, an altimeter (even a wrist version) and the right maps for the area (1:25,000 scale). Maps can readily be purchased in bookshops, newsagents or tourist information offices in mountain resorts.

Above left: avalanche beacon.
Opposite: the correct way to protect your avalanche beacon is to wear it under your jacket.

HOW TO GO ABOUT IT

How do you become a ski tourer/mountaineer? The best way is to sign up for a course in ski touring/mountaineering; you will find that all ski touring/mountaineering schools organize at least one a year. Apart from the technical aspects of skiing, the courses include sections on meteorology, snow conditions, first aid, and rescue. They cover first the theory and then the practice during excursions organized and led by qualified instructors.

Anyone wanting to get into this sport must necessarily go through the best-qualified channels if safety is to be guaranteed. Let us underline things once again. Ski touring/mountaineering is within many people's grasp (at least after the correct amount of basic training and fitness), but it has got absolutely nothing in common with skiing down groomed runs serviced by lifts backed up by all the comfort and the best safety organization you can imagine.

Above: the best way to get into ski touring/mountaineering is to sign up for a specialized course and benefit from an instructor's experience.

Ski touring/mountaineering takes place far away from mountain restaurants or huts and, what is more pertinent, out of reach of the rescue services. It follows, therefore, that the main quality you need to acquire before setting out on even the simplest excursion is caution. On the open mountain "skiing is no longer a game."

The pointers set out below must not be read as a "manual" for a would-be ski tourer/ mountaineer. There is no manual that can replace training and experience. All they can do is give a simple description of the basic techniques that are currently used.

First lessons: On-trail exercises

It is better to start any lessons in ski touring/mountaineering on trail. Here you can test your gear and basic climbing and downhill techniques. Try to find a quiet run that is not much used, far away from the crowds and possible dangers from reckless skiers. Then choose the outer edges of the trail, where you can still see the run but well away from the middle, especially if the trail is very steep. Above all, never choose a place that is just below a change of incline.

Once you have found a safe place on the trail, you can use it to practice the range of techniques needed for ski touring/mountaineering, namely:

• Putting your skis on and off both on flat ground and on a steep slope, on soft snow and on ice

• Adjusting your boots for downhill and climbing

• Adjusting your telescopic poles

• Trying out your technique for turning to face the other way on the flat and on a steep slope

• Uphill walking technique

• Using *Harscheisen* (metal spikes or crampons)

• Roping techniques

YES: Practice climbing uphill alongside the trail.
NO: Do not attempt to climb up the middle of the trail.
Below: step turn.

Walking uphill on skis uses the uphill gliding technique on alternate skis (see the chapter on "Cross-country skiing"). The skins stop the skis from slipping backwards. You can simulate a proper ascent on trail for at least several minutes. This will give you an idea of the effort involved and the probable difficulties you will encounter during a trek, without incurring the risks of going off trail.

This type of experiment will make you aware of the true physical exertion required for ski touring/mountaineering. Indeed, the fatigue of the ascent should be viewed as a basic ingredient of the overall satisfaction.

Ski tourers/mountaineers appreciate the uncontaminated environment the mountain offers. They use the slow and arduous ascent as a time to contemplate, observe, and reflect. The constant effort required (although not intense) comes to represent the elevation of their will over their bodies. Even though climbing uphill is more pleasurable on skis, when you encounter certain types of hard snow or the terrain is especially steep, it is easier and safer to continue on foot (possibly even wearing crampons). On these occasions you stow your skis in your rucksack. In this connection, it is important to remember that you should anticipate this type of difficult terrain in advance and have planned your course of action. Spikes should be inserted before you traverse a glacier. You should take your skis off before you get to a tricky bit of terrain. If you leave it too late, it becomes more difficult and even dangerous to undo your bindings.

This is another reason why the beginner ski tourer/mountaineer must first master the technique of putting both skis and crampons on and off in any situation.

Kick turn.

No good skier encounters difficulty in a downhill run on a groomed trail, however steep it may be. But you still have to practice all the turns you know while wearing all the clothing and carrying all the gear and equipment you will need for ski touring/mountaineering. If you are not used to wearing a rucksack, you can easily find yourself off balance in the turn. At a more basic level, you should get used to the feel of skiing in ski touring/mountaineering boots. Because these are less rigid than downhill boots, you need to adapt your style, especially when edging your skis or bending and straightening your knees. It is a good idea, therefore, to do a few runs on the trail (using the lifts) to get used to your new center of gravity and your new gear.

Try to avoid wide turns or high speeds. Concentrate instead on narrow turns. Each turn must be properly controlled and finished, almost as if you wanted to stop at the end of each one without any desire to go into the next. This exercise simulates off-trail conditions over terrain that does not allow you to ski a neat sequence of turns—the type of terrain where each turn has to be thought through and carried out with the utmost safety in mind.

NO: The skier is leaning too far forward because his boots are too soft.
Opposite, above: basic turn; center: advanced turn; below: narrow, tight turn.

First ventures off trail

Once you have practiced thoroughly on trails, it is time to move onto ungroomed snow. And the ideal exercise yard where you start is close by. It is the off-trail area right next to the groomed runs. In general, these areas provide exactly the same kind of snow conditions that you will meet during ski touring/mountaineering treks. All you have to do is to move a few dozen meters off the edge of the run to recreate the kind of difficulties you will typically encounter on ungroomed snow. The actual technical difficulties inherent in these situations are often magnified by the muscular rigidity of the skier that is so frequently found in people who have never skied fresh snow. You will find a description of the downhill techniques you need to ski ungroomed snow in Chapter 3. But let us

underline once again that you really must adapt your technique to every type of snow condition (cold and soft snow, wet spring snow, crusty wind-blown snow). Simply put, ski tourers/mountaineers need to practice on every type of ungroomed snow. You need to start with simple sliding exercises, or with turning round to face the other way, and go right the way through to practicing a sequence of turns. The one technical adjustment you need to make for all off-trail snow conditions is to shift your center of gravity slightly backwards. This stops your tips digging into the snow. But do not overdo it. The fact that you have a rucksack on your back already tends to shift your balance backwards. You should also practice using your avalanche beacon, try out risk limitation, first aid and rescue techniques, and orienteering using maps, compass and altimeter (see p. 194).

NO: The skier is leaning too far back because his rucksack is too heavy.
YES: Exercises performed on the edge of the trail on ungroomed snow.

THE SKI MOUNTAINEERING TOUR

Your first outings (but it would be better if it were all your outings) must be done with an expert guide. The choice of itinerary must principally be made on the basis of a logical progression in the degree of difficulty encountered. The first outing must therefore aim to reach an easy and well-known objective. If you do not know the area yourself, you will find that for many places ski touring/mountaineering guides are on sale. Even if you have been there before, these publications are always a useful supplement to direct experience. Apart from topographical detail, they tend to include the time each climb takes and the degree of difficulty (see Table 1) of the routes described. Purchasing these guides is invaluable for everyone, but an absolute must for beginners setting out on an itinerary in a place they do not know.

The day before setting out, gather all available data on meteorological conditions and weather forecasts as well as avalanche risks in the area chosen. This information is quite indispensable to a safe tour. Owing to their frequency and seriousness, avalanches are the gravest danger that the ski tourer/mountaineer will ever encounter. Allow plenty of time for the route you are hoping to cover. It is wise to add half an hour to every two hours shown in guide books for unexpected hold-ups and rest periods. But you must also adjust the time you allow to take account of the season, the direction of the route, and the downhill slopes. You must always put safety before your search for the best downhill skiing conditions. Above all, avoid places where there is an avalanche risk when the sun is high.

Preferred routes
A Ridges and crests
B Flatter areas
C Change direction in the lee of rocks
D Fall line close to rocks

Routes to avoid
E Slopes unbroken by rocks or trees
F Slopes in the shade

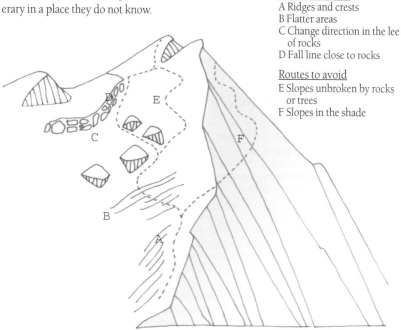

HOW TO READ A MAP

In order to enjoy a ski touring/mountaineering trek safely, it is indispensable to know the lie of the land, either through first-hand knowledge of the area or by researching it on a detailed map. What you are looking for are the differences in height, the length of the route, how steep the various sections are, the presence of rocky areas and the possible risk of avalanche on certain slopes. It is also necessary to ascertain the existence of mountain huts and refuges.

The best maps for this purpose, which are generally available for all areas in which ski touring/ mountaineering occurs, are to a scale of 1:25,000 (2·5 inches to 1 mile). This means that a centimeter (0.4 inches) on the map corresponds to 25,000 cm (9,800 inches) on the ground, i.e. 250 m (820 feet). However, you must be aware that the linear measure only conveys the distance between two points as the crow flies. You must cross-reference this information with the contour lines that show how steep the land is (the closer together the contour lines are, the steeper the terrain). Contour lines also allow you to distinguish the topographical features of the area (valleys, ridges, etc.). Once you have all this information, you can choose a route that requires the least effort and keeps well clear of areas where there is a danger of avalanches. Special symbols are used to indicate rocky outcrops. This means not only that you can avoid crossing them but also that you can evaluate the risk of avalanches on the areas beneath them. This scale of map also shows paths over the mountain. Remember, though, that it is often difficult to spot the paths when they are covered in snow and that summer routes are not always feasible in winter. Information provided by maps must be related to the ground during the trek. To check that you are still following the right route, find where you are on the map (see diagram). This means drawing imaginarylines (at least two, better three) that unite clearly identifiable points (refuges, churches, mountain peaks) on the map and then working backwards from their intersection to find exactly where you are.

The climb

Always ascend in single file, keeping a few meters (yards) distance between yourself and the skiers in front and behind. The most experienced member of the group, who knows the route well, should lead the column. This is particularly important over steep slopes, in places where there is no trace of anyone else's passage, over rough ground or tricky areas. In fresh snow conditions, however, it is extremely tiring to be the trail-blazer and it is therefore a good idea for people to alternate regularly in the role. When crossing slopes where there is a risk (however minimal) of avalanche, it is important that you make your preparations in advance. Check your avalanche beacons beforehand and then spread the line out more (but without ever losing sight of the skier in front and behind), undo the safety straps on your binding and

grip your poles without threading your hand through the straps (skis and baskets tend to sink in avalanches).

Once you reach your target, it is essential to stop for a while and rest (and take the ritual photograph of you all). But make sure the break does not last too long or your muscles and mind will relax too much. Your body must remain toned and alert, ready to tackle the descent in complete safety. From this moment on, in fact, you must keep all your wits about you if you are to remain in control, able to make strong and instantaneous decisions. If there was time for contemplation and meditation during the ascent, in the descent mind and body must work rapidly and accurately. If not, you risk losing the level of safety that is necessary for any enjoyment of the situation. Once this goes the descent is "endured" with anxiety and apprehension.

Left: two separate moments during the phase of leaning on the boots when climbing uphill; above: one foot rests on the binding completely; below: both heels are raised.

The descent

After a very light but energizing snack (chocolate, fruit purée or juice), remove your skins and stow them in your rucksack. Put your skis back on and lock the bindings into the downhill position. Put your windproof jacket and hat on and make sure you wear your heavy-duty gloves. This is not just a precaution against the cold, but also a way of protecting your hands should you, as is always possible, fall. Nor must you ever forget safety during the descent. Wherever the terrain allows, always choose the safest route. If you encounter high-risk situations, make sure you spread out, but never lose sight of each other. When skiing down open and steep slopes, make sure you turn tightly across the fall line. You alternate this with short traverses across the fall line in order to minimize the risk of your presence detaching build-ups of snow. When skiing through woods, be very careful to avoid small hillocks of snow that all too often hide roots or fallen branches. This type of obstacle means that you have to make an instant decision on which way to go and they are often the cause of disastrous falls which can prove dangerous, especially if your skis fail to come off automatically.

Downhill technique must be adapted to the prevailing snow conditions. Below: skiing downhill over spring snow; bottom: completed turn on crusty or wind-swept snow; left: skiing downhill over hard, compacted snow, similar to conditions on a groomed run.

TABLE 1. DIFFICULTY SCALE

There are currently two scales in use to grade the difficulty of ski touring/mountaineering routes. Each was created by a great French skier-climber whose names they respectively take. The first scale classifies technical difficulty, while the second, which by and large tends to be used more in publications and by guides, categorizes the type of skier and takes account of difficulties in the ascent phase and of a mountaineering nature.

Traynard's technical difficulty scale

S1. Wide, open, slightly sloping ground, where descent does not need to follow a set route.

S2. Steeper slopes, but not excessive incline, presence of moguls or bumps, which allows a free downhill run.

S3. Consistently steep slope that calls for short turns but still allows the possibility of choosing your own route.

S4. Very steep slope (30°–35°), often exposed, with downhill run dictated by the difficulties and lie of the land.

S5. The same characteristics as S4 but pushed to the very limits of a perfectly fit and trained skier.

S6. Slopes with gradients steeper than 45°–50°, very exposed, which require acrobatic feats to ski them. Exclusive territory of a small band of skiers, falls outside terrain of ski touring/mountaineering and definitely classed as "extreme skiing."

Blachère's classification scale

IS. Intermediate skier: well able to ski downhill with difficulties of the S1 or S2 types; only able to tackle S3 for short spells.

GS. Good skier, perfectly able to handle S3 conditions, can ski downhill over S4 terrain without any problems provided it is only for a short time and the slope is not too exposed.

ES. Excellent skier: can ski downhill over any terrain provided no acrobatic feats are called for.

The addition of "A/M" (Alpine/mountaineering) means that, even if only for a short stretch, the route includes terrain that calls for specific mountaineering skills. For instance ESM (Excellent Ski Mountaineer) denotes a route that only excellent skiers with proven experience of winter climbing should tackle.

Avalanche danger

We are not trying to be unnecessarily alarmist, nor do we want to curtail your enjoyment of what is a wonderful pursuit. But we really must underline yet again that as soon as skiers go off trail they remove themselves from the safety guaranteed by groomed runs. We want everyone who thinks about venturing into the world of ski touring/mountaineering (or even just skiing off trail) to fully grasp and understand the risks involved and to accept the proper guidance offered by competent ski touring/mountaineering schools, associations, and clubs. Furthermore, we really must advise anyone thinking of starting out to hire the services of properly qualified, expert, and professional guides at least for the first few ski treks.

The risk of an avalanche is undoubtedly the greatest danger faced by ski tourers/mountaineers and indeed by anyone skiing off trail. In the Alps alone, avalanches kill an average of 130 people each year. Nearly all of them are expert skiers who had not, however, properly evaluated the danger of snow falling away in an avalanche. The most worrying fact of all is that, in 80% of cases, the avalanche was provoked by human activity in the area. Over half of all skiers caught in avalanches do not survive. The probability of finding a person alive under the snow is 40% after one hour but only 10% after three hours. It follows, therefore, that immediate help is of fundamental importance. The life expectancy of someone completely buried under an avalanche (always assuming that they have not already suffered serious injury) is 15 minutes. After this time, the possibility of not suffocating depends entirely on the fortuitous presence of small pockets of air close to the victim's face. Suffice it to say that 15 minutes is not a long time to get a rescue operation both under way and completed. In the best possible of circum-

stances, you have five minutes to pinpoint the victim's avalanche beacon and a further ten minutes to dig them out with your avalanche shovel. This is why it is best that a trekking group has a large number of people in it, each of whom carries his or her own shovel. This considerably cuts down on the digging time.

Above: rescue team in action
to save avalanche victims.

205

OFF-TRAIL RULES

Here is a summary of a few basic rules that all ski-mountaineers, ski-tourers and, more generally, off-trail skiers, should follow:

• Never go out alone.

• Let someone trustworthy know exactly where you are heading (if you are staying in a hotel, let the hotel keeper know).

• Avoid deep snow for at least three days after a heavy snowfall.

• Be prepared to change your plans after hearing the weather forecast or avalanche warnings.

• Never forget to carry an operational avalanche beacon, an avalanche shovel, and a probe.

• Never undertake off-trail treks or runs without first practicing how to use the avalanche beacon and the necessary rescue and first aid techniques.

• Use an airbag (but do not have blind faith in it).

• When touring, make sure that the members of your group spread out in a line, both uphill and downhill, so that no more than one member of the group could be caught in an avalanche.

• Avoid wind-blown snowdrifts in windswept bowls and slopes.

• Try to ski downhill following your uphill route so that you already know the lie of the land and the snow conditions.

Basic precautions, such as never skiing off trail alone, apply to everyone and not just ski mountaineers/tourers.

DOS AND DON'TS OF AVALANCHES

• Snowfall of more than 50 cm (20 inches) brings with it the danger of avalanches regardless of the height or exposure of the slope. When the wind blows, however, slabs of snow may build up that can be broken off by a snowfall of only 20 cm (8 inches). The danger subsides as the snow settles, which is helped by a rise in temperatures.

• The composition of the snow mass plays a determining role in creating avalanches. Most slab avalanches occur when blocks of compacted snow slide over the unstable snow beneath.

• Skiers trigger 80% of avalanches. Cautious and prudent behavior on their behalf would avert major accidents.

• Avalanche victims rarely survive. It is therefore of fundamental importance to try to avoid triggering an avalanche. This means checking the avalanche reports and warnings in advance and, if need be, aborting the trek.

• You cannot always predict an avalanche. It is therefore essential to behave as though every slope, however low the risk, involved a serious avalanche danger. Keep to ridges and flat terrain and avoid long traverses. If traversing is unavoidable, then do it as high up the slope as possible, move from one safe point to the next (a tree or a rock) and only stop in these places. If need be, remove your skis (which reduces the risk of your triggering a slab movement) and descend wherever possible along the fall line. Avoid leeward slopes where snow tends to build up more than elsewhere. Make sure that everyone's avalanche beacon is fully operational.

• If you find you have to traverse danger areas:
 – Keep a distance between you so that only one skier at a time is exposed to the danger, but never lose sight of each other
 – Undo the safety straps on your bindings, slip your hands out of the pole straps, use one strap only to hold your rucksack in place.

• When traversing, take note of a safe place to make for using a diagonal descent.

• If you are caught in an avalanche, this is what you do:
 – Try and get rid of anything that would drag you down (poles, rucksack, skis)
 – Keep your mouth closed
 – Make an effort to stay afloat in the snow by "swimming" with your arms and legs, trying to direct your movements toward the edge of the avalanche.

• If you witness an avalanche accident, this is what you do:
 – Keep looking to see where the person is swept and memorize the spot where they end up
 – Call for help immediately (mobile phone)
 – Find the victim, free their nose and mouth but under no circumstances try to move them (unless they are able to move themselves), keep them covered with dry clothing, and wait for help to arrive.

TABLE 2. EUROPEAN AVALANCHE DANGER SCALE

Stability of snow cover and probability of avalanches occurring (*).

LOW. The snow cover is generally well compacted and stable. An avalanche would generally only be triggered by a large load (**) on a small number of extremely steep slopes (***). The only real danger comes from small, spontaneous avalanches (in other words not triggered by people, so-called slippages).

MODERATE. The snow cover is fairly well compacted on a few steep slopes and elsewhere is well compacted. Avalanches are most likely to be triggered by a large load applied to the steep slopes in question. Large spontaneous avalanches are not forecast under these conditions.

MARKED. The snow cover is only moderately or poorly compacted on the steep slopes. An avalanche can be triggered by a small load, especially on the steep slopes in question. Given the right circumstances, you can also expect fairly large spontaneous slippages and, in individual cases, major avalanches.

HIGH. The snow cover is poorly compacted over nearly all of the steep slopes. A small load could trigger an avalanche on most steep slopes. Under certain circumstances, you should expect a lot of fairly large spontaneous slippages and sometimes a major avalanche.

VERY HIGH. The snow cover is generally badly compacted and mostly unstable. You should expect a large number of major spontaneous avalanches, even on not very steep slopes.

Notes

This scale is used in Austria, France, Germany, Italy, Scotland, Spain, and Switzerland.

(*) Bulletins describe this in greater detail (height, exposure, lie of the land, etc.).

(**) Large load (group of skiers bunched together, trail-maintenance machines, explosives). Small load (one skier, people walking without skis).

(***) A steep slope is more of than 30°. An extremely steep slope is one the skier finds hostile with regard to profile, lie of the land, proximity to the summit, and the roughness of the terrain.

TABLE 3. CANADIAN AND USA AVALANCHE DANGER SCALES

Danger level (and color). Canada.

LOW (green). Natural slippage very unlikely. Avalanche triggered by people unlikely. Routes generally safe. Adopt normal safety procedures.

MODERATE (yellow). Natural slippage unlikely. Avalanche triggered by people possible. Use caution on steep slopes.

CONSIDERABLE (orange). Natural slippage possible. Avalanche triggered by people probable. Use utmost caution on steep slopes.

HIGH (red). Natural slippage and avalanches triggered by people possible. Advised not to go onto slopes where there is avalanche warning.

EXTREME (black). Certain risk of generalized natural slippage and avalanches triggered by people. Essential to avoid all areas at risk.

Danger level (and color). USA.

LOW (green). Natural slippage very unlikely. Avalanche triggered by people unlikely. Snow cover generally stable. Possible isolated areas of instability. Routes generally safe. Adopt normal safety procedures.

MODERATE (yellow). Natural slippage unlikely. Avalanche triggered by people possible. Possible slippage confined to steep slopes. Use caution on very steep slopes.

CONSIDERABLE (orange). Natural slippage possible. Avalanche triggered by people probable. Probable slippage on steep slopes. Use utmost caution on steep slopes.

HIGH (red). Natural slippage and avalanches triggered by people possible. Snow cover unstable on many slopes of varying steepness. Advised not to go onto slopes where there is avalanche warning. Possible to go on routes where the slopes are not steep and that are not downhill of steep slopes.

EXTREME (black). Certain risk of generalized natural slippage and avalanches triggered by people. Snow cover is generally highly unstable. Possible trigger of large and highly destructive avalanches. Essential to avoid all areas at risk. Possible to go on routes where the slopes are not steep and that are well away from the route of any avalanche.

7
CROSS-COUNTRY SKIING

How equipment and techniques have
evolved. The basics of balance and gliding.
The search for maximum performance. Classic
and skating techniques.

INTRODUCTION

Alpine, or downhill, skiing and cross-country (Nordic) skiing share certain characteristics, but at the same time they are poles apart. They have the same origins, but the "philosophy" behind their development is completely different.

Talking about Nordic skiing, or cross-country skiing, is to talk about the origins of skiing. Anyone who practices this sport is choosing to get closer to nature, to rediscover the original power in their own body, and to rediscover their feet as the means by which people were able to get about, in areas covered by snow for many months of the year, in order to explore them and get to know them.

In recent years we have seen these two sports gradually drawing closer together again, owing partly to technical innovations, but mostly to an increased recognition that they complement each other

perfectly for people who want to savor the whole range of experiences that mountains offer in the winter. This leads on naturally to ski-touring.

How equipment and techniques have evolved

The origins of skiing can be traced back to the first decades of the 20th century, when the equipment used for downhill skiing was not much different from that used for cross-country skiing. As late as the 1940s skiing manuals presented the techniques for the two sports side by side. Then, as the use of ski lifts for downhill skiing became more widespread, the gap between the two disciplines became more obvious, and the technology used to manufacture their respective equipment developed in different ways.

The need to reduce the effort involved in covering long distances has meant that

Cross-country and downhill skiing come from the same origin, and were only later differentiated by their equipment and technique.

the shape of cross-country skis differs from that of downhill skis. The fact that advancing uphill or on flat ground plays such a large part has meant that the weight of skis has been reduced and they are narrower, while they are kept as long as possible so as to provide an adequately large surface in contact with the snow. Lighter and more resistant materials have made it possible to produce extremely light skis with excellent performance.

EQUIPMENT

Cross-country skiing equipment can be divided into two groups: that for the traditional, or classic, style and that for skating style. The first distinction concerns the skis: classic skis are longer than those for skating technique, while the latter are thicker at the waist and have more rigid edges. Boots also vary according to which technique is involved: skating boots are a

bit taller and more rigid than classic boots. Lastly, skating bindings grip more to support the foot during the pushing phase of skating.

Above: skating-style boot and binding. Left: classic-style boot and binding.

Preparing the skis

When snow is very cold, frozen crystals stick to the base of the ski; these crystals, being rough, attach to the surface of the snow underneath, and thus prevent gliding. Even before you reach this extreme, the abrasion of snow crystals on the ski's base is still the main source of friction. On the other hand, when the snow is very damp, it is the suction effect, produced by the water that forms between the ski and the snow, that causes loss of speed. What actually promotes easy gliding is the lubricating action of a thin layer of water, produced by the snow melting on the ski base. However, this film of water must be neither too thick nor too thin: by using the correct treatment on the base of the ski it is possible to create optimum conditions for any type of snow or weather. There are basically two main elements involved in achieving this: getting the right pattern impressed on the base of the ski and applying the right ski wax.

The pattern, or design, on the base is

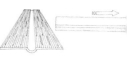

made up of an infinitesimal number of microgrooves, which help to form the film of water when you are skiing on very cold snow, and enable excess water to be eliminated in damp snow conditions.

Left: "fishscale" base which causes greater friction and is generally used by beginners and intermediate skiers. Above: patterned base for expert skiers; it creates less friction but needs to be waxed.

CLOTHING

Cross-country skiers' clothing is simple, basic, and practical. The undergarments consist of a vest (wool or cotton, but better if made of a synthetic material or even a string vest); ordinary underpants, which can be exchanged for thermal ones on cold days, then a pair of leggings (tights) of the Norwegian type and a high-necked jersey or top. Socks should be short and elasticized. Depending on the outside temperature, the following may also be worn: a padded jacket with a zip fastening at the neck, a fleece waistcoat, or a jacket in a modern breathable material. Waterproof trousers with a dungaree top to protect your back can sometimes come in handy. Protect your head from the cold with a head-band or a hat, and your hands with lightweight fabric or fleece gloves with leather reinforcement at the palm. You should always wear sun glasses.

SKI WAX

Applying wax serves several purposes. Firstly, it prevents dirt particles from being absorbed by the base of the ski. Ski bases are made of polyethylene, made by a process of sintering or extrusion, often with the addition of graphite. This process results in a porous substance, that can vary in density to better suit the different types of snow. Although the insertion of graphite is intended to make the material a conductor, in order to eliminate the static electricity that is responsible for attracting dirt particles, unless the pores are filled dirt particles will inevitably penetrate. Of all the possible causes of friction, dirt is most definitely the greatest. When hot wax is applied the pores dilate, allowing the wax itself to penetrate deeply, thus saturating the ski base. Excess wax is then scraped off.

A second motive for applying wax is to make the skis more water repellent. The higher the water content of the snow, the more important it is to use materials that make the water droplets run off quickly. If you want to get an idea of how effective wax treatment is, try putting a few drops of water on a treated ski and on an untreated ski: if you tilt the skis the drops on the treated ski will run down much faster. If the opposite happens, you have used the wrong type of ski wax! In recent years, owing to its water-repellent properties, fluorine has become widely used, either mixed in with the wax, or in the pure form of fluorine carbonate.

A third reason for wax treatment is to create optimal abrasion between the ski surface and the snow. If the surface of the ski base is too hard it will transmit too much heat to the snow, resulting in too thick a film of water. On the other hand a surface that is too soft will allow the snow crystals to penetrate. Ski wax is thus useful in modifying the surface of the ski base to suit snow conditions. Snow slightly harder than the ski base is the prerequisite for the optimum film of water and thus for optimum gliding.

Influence of temperature and humidity

Which wax to choose depends on three main factors: temperature, humidity in the air, and the type of snow.

The temperature that matters is that of the snow's surface. If the air temperature is very high (above 5°) you will also have to take into consideration the fact that the snow will be very wet. A rough categorization of air humidity is as follows: 1) below 50%; 2) between 50% and 80%; 3) above 80%. Correct identification of the type of snow is vital, and at the same time difficult. Fresh or falling snow when the temperature is low is made up of very sharp crystals, and requires a wax capable of preventing them from penetrating the sole. The conformation of artificial snow is similar, and requires the use of synthetic paraffin. When the air temperature is higher than 0°C (32°F) the temperature of the snow itself stays at 0°C, and the amount of water that is present between the snow crystals increases, until saturation point is reached. In these sorts of conditions it is better to use fluoridated wax that is highly water repellent.

Applying the wax

The ski should be dry and clean. Applying hot wax needs careful attention, and you should always follow the manufacturer's instructions. Bear in mind that if the wax is heated to 120°C (250°F), in six seconds about 18–19 g (just over half an ounce) of paraffin will be absorbed, while at 70°C (160°F) not even 1 g is absorbed. Above 130°C (265°F) most types of paraffin deteriorate. Make sure that you spend enough time waxing to allow the wax to penetrate well. Before carrying on with further maintenance work (scraping off excess wax or polishing) allow the skis to cool down to room temperature.

Gripping wax

Besides helping skis to glide, in cross-country skis wax treatment is also intended to provide sufficient adhesion during the pushing phase in the classic technique. In fact, this was the only purpose that wax did serve in the past, covering the entire length of the ski. Nowadays it is only used on the section of the base underneath the "camber," i.e. the section that comes into contact with the snow when it is weighted by the skier as he pushes off. The current trend is to keep this section as short as possible, which corresponds, of course, to the demand for more precise control in technique.

How does Gripping wax actually work? The substances used now (synthetic hydrocarbons such as wax and resin) provide a dense structure, which is extremely resistant when the ski is in contact with the snow and glides beautifully. Furthermore, the low level of penetration by the snow crystals eliminates the danger of the ski wax itself actually freezing. When the camber is loaded down by the skier's weight, it comes into contact with the snow crystals which penetrate it, but do not attach themselves. Once the weighted phase is over, the crystals, which are not linked in any structural way, are easily expelled by the surface as soon as the gliding phase begins. If the ski wax were to freeze, the snow crystals would no longer be able to be shifted, and would then act as gathering points for other crystals, thus forming so-called "clogs" of snow. As a general rule, as the temperature increases the snow crystals become rounder, and so the wax needs to be softer. On crystalline, cold snow, sticks of solid ski wax are used.

TECHNIQUES
The "driving power" of a cross-country skier

In cross-country skiing you nearly always have to cross large stretches of flat or slightly uphill ground, while downhill stretches become almost like resting periods, where you can catch your breath again, always assuming that you are skilled enough to keep your balance without effort. In these circumstances your muscles are the only source of power for forward motion: there are no ski lifts to transport you to the top and often there is not even gravity to pull you forwards, as in downhill skiing. This is why technique is so important in cross-country skiing, because it is the only way that you can make optimum use of your efforts, in such a way that the energy used by your legs and arms is translated efficiently into forward motion. Cross-country skis need to fulfill two apparently contradictory needs at the same

time. On the one hand you want to make the most of the gliding motion so as to reduce the muscular effort needed to advance. On the other hand you must be able to transmit to the ground the impulse

Left and above: simultaneous planting the foot and pushing constitute the "motor" of the cross-country skier.

necessary to push off forwards, without which there wouldn't be any gliding at all. But how is this possible if, the moment you put on your skis, you realize that every time you try to step forward on one foot you make the other foot slide backwards? When we walk, it is the friction between foot and ground that provides the grip that is used to propel the rest of the body forwards. Once you get rid of this grip, there seems to be no way of advancing at all, let alone at a greater speed than a man walking. This is where man's ingenuity comes into it, combining technique and technology in an effective manner.

The mechanics of cross-country technique explained

By reducing to a minimum the time that the "pushing" ski is weighted, it is possible to make the most of that brief moment when the skier's weight is directly over the ground, so canceling out the factors that make the skis glide. If at the same time a part of the weight can be planted at a separate point (the opposite pole) which is then also used for pushing off, the trick is complete! Cross-country skiing is a "four-wheel drive" sport.

Obviously it is not all quite this easy. At one time the entire base of the ski used to be treated with gripping wax that adhered to the snow. Nowadays, in the effort to obtain maximum speed with minimum effort, this trend has been reversed: application of gripping wax is limited to only the very center of the ski, right under the foot. By starting from these assumptions, the American William (Bill) Koch introduced, at the start of the 1980s, the skating technique which enabled him to win the cross-country World Cup in 1982. This new technique in fact made it possible to dispense completely with the use of gripping wax. As a result the skating technique became a separate entity (as freestyle technique), but the principle that it originated from still remains valid in classic crosscountry.

Without friction (right) the foot would slide in the direction shown by the arrow.

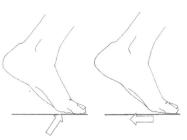

From balance to gliding

The physical principle

In cross-country skiing today there are two main techniques in use: classic and skating, but in the initial learning stages your experiences will be identical for both techniques.

The first important experience is without doubt learning to glide, which can be seen as a sort of dynamic equilibrium, but it also feels odd if not downright unnatural.

Right from our earliest years we are in fact accustomed to walking on more or less flat surfaces, that provide sufficient friction to allow us to move forward at a modest speed. By planting our feet on the ground we move without even paying attention to the movements that our body is making.

Putting skis under our feet means getting rid of that safely planted grip on the ground. Furthermore, having to tackle routes where the slope of the ground is always changing, with accompanying changes in the angle at which we are standing vertically, results in a sensation of clumsiness (often more than just a sensation!) and inability to properly control our own movements.

The experimental method

The first thing that beginners should do is "experiment," without being afraid to make exaggerated movements and gestures (too wide or too tight, too quick or too slow, etc.). In this way it is possible to work out the relationship between actions and their effect, and to memorize the correct "steps" needed to enter into the world of skiing, just like a child that is learning how to move about and walk. Once you have put your skis on, the first thing that you must do is take careful note of the new conditions required for balance. Exercises that can help you in this are walking slowly, sliding a little on flat ground, alternately raising the skis with or without actually moving to a different position,

Left: your first experiences of gliding should be carried out on fairly level ground, with the help of a push from the poles.

always keeping in mind that it is precisely by making mistakes that you learn the most.

To start with you will inevitably fall over numerous times. When you need to stand up again after a fall, remember that if your center of gravity has fallen outside the vertical line that passes through your feet, your body will be affected by transverse forces which, in the absence of friction on the ground, will make your feet slide even further away, resulting in a series of useless and frustrating efforts to get up again. So

Facing page, left: alternately raising the skis; right: gliding on parallel skis.
Below: to get up after a fall, you must bring your body back in line with your feet, so as to avoid your skis sliding forwards.

you must bring your body back in line with your feet as much as possible, and while you are getting up again you should try to keep your head a bit in front of your feet.

Once you have gained a sufficient mastery of balance, you can then practice your agility by trying out some short glides. It is obviously a good idea to choose a fairly flat piece of ground, ideally one that ends in an uphill slope. It is quite pointless to think about possible dangers, which are anyway almost non-existent; you should concentrate your attention more on the pleasant sensations of speed, acceleration, and the vibrations transmitted from the ground.

Basic movements

First steps

The first thing to do is to learn the basic step, a movement that is very similar to an ordinary walk. It is an easy and elegant movement, but you need to pay careful attention to coordinating the action of your arms and legs.

Set one ski forward, slightly bending your knee in a natural way, and at the same time swing the opposite arm forward, planting the tip of the pole wide of the skis and level with the forward foot. Planting the pole too far forward, besides involving an awkward arm movement (you will be forced to raise your arm in an exaggerated manner), generates a force that opposes advancement, and demands pointless effort from the upper body.

Bringing your foot back should be done a natural way, by raising the heel. While you are performing this movement you may also try to find out how long you can leave your weight on the weighted ski without it sliding backwards. Try doing this either by keeping your heel lowered (i.e. resting on the ski), or by taking advantage of the flexibility of the boot to get a grip with the front part of your foot. Your poles should be held with the strap to the

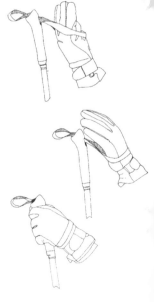

Left: correct stance for gliding. Below: the correct way to take hold of the poles.

front, threading your hand into the loop from underneath, and holding it between your thumb and index finger. This will make it much easier to bring the pole back as you start the next set of movements.

You should also have a go on a bit of uphill ground, noting the effect that varying the length and frequency of your steps makes.

Your arms should not only support the movement of your legs, but should also help to produce a real proper push forwards. To accompany the basic step you should .also practice the basic push, achieved by using only the pushing action of your poles and arms.

You should choose flat or slightly sloping ground.

NO: Try to avoid stiffening your legs and stretching out the pushing arm (left).
NO: Wrong coordination between arms and legs (below).
YES: The first steps should be very similar to an ordinary walk.

METHODS OF ASCENT

A route through the mountains is not of course completely flat, and you also need to know how to negotiate slopes, both uphill and downhill. To climb a slope you will need to use the side-step or the herringbone.

The side-step is performed with the skis parallel and at right angles to the fall line, and edged on the uphill side. Lean your weight first on the downhill ski (while keeping it edged) and raise the other and move it sideways uphill together

In the side-step the skis are kept at right angles to the fall line.
YES: Skis correctly positioned.
NO: Do not point your heels or tips downhill in case they start to slide downhill.

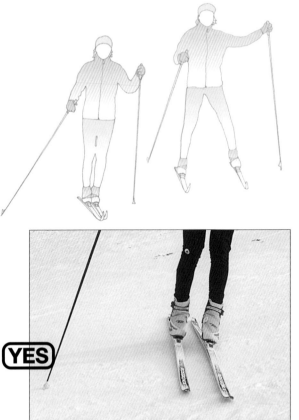

with the pole on that side. Then bring the downhill ski up to join it, together with its pole, and so on.

A variation on the side-step is the diagonal side-step, in which the raised ski is also moved forwards. In the herringbone the skis should be placed with their heels together and their tips apart, edged along the inside. You advance straight up the fall line by lifting and moving each ski in turn, using the ski poles to help you by planting them in the snow just behind your feet. It is easier to edge your skis and plant them if you bend slightly at the knees and ankles.

YES: The skis are positioned with their tips apart and are edged on the inside.
NO: Avoid crossing the heels.

DESCENDING

Descent can sometimes be the real bugbear of beginner cross-country skiers, who very often, especially if no longer very young, choose cross-country instead of downhill skiing precisely because they are scared of falling on steep slopes. In fact, not paying enough attention to the problems involved in descent can mean that cross-country skiers find themselves in difficulties. For this reason you should devote enough time to learning technique so that your first experiences of fairly demanding runs are not ruined by being scantily prepared for tackling the inevitable descents.

The problems linked to descending are:
- variations in gradient
- changes of direction
- controlling speed.

These three factors all demand excellent balance, coordination of movement, and a sensitivity to the route chosen, and for this reason you should not expect to succeed in a very short time in gaining mastery of your skis in every situation.

In the sketch: the correct basic position, to be maintained even during gentle descents. Below: how to tackle a change in gradient.

Variations in gradient

You should start by gliding on parallel skis down increasingly long stretches of gentle slope, ending either in level ground or in an uphill slope, and including changes of gradient; it is better if this is actually a prepared cross-country loipe (a machine-ski trail) and you are able to follow tracks.

The stance to adopt is with your legs slightly bent, your arms out ahead, parallel and partly flexed. Your torso should be at right angles to the slope and your poles should be held raised from the snow and pointing backwards. Your body should be relaxed, especially your shoulders and the base of your feet, in which you need maximum sensitivity. Greet each change in gradient by adapting the position of your body to the shifts of the ground.

Frequent bending and straightening, at first over a limited range and later more extensively is useful for acquiring a better control of your skis. Another thing that you can try out during these descents is to practice gliding the skis alternately and shifting your weight from one to the other.

Once you have gained some familiarity with the movements on the loipe, you can try out some descents off-track, perhaps even making small sideways movements with the skis.

This exercise introduces a possible solution to the second problem: changes in direction.

Below: on any cross-country run there are frequent changes in gradient and your movements must be continually adapted to suit different situations.

CHANGING DIRECTION

There are a number of ways of changing direction:
- using a succession of steps
- using different types of turn.

Forward steps are the simplest way to change direction and sometimes the only way, such as in crusty ungroomed snow. This can be done either on flat ground or going downhill. The movement involves putting all the weight of your body on one ski and raising either the tip or the heel of the other, and then placing the weight of your body onto it The action is repeated until you have completed the turn. It is a good idea to try out changes of direction in spaces of different width, on either flat or slightly sloping ground. During the exercise you should take the opportunity to note how much hindrance your heels are and what is the correct balance to give to the ski at the moment when you bring it back; both of these will be very important factors in skating technique.

Turns can also be carried out:
- in a snowplow (wedge)
- with parallel skis
- with Telemark technique.

To change direction with a series of steps you must shift your weight onto one ski and point the tip of the other one away, and then bring the skis together again, and so on.

The snowplow (wedge)

In this early stage of learning only snow-plow turns will be dealt with, leaving the study of other methods for when you have acquired a better control of your equipment. Leaving aside the use of the poles as a brake, a rather rudimentary but effective method, in use since the early days of skiing, the snowplow is the main method of controlling speed when descending the fall line.

The heels of your skis should be wide apart, and your weight should be firmly on the inside edges. Your torso, just as in the parallel glide, should be held perpendicular to the slope, with your knees and ankles slightly bent. You should keep your knees apart so as to place your weight properly on the skis. By varying the distance between your heels and by adjusting the angle at which your skis are edged on the snow to suit the circumstances, it is possible to adapt this method of speed control to slopes of different gradients.

The snowplow (wedge) is the main method of controlling speed; the weight of your body should be spread equally on the edged skis.

To control speed when descending on a track only one ski is put in the snowplow (wedge) position, while the other continues to run in the track.

The wider apart your skis, and the more edged they are, the more effectively they will brake.

The things that you should be continually checking while doing a snowplow, until you are able to come to a complete stop on slopes of different gradients, are the positioning of your arms, the tilt of your torso, and the angle of edging your skis. Increased edging should be obtained not by bringing your knees together, but by pushing your feet further apart: if you do bring your knees closer together your ski tips will tend to cross.

You should then try downhill sections alternating between snowplowing and parallel skis.

Points to note

When you need to control your speed while descending a prepared track, you should move only one of your skis out of the loipe, with its heel pushed outwards and weighted on its inside edge, gradually transferring your body weight to it. Practice this until you can come to a complete stop.

Careful: too much edging could make your skis cross.

NO: Skis too parallel (top).
NO: Knees too close together (center).
NO: Skis not held apart, resulting in tips crossing (bottom).
YES: Correct position for the snowplow (wedge).

Snowplow (wedge) turns

From the position for descending in a snowplow it is easy to initiate a change of direction. Friction on the snow from both the skis, if totally symmetrical, allows you to proceed in a straight line. All you have to do is reduce the pressure on one side in order to start a shift in that direction.

Try making a snowplow descent while flattening alternately, first one ski and then the other. Flattening one ski can be achieved by keeping your torso steady and turning your knee outwards on the side that you have chosen. Once you start to turn, shift the weight of your body so as to put more weight on the opposite ski. You can also bend your legs while you are doing this, so accentuating the change of direction and the turn.

The ski that is flattened and becomes

the inside of the turn should be kept slightly ahead of the other and completely flat, so as to avoid cutting into the snow and hindering the movement.

At the end of the turn, by lessening the degree of edging and by returning to the basic position, you can once more point your tips down the fall line to start the next turn in the opposite direction.

Left: before the turn you must adopt the correct snowplow (wedge) position.

NO: Do not turn your shoulders into the turn (facing page) and do not flatten the outside ski (the one on the right in the photograph).
NO: An incorrect snowplow (wedge) position will make it difficult to start the turn (right).

TORSO
SLIGHTLY
INCLINED

ARMS HELD
FORWARD AND
WIDE OF THE
BODY

POLES RAISED FROM
THE SNOW AND HELD
POINTING
BACKWARDS

LEGS SLIGHTLY
BENT

HEELS APART

TIPS CLOSE TOGETHER

THE SNOWPLOW (WEDGE)

THE SEARCH FOR MAXIMUM EFFICIENCY

Once you have a good grasp of the basics you can choose whether to proceed with classic or skating skiing.

In the classic technique, as has been explained, the push given by your legs is effective because of the gripping wax, and results in a gait in which the ski is at a standstill at the moment of pushing off.

Skating skiing, on the other hand, does not need gripping wax; the pushing phase is longer and is carried out with the ski always in motion, resulting in greater efficiency of muscular effort. Choosing one technique does not necessarily exclude the other. All the experience that you gain, with whatever equipment and in whatever style, creates your "portfolio" of skiing experiences, and can be very much to your advantage in different situations.

The next stage is to examine how to get maximum efficiency out of your movements, in order to be able to successfully tackle any type of run with minimum expenditure of energy, so that you can extract the maximum enjoyment both from the physical exercise itself, and from the natural environment around you.

CLASSIC TECHNIQUE

The classic technique consists of a set group of steps for advancing on flat or rising ground. The most commonly used steps are:
• diagonal gait
• diagonal gait uphill
• double pole with leg kick
• herringbone
• double pole

By using these steps correctly it is possible to ski any sort of track successfully, and choosing the most suitable step depends on the type of terrain and the type of snow. Until fairly recently the choice of which of the different steps to use depended solely on an analysis of the terrain: flat, uphill or descending. Nowadays the determining factor has become speed: taking into account how well the skis glide, the individual's ability and fitness levels, it is quite possible to cover the same piece of ground using a variety of steps.

Left: skating technique.
Above: classic technique.

Diagonal gait

In the diagonal gait the movements of legs and arms must be perfectly synchronized; as one arm goes forward the opposite leg goes forward as well, and it is this combined action that provides the push.

With the weight of your body on one ski alone (the right ski for instance) swing forward the arm on that side (right) together with the opposite ski (left). At the same time the opposite arm (left) must plant its pole in the snow level with the binding of the other ski (right). With your weight on this pole you achive the forward push, while the ski that has finished its push is now brought forwards, taking

advantage of the gliding motion.

The weighted leg starts to push when both legs are more or less at the same level, making use of the effect produced by the gripping wax.

As the weighted leg finishes its pushing action, your weight will end up completely on the ski that you have moved forward, which is kept flat on the snow by the advanced position of your torso.

Once finished pushing with the pole your hand should open, keeping the grip between your thumb and index finger.

The diagonal gait can be adapted to suit particular situations as follows:

• the triple step, in which you push twice

Side and front view of the diagonal gait at the moment of pushing off.

with each arm and then hold the poles out in front of you instead of the third push
• the Finnish step, in which you alternate two whole diagonal strides with two gliding steps without poling

Above: front and side view of the diagonal gait at the moment when one arm is pushing and your weight is on the opposite foot.
Right: pushing phase of the left foot.

A more detailed look

Detailed analysis of the movements involved in the diagonal gait reveals how the leg push starts when the arm push finishes, i.e. at the moment when, owing to

the friction produced by the load upon the weighted leg, the ski stops gliding.

To get the most out of the leg push, your foot, at the end of the pushing action, should be almost at right angles to the ground. This reduces the adhesive tendency of the ski wax, and results in a better glide. You should start the arm pushing movement with your elbow slightly bent, so as to involve the shoulder muscles as well; this flexed position is maintained until your arm is level with your leg, after which the pushing motion is provided by your extended forearm (with your elbow straightened) and lastly by your hand (with your wrist straightened). Pole length is very important. To keep to a minimum the time lapse between the moment when the pole is planted and the moment when the push actually begins, the pole grip should not come higher than your shoulder.

YES: At the moment of pushing your foot should be almost at right angles to the ground.
NO: The pole is being planted too far forward (top).
NO: The arm is too flexed before planting the pole (center).

Diagonal gait uphill

When climbing, the joints in the lower limbs must be much more bent. The arms push until they are beyond the outline of the body, in order to make the most of the muscles of the shoulders. The gait is similar to that of the uphill walk, with sliding reduced to the minimum. The frequency of movements increases, while the size of the paces is reduced as is the time spent with the weight on the pushing ski. The adherence of the weighted ski to the ground becomes more important as the gradient of the slope increases. A good technique in the diagonal gait uphill allows you to obtain a good pushing

motion even on quite steep slopes, but when the force needed for you to make sufficient forward progress becomes excessive it makes sense to gradually open out the points of the skis, changing to herringbone. Edging uphill in this way allows you to climb up tracks which are so steep that the gripping power of the wax is not sufficient to let you push forward.

Top: uphill steps are shorter and more frequent.
Right: as the gradient increases, you will gradually switch to the herringbone step.

Double pole with leg kick

In this step you combine pushing off with one leg with swinging your arms forwards; they should move parallel in the same direction. While you bring one ski forward, plant both poles together almost level with your ski tips. The pushing action of the arms takes place while you are bringing the rear ski forward.

A variation of the double pole with leg kick is to make two or more such steps and the diagonal gait, in which your legs follow the rhythm of the stride, while your arms are brought forward to push simultaneously.

In this variation, while your legs push off twice your arms only push once.

NO: Arm push accompanied by an over-exaggerated leg bend.
YES: Arm push with correct leg positioning.

Above, the two key moments of the double pole with leg kick: the start and end of the arm push.

Double pole

In this step the skis remain side by side and you do not push with your legs.

Starting from the basic position, with your knees and ankles slightly bent, throw both arms forward and plant both poles simultaneously. Weight them with your whole body weight and push off, prolonging your action until your arms are extended to the maximum behind you. It is important to keep your weight centered during the push, and to do this you must have a clear sensation of supporting the weight of your body on the poles. When you plant the poles in the snow, you should lean your torso forward, pushing with semi-flexed arms, which should pass as close as possible to your body. Before bringing your arms forward again you should straighten your torso up slightly and then, as your arms come forward, straighten your legs in preparation for the next push.

How to adapt to different types of terrain

On flat ground beginners mostly use the diagonal gait, while more experienced and fitter skiers prefer the double pole or, to go faster on very slow snow, the double pole with leg kick.

On uphill sections every skier uses the step that is best suited to his levels of skill and fitness. Hills that more able skiers will tackle using the double pole with leg kick are usually tackled by beginners using the diagonal gait or even the herringbone.

As a general rule, the greater the speed, the more the expert skier will rely on pushing with his arms, thus avoiding the slowing down that arises from leg pushes.

YES: Last stage of a dynamic push, prolonged until the arms reach their maximum backward extent.
NO: Do not plant your poles pointing forwards.

Left: a comparison of the classic and the skating technique. The two techniques are used in different situations. Generally the former is better suited to beginners, whereas with the skating technique greater speed is possible.

THE DIAGONAL GAIT

LEFT ARM
STRETCHED OUT
BEHIND AT THE END
OF PUSHING ACTION

RIGHT ARM
FORWARD AND
SLIGHTLY BENT

TORSO LEANING
FORWARDS IN THE
DIRECTION OF THE
GLIDE

RIGHT LEG
EXTENDED

RIGHT POLE
BEING BROUGHT
FORWARD

LEFT LEG
SLIGHTLY BENT

ROSSIGNOL

RIGHT FOOT AT THE
END OF ITS PUSHING
STAGE

BODY WEIGHT
ON LEFT FOOT
IN GLIDING
PHASE

SWITCHING TRACKS

Switching tracks becomes a very frequent operation whenever you are skiing in crowded areas or on busy days. It is useful when for instance you need to overtake another skier or when the condition of the track makes it necessary. Switching tracks is not a difficult operation, but you need to be careful to keep your balance, owing to the changes in the snow's surface.

Both skis are in the tracks.

Point the tip of one ski in the new direction.

Bring the other ski to join it and glide until you cross the other track.

Raise the ski tip (right in the picture) and place it in the new track.

Raise the other ski (left) and place it in the track.

Carry on with both skis in the new track.

SKATING TECHNIQUE

In skating skiing only gliding wax is applied to the base of the skis. Your skis should be positioned on the snow with their tips wide apart, and as you push off your weight should be on the inside edge. The ski with your weight on it is thus moving and not stationary as in the classical technique, giving you more time to apply force. Depending on the type of snow, the gradient and your speed, you will need to vary the amount of edging. Unlike classic technique, where at high speeds it is your arms that do all the work (double-poling), in skating technique it is your legs that are responsible for most of the pushing work. With the skating technique it is possible to reach higher speeds. The following are the different steps that are used in this technique:

• single leg skating
• double-sided skating
• double-sided skating with double pole every two steps
• double-sided skating with double pole every step

YES: The pushing ski must be well edged.
NO: If the ski is flat it cannot push effectively and slips on the snow.

Above: the skating technique is different from the classic technique in that the main push is provided by the legs. In the sketches: one foot is gliding (the right foot) while the other is the middle of the pushing phase.

Single leg skating

This type of step is used on prepared tracks and enables skiers to attain good coordination while pushing. The ski that is gliding remains in the track, which prevents it from skidding out to the side.

Using the tracks means that you can concentrate more on the pushing action, and makes it easier to keep your balance on the other ski. This is why single leg skating is frequently used in long-distance competitions, now a staple event, such as the "Marcialonga". Keep one ski in the track and raise the other, opening its tip out wide. Plant both poles simultaneously together with the open ski, edged on the inside, and then push off with the combined force of this leg and both arms.

When the action is complete, bring the foot of your pushing leg forward again and place it alongside the other foot. When you are going at a low speed this will be on a level with the other foot, at increased speed it will instead be placed in front.

NO: Torso leaning too far forwards.

Points to note

You may try to vary the angle at which you edge your ski, and experiment with bending and straightening your legs as you shift the weight of your body from the pushing ski to the gliding ski.

To avoid tiring out one leg and arm by only using that side, alternate the side on which you perform the push. Depending on the depth of the snow at the side of the track, you may open the tip of your pushing ski wider (little snow) or less wide (deep snow).

On turns you should push with the leg on the outside of the turn.

When traversing a slope you should push with the downhill ski.

Above: final stage of single leg skating, done with the right leg and both arms.

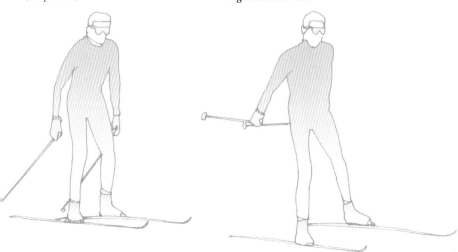

Double-sided skating

The position that you should take for this step is similar to that for the herringbone, but the skis are always kept flat, so that they can slide. Propulsion is obtained from the action of the arm and opposing leg. While pushing with for example the right arm, the opposite ski (the left), against which you are pushing, slides flat over the snow, and the weight of your body is gradually transferred onto it. When you start to run out of arm action, you edge the ski on its inside edge, by bending your ankle and knee. This produces the reaction needed to start off a new push.

At the same time as you push with one arm the opposite arm comes forward, in readiness for the next phase of leaning on the pole, which is planted a little forward of the ski binding.

When the ski with your weight on it begins the pushing phase, the other ski is ready to begin the next cycle.

The position of the ski in double-sided skating is similar to that in the herringbone, with the difference that the ski is always gliding.

Double-sided skating with double pole every two steps

This is the most natural step in skating technique. Forward movement is obtained from pushing the lower limbs in a skating action, coupled with one push of the arms for every two skating steps. As the speed increases distance between the tips of the skis reduces. You must shift your body weight from one ski to the other rapidly and completely, in order to make the maximum use of the phase when you are gliding on a flat (unedged) ski. The speed with which you transfer your body weight from one ski to the other is very important for keeping to a minimum the time during which you are moving along with your body weight spread over two skis which are traveling in different directions. In essence this results in an efficient use of the upper limbs which, by pushing hard against the sliding ski, help you to keep your pelvis in the correct position, that is forward and centered above the ski.

The most critical phase in double-sided skating with double pole every two steps is the gliding phase itself, during which you must take on a natural and relaxed position. The forward position of the pelvis allows you to keep your body's centered alignment, your balance, and your muscular relaxation, allowing you, as you come to the end of the gliding phase, to prepare for the pushing phase by bending the ankles, knees, and hips. The shifting of weight ends when you realize that all your body weight is on the forward foot. Your torso should lean forward. This, and your shoulders, should face the direction of the gliding ski.

As in all steps used in cross-country skiing, as soon as your legs have overtaken the poles in the pushing phase you should hold the poles with your thumb and index finger, pushing them so that they, and your arms, end up behind your body.

Double-sided skating with double pole every two steps and double-sided skating with double pole every step differ only in the rhythm of the coordination of the arms and legs. In the first, the arms push at the same time as one leg only; in the second case the arms push at the same time as both legs.

Double-sided skating with double pole every step

The movement of the lower limbs is like that for double-sided skating with double pole every two steps, while the arms push once for every push with the legs. As you are doubling the number of upper-limb movements per cycle, you have to bring your arms back extremely quickly; in this way you also obtain greater acceleration, which is encouraged by the momentum of your forward movement. The unweighted ski must be brought back in line with the other to keep a well balanced position.

Adapting the skating technique to different terrain types

As in classic technique, also in skating you use different steps, or adaptations of the basic steps, according to variations in the terrain and snow conditions. In general it is preferable to use double-sided skating with double pole every two steps, adapting it for traveling uphill or gently downhill.

When going uphill the weighted ski must be edged, instead of flat, the torso leans forward less, and you lean on the poles earlier. When tackling a steep uphill stretch the pole is planted further forward and a little later than the other. You get up particularly steep prepared tracks using the diagonal gait, which is also useful for allowing you to continue to make progress in tiring conditions. To increase your speed on the flat or on a gentle downhill slope, you use double-sided skating with double pole every step. You will have a problem with keeping your actions coordinated at high speed as once you have accelerated you almost always revert to double-sided skating with double pole every two steps. When traveling down a gentle slope off track the skating can be done without using the poles, while your upper limbs coordinate the movement through alternate swinging motion.

YES: Correct position of arms and legs.

DOUBLE-SIDED SKATING, WITH DOUBLE POLE EVERY TWO STEPS

ARM STRETCHED BACKWARDS AFTER THE PUSHING PHASE

TORSO LEANING SLIGHTLY FORWARDS TO KEEP THE BALANCE ON THE RIGHT LEG

LEFT SKI AT THE END OF THE PUSHING PHASE AND ABOUT TO BE PUT BACK DOWN AGAIN

RIGHT SKI FLAT, IN GLIDING PHASE

DOWNHILL TECHNIQUE

We have already mentioned the snowplow (wedge). It remains to be said that with cross-country skis it is possible to carry out many of the turns typical of downhill (Alpine) skiing, such as *wedel* (short-radius linked turns), parallel turns and even turns taught in schools of the past, such as the stem Christie and Telemark. Off-track, where you can come across any sort of difficulty or eventuality, a skier will be so much more capable of success in every situation if he has learnt to apply many possible solutions. You must nevertheless bear in mind that the mechanical properties of cross-country skis are very different from those of downhill skis; because of these you can't make the sorts of turns which need you to set edges and bend the skis and boots. Even in fresh snow the reduced buoyancy of cross-country skis limits your choice of technique, forcing

you to have recourse to solutions that seem rather inelegant to modern skiers, such as the schuss technique. The cross-country skier should practice downhill skiing, using occasionally downhill (Alpine) or Telemark equipment in order to improve his downhill technique.

Below: adopting the schuss position for downhill; above: descent with parallel skis. In the sketch above: the schuss technique for coming downhill; right: descent with Telemark turn.

COMPETITION

The technical skills of cross-country skiing needed in competitive sport are the same as those which a good skier should have in order to be able to manage any course with total confidence. Obviously, a competitor will tend to perfect his technique in order to bring him to perform at the highest level. For this reason, as opposed to what happens in many other sports, the most distinguished sportsmen are those who are the best exponents of the sport at any level.

The competitive skier must therefore turn his attention towards the development of bio-mechanical and athletic qualities, in order to improve his own performance. Furthermore, he must take into consideration various competitive tactics, factors which do not interest the recreational skier, in order for him to obtain the best possible results with the means at his disposal.

Bio-mechanical aspects

Even the slightest waste of energy at every step will eventually, after several kilometers (miles), reduce your performance, while perfect technique will prolong the phase of maximum efficiency and so reduce the causes of the friction which hinder your progress.

The sportsman must therefore train, repeating to the point of boredom the same movements, either in the same conditions, in order to improve the execution of the technique, or in different conditions, in order to learn how to adapt his technique most appropriately and effectively. Above all, the capacity to adapt oneself quickly to different situations requires a complete mastery of different steps in all types of terrain and snow conditions.

It must not be forgotten that fatigue uncovers faults that are hidden when skiing at a gentler pace. Improvements in technique can be obtained more effectively with the intervention of a coach, ski instructor or personal trainer who, using video replays and other means, can diagnose any problems and suggest the most appropriate solutions.

8
TEACHING
CHILDREN

From snow games to ski school. Sharpening children's skills and spirit of adventure. Getting started in the sport.

INTRODUCTION

When we talk about children, we really have to talk about play. Of course adults play too, but for kids the role of play is far more significant. Its role will never be the same again as the child grows up. Because for a child, play is also learning. Play is the entirely unconscious mechanism by which kids learn to navigate their way around our world. Indeed, movement and play are so bound up together as to be inseparable. We do not really know if a child moves whilst playing or vice versa.

If properly introduced, the mountain can become a wonderful play area, especially in winter. Snow is, in fact, the most marvelous of elements both because of the way it falls and because of the wide range of opportunities it provides for playtime. You can slide on snow in a thousand different ways using dozens of different means. You can slide on a sleigh, a bob, a sled or on a humble plastic garbage bag. You can

use downhill skis, snowboards, cross-country skis. All of this means that the snow and the slopes become a fantastic play village where kids can enjoy themselves and get to know the mountain together with their parents, play with other children, and learn from instructors. Kids must get to know every possible different way of sliding and they need to learn to experiment properly with all kinds of equipment. This helps to extend their basic motor skills and improves their overall awareness of the relationship between their own bodies and the environment.

Below: snow itself is a plaything; you have to let your kids gain in confidence in a really natural way.

THE AGE OF PLAY

The type of game played really depends on the age of the child. Up to about four or five, solitary games are the norm. At this age, it is more usual for a child to turn to adults for affection because he or she still needs their approval and support. During these years, children's moods change quickly and they live their playtime in a very emotional fashion. From five there are phases during which physical characteristics leapfrog over each other and take turns in changing. For instance, during one growth phase, we spurt up in height but do not put on any weight. In another, exactly the opposite happens.

What is even more pertinent to the case in point is that the proportions of the body never remain the same. During the early years of life, the proportion of the head is

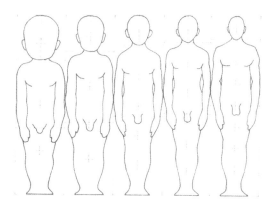

The proportions of the human body as it develops from infancy to adulthood.

onwards, the number of games involving other children increases rapidly, as does the child's sense of collaboration. This in turn calls for the rules of the game to be defined and respected. By this age, children are more emotionally stable since they have come to know themselves better and value themselves more.

The range of snow games is broad and depends largely on the child's physiological maturity. But before going into the detail of games, let us first glance at the developmental stages between childhood and adulthood.

If we look at physical development, one of the basic principles is that there is no smooth or constant rate of growth. Rather, considerably greater than in later developmental phases. Similarly, the torso is longer than the legs. These basic physiological facts mean that children have a different center of gravity at different ages. In turn, this is the main reason why (as in all sporting disciplines) the technique taught must be appropriate to the age of the child.

Now let us take a look at how kids behave on the snow. For clarity's sake, we will divide the comments according to age. But please bear in mind that this is a very rough and ready division, because all children grow according to their own biology and environment and not just as their chronological age might suggest.

From two to five years: snow play

At this age, it seems that children are mainly driven by their curiosity. The natural desire to learn and experiment makes children play in the snow in every way imaginable. And this includes tasting it. Sometimes this action seems akin to a regression to the "oral phase" during which children put everything they come into contact with into their mouths. But frequently, all they are expressing is thirst or hunger. The early outings on the snow should be done without skis. Children should be allowed to walk and run, fall and play in the snow in just the same way as they do when they first go to the beach. The way kids move on snow expresses both enjoyment and surprise. They grow curious about the feeling they get when going up or down even the slightest slope because of the instability of the slippery snow beneath their feet. But they enjoy their play more and are more comfortable with it if at least one of their parents is

there to guide them and help them discover and experiment with new sensations. It is then that the game assumes an emotional value, since the adult imbues the child with a sense of protection and safety, even in the most adventurous of situations. This period of getting to know the snow and the slopes (and the mountain environment in general) can last several days. During this time, it is inevitable that one of the ways the kids get to know

their environment is through sliding and slipping.

When can a child start skiing? If skiing simply means slipping, then any kid who has spent a few days on the snow sliding around has already started skiing. The important thing is that he or she has already started trying to slide (if only whilst wearing boots) while standing up, perhaps with the help of his or her parents or elder sibling. At this age their attempts to get their balance right are neither fast nor accurate. Their muscular force is mainly in their arms (children are far stronger at climbing) rather than in their legs.

In their earliest years, children need to explore the reality of the world in which they live safe in the knowledge that their parents are close at hand. At this age they prefer solitary games. Only once they have grown enough in self-confidence do they start sharing games and new experiences with other children.

First skis

Once a child has made friends with the snow itself, then you can put him or her on skis. It doesn't matter whether you opt for downhill or cross-country. The most important thing is the length of the skis. They must be short, 60–70 cm (24–28 inches) at the very most. Above all never let a child wear ski boots that are too large. The child's first attempt at sliding with skis on his or her feet should be guided by a parent who

knows how to ski because they will be the best person to help the child enjoy the adventure of skiing, especially on an emotional level. If, however, neither parent skis, then it's best to put the child into the hands of a ski instructor. By the age of three or four, kids are already able to learn the key concepts of how to control their skis, from snowplows (wedges) to steering with parallel skis. Adopting the correct stance also comes easily to them as they instinctively lower their center of gravity to improve their balance. On the other hand, they are not able to objectively evaluate the speed at which they are traveling. Very often they are enjoying themselves so much that they pick up speed and end up losing control of their skis. Falls are harmless and frequent and it's best to let the child learn how to get up on his or her own. Nonetheless we cannot emphasize enough that a child of this age should be accompanied by a responsible adult at all times when out on the slopes.

Ski school and play park

An excellent way of working things is to sign the children up for ski school, which are often equipped with specialist areas for kids. These are usually special sections of the slopes, closed to other skiers, open only to children and authorized staff and equipped with all you need to teach skiing. There are cut-out fairytale figures, slides, and all kinds of teaching materials that are used to stimulate creative play for long spells during the day. The ski instructors and kindergarten teachers work together in an environment where sliding is encouraged in a safe and protected manner.

Very young children should not be forced to carry out rigorous exercises. Their first steps on skis should be in the company of their parents or an older sibling.

From six to eight years: ability and discovery

It is during these years that the child's body lengthens and assumes proportions similar to those of an adult. This rapid growth often goes hand in hand with a marked skeletal suppleness since the child's frame is not yet supported by sufficient muscular development. This means that kids sometimes go through a phase of insecurity in their movements and psychology. Nonetheless, children can rely on being better balanced and coordinated than adults, which means they are quicker at learning the techniques of how to control their skis. Their obvious ability to learn new movements fuels their enthusiasm for tackling new situations. Furthermore, their social skills are now far more advanced and they are able to accept rules (although these have to be fairly general). So now the play can become more adventurous. The runs become an enormous play area to explore, to discover new routes, new types of snow, new slopes. All the while, the children enjoy sharing this experience with their classmates and their instructor, whose role assumes a fundamental importance. For as in all adventure games, there are moments of joy but also "dramatic" moments where fear must be overcome. It takes a very observant person to notice the different types of behavior typical of this age. Some children have no problem opening up emotionally to adults, others naturally turn to their classmates, while some go through tense times as they sense the possibly competitive nature of snow play.

By about seven to eight years, it is quite clear that children are developing both physically and psychologically. They begin to want to try new things and to compete with their peers. Their bodies are becoming more similar to those of adults, allowing coordinated movements, but they do not yet have sufficient muscular development to support their skeletons.

Downhill and cross-country skiing; snowboarding

This is easily the best age to let children try out the different types of equipment. It is very important, in fact, that their experiences of motion on snow are not limited to any one discipline, but that they try out downhill skiing, cross-country skiing, and snowboarding. This "multi-disciplinary" approach will guarantee the acquisition of a thorough mastery of movement on the snow and an attitude of confidence in and respect for the mountain. It is as well to allow a few days for each discipline, without letting the child sense that there is any hurry to change equipment or runs.

Equipment

Children aged between six and eight years who are skiing for the first time should use short skis: the ideal length of a downhill ski is less than the child's height; that of a cross-country ski should be around the child's height; a snowboard should at most reach the level of a child's chest. If the skis/board are too long the child's capacity for movement will be limited and the time it takes to learn the basic techniques will be lengthened. Boots must be absolutely the right size, and not too big. If the boots are too big the child will not be able to control his movements precisely, which will also tend to increase the learning phase besides encouraging poor balance. You should use a ski hire outlet which has children's equipment available.

It's a good idea to allow children to try out the various glisse tools, one after the other: downhill skiing, cross-country skiing, and snowboarding.

From eight to 11 years: introduction to the sport

The main physiological principle of this age group is that their body proportions are very similar to those of an adult. For the first time their capabilities as regard coordination and movement are very high and the child is naturally ready to learn really quite difficult motor skills. This is proved by the fact that in some sports, such as gymnastics, children exhibit very high skills in their movements. Children of eight to 11 years also have a greater readiness to learn new skills and to perfect those that they have picked up along the way. All this is thanks to the child's increased levels of concentration: the child is now able to analyze movements in the tiniest detail, and not just at the whole-body scale, as he did previously. At this age it's acceptable to think of an introduction to competitive activities, but in a manner and with systems appropriate to the age of the child. Indeed, it's acceptable to think that one discipline will take precedence over all the others, without however ever abandoning them altogether.

All three disciplines (downhill skiing, cross-country skiing, and snowboarding) can be considered as valuable introductions to any one of them.

Equipment for this age group must be chosen with care. We must stress again the need to have boots that are exactly the right size, and not too big. For more skilled children the equipment should be robust and of the best possible quality, given that they are likely to want to tackle challenging runs.

An introduction to competition can take place at a very young age. But it requires a high level of diligence, which cannot be valued too highly.

9
FITNESS TRAINING

Physical fitness for health, injury prevention, and overall performance. Exercises to do at home, at the gym, and in the open air, for all different types of skiing.

INTRODUCTION

If you want the time that you spend skiing (or snowboarding) to be a totally carefree experience, you must always set aside some time for getting in shape. You must not forget that skiing is a high-energy sport, extremely demanding physically, and that the risk of injury increases dramatically when you are tired. It is an accepted fact that most accidents on the slopes happen either first thing in the morning, when the muscles are still cold, or (and this is the majority) in the afternoon, when physical exhaustion causes reflexes to slow down and overall performance deteriorates. This is where adequate fitness training comes in, to prevent accidents and injuries that occur when the body is worn out and stretched to its limit by numerous descents.

PHYSICAL FITNESS

If you wish to stay in good health, physical fitness is an absolute must, on a level with nutrition and rest. Taking a little exercise every day ought to mean that you are sufficiently prepared to take on any sport, assuming of course that you follow the

Right, a few minutes of stretching before starting to ski can greatly reduce the risk of muscular injury. Even competition skiers, who have obviously done a lot of fitness training, react less quickly and are more likely to fall after very lengthy and tiring demands on their body.

268

right step-by-step approach. But modern life is often diametrically opposed to physical activity, so much so that it becomes necessary to deliberately program it into your life. The demands of work should never be used as an excuse to justify a sedentary lifestyle, since being in good shape physically is something that you cannot do without, and which can also have a very positive influence on your work. Besides, getting yourself physically ready for skiing, or indeed for any other sporting activity, can be done anywhere: out in the open, at home, or in the gym; the only thing that you need is a little willingness to overcome sloth.

How often and how much

There is no limit to how much exercise you can take: our bodies are designed to tolerate increasing demands. At any rate, let's say that one hour of physical activity every day would be the ideal, for being in good shape generally as well as for getting fit for skiing, but it is not always easy to fit it in. Three days a week is a reasonable

compromise, two days is already too little, while only one day a week is likely to do more damage than good, because you would be trying to make up in one go for what you have not done the whole week, and this is obviously an overload of exercise. To sum up: if, for example, Sunday is the day you go skiing, you should be exercising on Monday, Wednesday, and Friday, devoting the first two days to more strenuous exercises and the third to more technically specific exercises.

The body's muscles need to be continually toned, either by outdoor activities, or by exercises at home or in the gym.

DIFFERENT TYPES OF FITNESS

Cross-country skiing

Cross-country skiing combines athleticism and skill: only if you are in very good condition physically can you develop your skills to a high level, just as you need a good level of skill if you are to make the most of the potential created by your fitness. One of the most important qualities is the body's overall ability to combat exhaustion, as in the case of marathon runners. Stamina, which is also called cardiorespiratory or cardiovascular capacity (the ability to deal with not strenuous but prolonged activity), is seen as the queen of all physical qualities, representing the very essence of good health. In reality, what is most important for the cross-country skier is localized stamina: just think of the arm movements, where a very few, specific muscles (shoulder, back, and pectoral muscles) are required to repeat the same type of work over a prolonged period of time. So cross-country skiers must have great muscular strength, or rather, they must be able use their strength for long periods. Strength of this sort, however, should not mean a huge increase in muscle size, which would be at the risk of reducing stamina. Lastly, cross-country skiing demands flexibility. This means being able to make very broad movements with arm, hip, and leg joints; this allows skiers to make wide, natural and fluid movements.

Fitness training for cross-country skiers therefore comprises a number of aspects, which can sometimes contradict each other, but which, if developed in a balanced and coordinated manner, form the basis of one of the most all-round sports.

Downhill skiing and snowboarding

From a point of view of the physical demands and the energy involved, these two sports are very similar. They both entail the use of ski lifts, which save skiers the effort of getting themselves to the top of the mountain by their own means, while the greatest effort is concentrated in the descent.

The effort involved in descent is made more intense by three factors: 1) speed, 2) radius of the turn, 3) gradient of the slope. Increased effort is demanded by turns at greater speed, with smaller radii, and down steeper gradients, and having strong muscles in the legs and torso is therefore a very important physical quality in skiers.

There is another physical quality that skiers cannot do without: ability to react quickly. They need to be able to perform a variety of movements at great speed, as the descent is full of continually changing conditions, starting with the snow surface. Skiers must always be able to move with agility, in a coordinated and efficient manner, when faced with the variations in surface, gradient, trajectory, and other "traffic." This ability depends on your genetic make-up, and also on your experiences of movement starting from childhood; not everybody has this ability to react quickly, in a cool-headed and effective manner, when faced with possibly risky situations that can arise on the trails (pistes). In competition skiing quick reac-

tions, coupled with certain mental qualities, represent the difference between a competitor and a champion.

Finally it should not be forgotten that skiing and snowboarding tend to be whole-day activities. This is why a third quality is needed: stamina, which has already been discussed with regard to cross-country skiing.

The physical qualities needed for downhill skiing (on the page opposite) and for snowboarding (below) are identical; in both sports you must be able to adapt yourself quickly to changes in snow conditions and the gradient. The qualities needed for cross-country skiing (bottom) are very different; in this stamina is the deciding factor.

Knowing your own body

An essential starting point for any physical activity is awareness of your state of health and your level of fitness, which you can easily find out from a sports doctor, who can often be found at a gym. The basic assessment involves various measurements, such as weight, height and body-fat percentage. The first two are obviously easy to measure, but working out the body-fat percentage is a more complicated process, involving the use of calipers and a bodystat machine. Some very recently developed machines are even able to evaluate the level of "cellular hydration" (water content of the body), the most important statistic related to health.

Measuring how the body is made up in terms of muscle and fat helps to work out if weight loss needs to be included as part of fitness training, which will mean the prescription of a special diet. At any rate it is quite clear that a sedentary lifestyle and bad eating habits quickly increase the percentage of fat. The exact measurement of the body-fat percentage can only be worked out by a specialist, but on your own you can work out at least an approximate measurement. The weight:height ratio gives in fact a sufficiently accurate indication, and it is even better if this is coupled with the "pinch test," which means testing how much loose fat you can pinch between your thumb and fingers on the fatty zones of your body. Weight loss is not the same as fat loss: after you have exercised, for example, you weigh less because you have lost a lot of water. Besides this, if your muscle size increases as a result of exercise, your weight inevitably increases too.

To test your fitness levels, you should ideally use machines that are able to provide objective data, such as treadmills and exercise bicycles fitted with the appropriate measuring devices.

Working out your sporting ability

There are many tests to work out the level of your sporting ability.

• Measurement of cardiorespiratory (heart–lung) capacity: this test is done on a treadmill, a stepper or a bicycle, lasts a few minutes, and measures your heart rate.

• Measurement of strength: this test is carried out on apparatuses in the gym to determine the strength of the various muscle groups (legs, torso, arms …).

• Measurement of muscular potential: this test involves measuring the height and length of various jumps.

• Measurement of flexibility: this test involves measuring the breadth of movement of the various joints (usually shoulders and hips).

The best way of finding out your own sporting capacity is to get it tested by a sports doctor or fitness specialist; if you want a more in-depth report, you must consult a specialized center. But there is a way of working out your level of fitness right within your own home. Obviously it is not a particularly accurate test, but it is certainly the cheapest method and easy to carry out:

Do 40 squats in one minute, and then measure your heart rate straight after the exercise, and again after a minute's rest. By using the same test later on (for example once a fortnight) you will be able to compare your heart rate readings and evaluate your level of fitness.

It is also possible to test what sort of shape you are in at home, although this is not so accurate.

EXERCISING OUTSIDE

The best place to exercise is outside in a natural environment. If there are also small green areas in the city where you live, then it is time that you reassessed them as places where you could get into shape.

Running (cardiorespiratory capacity, or aerobic fitness)

The best of all outdoor activities is jogging (1) or running (2). Everybody is capable of running, even those who have not done it for many years. Running is a natural movement for humans, though we have rather abandoned it. However, it is not difficult to rediscover the pleasures of running if you adopt the right step-by-step approach.

Besides improving your cardiorespiratory capacity, jogging is the basic warm-up exercise for the next stages of a training session. Anyone who has no particular physical problems should run at least three times a week for at least twenty minutes each time (this is achievable within a month). Anyone on the other hand who has weight problems should be more careful, and should start with simple walking sessions, working up to running at a later date. Details are given below (Table 1) of an ideal step-by-step approach for anyone starting from scratch.

Jogging (1) or running (2) are the most important type of exercise.

TABLE 1 ALTERNATE RUNNING AND WALKING ("INTERVALS")

(for anyone who is taking up running again: to be done twice a week for the first two weeks, and then three times in the third and fourth weeks)

	running minutes	fast walking minutes		
First week	1	2	6	times
Second week	2	2	5	times
Third week		1	6	times
Fourth week	6		3	times

TABLE 2 CONTINUOUS RUNNING

(program to be followed after four weeks of alternate running and walking [Table 1])

	1st session minutes	2nd session minutes	3rd session minutes
Fifth week	13	17	15
Sixth week	15	20	17
Seventh week	18	22	20
Eighth week	22	25	23

Aerobic movements (strength, agility, flexibility)

This is a series of exercises to be done either on the spot, or while jogging, and is perfect for doing in the middle of a green area in a park. The aim of these exercises is to stimulate muscular reactions, to make your legs and feet more sensitive to different movements and weights, to encourage coordination between different parts of the body, as well as to develop rhythm and agility. These exercises should be done in the warm-up phase, in addition to running, before starting on the more strenuous exercises.

The most common movements are:
• Knees-up jogging (1): either on the spot or moving slowly forward, raise your knees up as high as possible towards your chest, making sure that you coordinate your leg and arm movements.

• Heels-up jogging (2): either on the spot or moving slowly forward, cast your foot up behind you until your heel touches your buttock; your knees should stay low, while your arms move as if you are running or remain level with your ribs.

• Sideways jogging (3): make a series of sideways leaps without jumping too high in the air.

• The "grapevine" (4): this is purely an exercise for agility and coordination: you cross one leg over, first in front of the other one and then behind, while keeping your arms wide to balance your body.

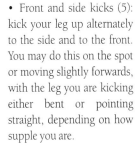

• Front and side kicks (5): kick your leg up alternately to the side and to the front. You may do this on the spot or moving slightly forwards, with the leg you are kicking either bent or pointing straight, depending on how supple you are.

Squats and lunges (strength)

Squats are mostly carried out on the spot. They are useful for strengthening all the muscles in your legs and back, and can be either of low intensity or of high intensity depending on how you do them. Squats are recommended for those who are at the beginner or intermediate level since these are not particularly strenuous exercises, but they can also be a worthwhile exercise for experts if they are done on one leg only, or if the squat position is held for a few minutes. In the latter case the way that the muscles work is called "isometric," since no movement is involved.

Two-leg squats:

• Half squat (1): This position is very reminiscent of the "egg position" used in downhill skiing, and involves bending and straightening your legs, having first adopted a stance with your feet apart (in line with your hips). This is the simplest of the squats, within the reach even of those who do little exercise. If you maintain the half-squat position for a minute or more, it becomes a high-intensity exercise, beneficial for expert skiers as well.

• Full squat (2): bending to the full squat should only be done when you are in good physical condition, as it puts a lot of strain

on the knees. For instance, it should be avoided by anyone who is a beginner or who has a weight problem. The leg muscles are contracted in a very intense manner, involving principally the adductor muscles.

• Forward lunge (Steps 3 and 4 on facing page) (3): Step forward with one foot and squat down on this front leg. You can control the intensity of this exercise by varying the degree to which you bend down: the lower you bend the greater the intensity of the muscular contraction. Lunges should be done in alternation as if you were making large strides forward. You can hold the squat position for a few minutes, making the exercise more intense.

• Sideways lunge (Steps 3 and 4 on this page) (4): Put one leg out to the side and squat down over it. Once again the intensity of the exercise can be controlled according to how low you squat. By lunging first to the right and then to the left you will be simulating the rhythmic action of skiing turns, which use in particular the adductor muscles of the thigh.

One-leg squats:

Squat down over one leg while the other is balanced on its toe slightly behind you. This is not far off the Telemark position, involving your knee very nearly touching the ground. This means that you can control the load with your rear leg: if you are solidly planted on your back leg, your front leg will be bearing very little load (1 and 2); if your rear leg is raised, your front leg will be bearing the entire load of the exercise (3 and 4).

Leaps (strength and power)

Leaping, however you do it, is the most natural expression of physical power. A leap involves muscular strength, neuro-muscular speed, coordination of movement, rhythm, and leg and arm control. It is especially beneficial for those who are already fairly fit, and inadvisable for beginners in the first stages of their training. So leaps should only be performed after at least two weeks of fitness training, involving running, aerobic movements, stretching and abdominal exercises. You should start with fairly easy leaps, limiting your spring and your arm movements at first. Besides this you should on no account bend your legs fully; you should stick to a 90° angle at the knee. A leap with a full squat is only advisable after many weeks of training. Some of the most important leaps are summed up below.

• Forward leap on both feet (1): this is easy to do, and is best when coordinated with an arm swing.

• Sideways leap on both feet (2): this is the exercise that most recalls the downhill skiing movement, which also involves small sideways shifts. You can either keep your arms at your sides, or swing them in a coordinated movement, or keep them in front of you as in skiing.

• Running leap (3): this means taking great bounds forwards as if you were jumping over a ditch or an obstacle; these leaps are high intensity, and should only be performed after a few weeks devoted to running and increasing the strength of your abdominal and torso muscles.

• Sideways leap on one leg (4): you push off sideways on one leg; the intensity of these leaps can be varied at will, going from small bouncing sideways steps right up to really wide leaps.

• Downward leap (5): use something slightly off the ground, such as a park bench or a tree trunk; to begin with it should be no higher than 40 cm (15 inches) – after a few months you can go as high as 80 cm (30 inches); you should on no account do a downward leap if you have muscular or joint problem, or if you are still in the early stages of training.

Exercises for abdominal muscles and arms, and stretching

Exercises for strengthening your abdominal muscles and for muscle lengthening (stretching) are dealt with in the section on exercises to be done at home. Arm exercises are mostly dealt with in the section on exercises to be done in the gym. All these exercises can also be done in the open air.

Typical program for outdoor training

Here are two examples of outdoor training, one for someone who is just beginning, and the other for an expert.

If you are just starting, after the first four weeks entirely devoted to running and stretching a typical program for a training session could be as follows:
• Running: 15 minutes, slow at first, then gradually building up speed.
• Aerobic movements: five different movements, with two 8–10-second sessions of each one.
• Abdominal muscles: two sets of ten curls (two different types).
• Arms: two sets of ten press-ups, with your body stretched out behind and your knees on the ground.
• Legs: hold the half-squat position for at least 20 seconds; repeat twice.
• Stretching: 10 minutes.

If you have been training for at least two months, three times a week:
• Running: 20 minutes, slow at first, then gradually building up speed.
• Aerobic movements: seven different movements, with two 8–10-second sessions of each one.
• Abdominal muscles: two sets of 20–25 curls (two different types).
• Arms: two sets of 15 press-ups.
• Legs: forward leaps on both feet, ten leaps, repeated three times.
• Sideways leaps on one leg, ten leaps, repeated twice.
• Running: five minutes at a very gentle pace.
• Stretching: 10 minutes.

EXERCISING IN THE GYM

The great advantage of the gym is that you have everything at your disposal. There are many different machines for fitness and for increasing your muscle power, covering every possible aspect, and they are increasingly equipped with electronic controls which give guidance to whoever is using them. And do not forget that there are always fitness and medical experts present who offer an individual training program service and physiotherapy sessions if needed. Compared to a few years ago, when gyms were only for muscle-building, gyms nowadays offer a wide variety of activities, from muscle building to aerobics, and include all the latest trends.

One thing that is certain is that in a gym the machines work as a catalyst of your attention and interest. These machines can be divided into two types; those for muscle building and those for aerobic exercise (exercise of a long duration, also called cardiovascular fitness). Muscle-building work can be extremely selective, as there are numerous machines designed to act upon one particular muscle group. Cardiovascular fitness work only involves a few types of machine, which are traditionally the treadmill, the exercise bicycle (the modern version is called a spinning bike) and the stepper to simulate the motion of going up stairs.

Muscle building with machines and weights

Anyone can use the machines and weights that are found in a gym, even those who are just at the beginning of their training. The intensity of the workout obviously has to be properly tailored to each person's fitness level. The advantage of machines is that they are able to work upon the precise muscle that you wish to strengthen; they are excellent for rehabilitation after an accident, and as part of a more general pre-ski fitness program. A somewhat artificial distinction may be made between the different types of muscle work for the upper and the lower body. Note that no indication as to the actual "workload" (the weight that you lift) is given, as this is entirely unique to each person and can vary enormously. The instructors in the gym will give you an indication of what is right for you.

Arm and shoulder exercises

• (1) Sitting on the bench, raise the barbell (you can also do this without weights) behind your back.

• (2) Sitting on the bench, lift two dumb bells, raising your arms high above you either out to the side or in front (deltoid muscles).

• (3) Sitting on the bench, with your back supported, lift the dumb bell to shoulder height (biceps).

• (4) With your arm resting on the slanting backrest of the bench, flex your arm, bringing the dumb bell up to your shoulder (biceps).

• (5) Standing up with the barbell (you can also do this without weights), raise it up as far as your chest (biceps).

• (6) With your hands on the bench behind you and your body stretched out in front, bend and straighten your arms (triceps).

• (7) Machine for triceps.

• (8) Machine for dorsal muscles.

Leg exercises

- (1) In a standing position with legs slightly apart and heels raised a couple of centimeters (inches), do squats and half squats.
- (2) In the same stance as in the previous exercise, do half squats with a barbell held level with your pelvis.
- (3) Same as the previous exercise, but with the barbell on your shoulders.
- (4) Leg press: flex your legs to a half-squat position.
- (5) Leg extension: raise your legs until they are level with your knees.
- (6) Machine for the muscles at the back of the thigh (femoral biceps): flex your legs.
- (7) Machine for the muscles on the outside of the leg (abductor muscles): open your legs.
- (8) Machine for the muscles on the inside of the leg (adductor muscles): bring your legs together.
- (9) Lying on one side on the slanting bench, raise your upper leg (abductor muscles). You can increase the intensity of this exercise by using a small weight.
- (10) Lying on one side on the slanting bench, raise your upper leg (abductor muscles). You may use a small weight.

Typical program for fitness training in a gym

The modern method of training in a gym involves the principle of circuit training, which means a series of exercises that work on different muscle areas, that you do in a set order one or more times. The circuit is made up of between six and 15 different "stations," between each of which you have a short time to recover.

Example of a typical circuit:

1st station	pectorals
2nd station	legs (quadriceps)
3rd station	triceps
4th station	legs (adductors)
5th station	dorsal muscles
6th station	abdominal muscles
7th station	biceps
8th station	shoulders

EXERCISING AT HOME

We are often led to think that we can only exercise in specific places, and sometimes forget that even at home a huge amount can be done. Some people have even equipped themselves, building a proper gym in their own house, and buying the right machines. Here, however, the only exercises considered are those that need no machines (the only thing that you are advised to buy is a mat, a pair of dumb bells, and a "Dynoband"). The biggest problem with exercising at home is having to do it alone, which can become monotonous; you can alleviate this by listening to the radio or to some good music.

At home, as in the gym, it is not possible to do natural exercises for aerobic fitness (running, cycling, swimming …). In the absence of other equipment you can use a skipping rope, though at first this can seem very tiring. The best thing to start with is running on the spot, moving on to knees-up running and then heels-up running (see the section on "Exercising outside"), and coming eventually to using the skipping rope after a couple of weeks. If you do happen to have an exercise bicycle it is excellent for warming up (8–10 minutes) or for aerobic fitness (minimum 20 minutes).

Leg and arm exercises

For building up leg strength, refer to the section on exercising in the open air and study the guidance given on all the

different squats and lunges. You can increase the intensity of these exercises by adding an extra load such as two dumb bells or a Dynoband (a piece of elastic) (1).
Squats and lunges for legs, using dumb bells and Dynoband.
While doing the exercises you should keep the dumb bells level with your pelvis or close to your body, but do not put too much strain on your back. The most strenuous of these exercises is squatting or lunging on one leg, while also using the dumb bells or the Dynoband, and while raising the other leg off the ground (2 a, b, c).

For building up strength in your arms, you should refer to the section on exercising in the gym, and study the guidance given for exercises with dumb bells. Besides these, you can also use the Dynoband for your arms.
Arm exercises with the Dynoband.
• (3) Standing up, hold the Dynoband under your feet and stretch it upwards with one or both arms (deltoid muscles).
• (4) Standing up, with the Dynoband under your feet, flex your arm (biceps).

Exercises for pectoral muscles
Lastly, work on your pectorals by doing press-ups. These are done in a prone position (face down), raising yourself up with the strength of your arms alone. Your body should remain straight behind you. If you lower your knees to the ground the exercise is less intense and is suitable even if you are just starting training.

Abdominal exercises

The muscles of the abdomen are extremely important in that besides containing and protecting the vital internal organs they hold the torso up straight and act as backup for all arm and leg actions. In skiing (downhill and cross-country) and in snowboarding the abdominal muscles help you to keep your center of gravity properly aligned. So you should devote

• Lying down, with your legs bent and your feet flat on the ground, and your arms by your sides, tense your abdomen while raising your head until your feet start to lift off the ground. Repeat the exercise until you begin to feel really tired (1).

• By altering the position of your arms, you can make the exercise harder: hands on abdomen, hands on chest or shoulders, hands behind neck. Carry out the exercise as before (2 a, b, c).

time to working on your abdominal muscles right from the very first training session, obviously making sure that you do it in a progressive manner and do not put too much strain on your back. The majority of abdominal exercises are done on the floor, so an exercise mat is an essential item. You should not wedge your feet under anything when you are working on your abdominal muscles. Here are the exercises in order of difficulty, from the easiest to the hardest.

• Lying down, with your legs bent and your feet flat on the ground, and your arms by your sides, tense your abdomen while raising your upper body and twisting it to the left and to the right (3).

• In the same position as for the previous exercises, raise your upper body slightly and bend it to the left and to the right (4).

Stretching

This is the best known and most widely used way of lengthening muscles. Muscles do in fact need to maintain a certain amount of elasticity, which gets lost if you lead a sedentary lifestyle. Besides this, strengthening exercises tend to keep the muscles fairly contracted and thus in a shortened state. Muscle lengthening therefore works to compensate excessive contraction, and improves suppleness. Stretching means remaining in a set position for at least 20 seconds without causing too much muscular tension. Here are the most important stretches for skiers; you should consult specialist liturature for a more in-depth treatment.

1 a, b Muscles down the front of the leg.
2 a, b Muscles down the back of the leg.
3 a, b Adductor muscles.

4 a, b   Muscles on the inside and outside of the thigh.
5   Biceps and muscles in the forearm.
6   Triceps.
7   Pectorals
8   Back muscles.

Typical program for fitness training at home

At home too you can use the principle of a circuit that you do a couple of times. Here is an example of a training session at home.

• Warm-up: 10 minutes
Abdominal muscles
Arm muscles
Leg muscles
Pectoral muscles
• Stretching: 10 minutes

10
EQUIPMENT

Technical features of downhill, cross-country, telemark, and mountaineering skis, and of snowboards. Boots and poles.

SKIS AND BOARDS

Glisse tools

Skis are continually evolving. Manufacturers and technicians are always looking for ways to improve the performance of skiing equipment and at the same time the image of their products. When skis were only made of wood, the manufacturers' main aim at the production stage was that they should be as robust as possible; they were not supposed to break and were supposed to last as long as possible. From the 1960s and 1970s onwards, the use of glass fiber, metal, and new assembly systems meant that solidity and durability were almost guaranteed. Finally, in the last few decades, materials such as aluminum, carbon, Kevlar, and titanium have made it possible to design skis and boards with specific characteristics for different types of skiers and riders. Today hundreds of different models are produced, whose flex, length, and shaping specifications vary according to the user that they are destined for. From a technical point of view, modern skis are easy to manage and therefore more fun.

As time has passed cross-country skiing has seen the advent of the "skating" technique, which has brought many innovations in technology, while the latest trend in

Below and facing page, some of the different types of boards and skis used in the various branches of skiing, such as snow blades (ultra-short skis, seen in action on the right).

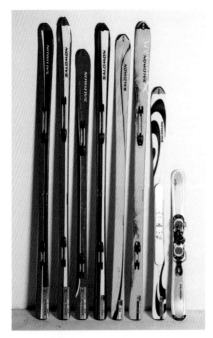

downhill skiing is carving: in just a few years skis have become shaped and also shorter than before. Ski-mountaineering has remained largely unaffected by the arrival of carving, while the old-style Telemark has seen great advances in technology.

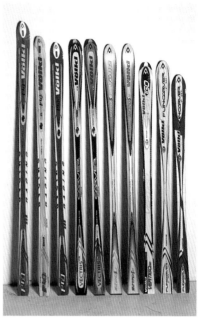

Shared characteristics of all downhill skis

Although the skis on the market come in many different shapes and forms, certain features are common to all downhill, Telemark, and cross-country skis.

A ski is essentially a narrow board that has a tip, a tail, and a central area. The tip curls up to prevent the ski sinking into the snow as it advances. The flat area of the ski, behind the tip, together with the tail form the constant point of contact with the ground. The central section is the part that, when there is no weight on the ski, has no contact with the ground and is seen to have a slight arch (bridge); this allows weight to be more evenly distributed over the whole ski when it is weighed down by the skier.

Downhill skis

A fundamental feature is their "shaping," which means the profile of their sides when seen from above; they are wider at the tip and at the tail, and narrower at the central section.

The sides of a ski are therefore shaped like the arc of a circle, and from this arc the radius may be calculated; sometimes the radius of the ski's shaping is specified by the manufacturer, and sometimes you have to calculate it yourself.

The more shaped (or waisted) a ski is, the smaller its curvature radius is. But why is shaping so important? To put it in simple terms, a ski will tend to perform a turn similar to its own geometric design; a ski with a radius of 20 m (60 feet), for example, will help the skier to perform turns with a radius of approximately 20 m.

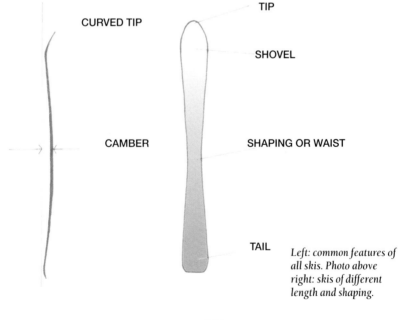

CURVED TIP

TIP

SHOVEL

CAMBER

SHAPING OR WAIST

TAIL

Left: common features of all skis. Photo above right: skis of different length and shaping.

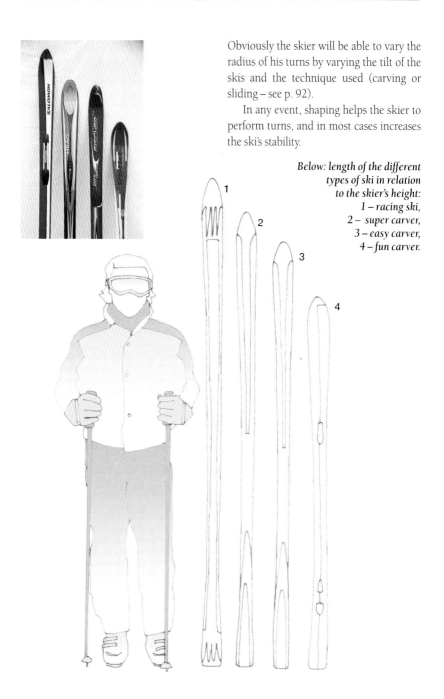

Obviously the skier will be able to vary the radius of his turns by varying the tilt of the skis and the technique used (carving or sliding – see p. 92).

In any event, shaping helps the skier to perform turns, and in most cases increases the ski's stability.

Below: length of the different types of ski in relation to the skier's height:
1 – racing ski,
2 – super carver,
3 – easy carver,
4 – fun carver.

Geometrical proportions certainly play an essential role in distinguishing between types of ski, and are the first thing that you will notice: length and shaping make it instantly obvious what use a ski is intended for, but they are not the only difference. As well as being shaped differently, the way that they are constructed and put together follows a different method according to the type of use that they are targeted at. Taking only shaping into consideration for the moment, here are the broad classifications of the different categories of skis.

Below, shaping means the different width of the board, narrower in the center than at the tip or tail.

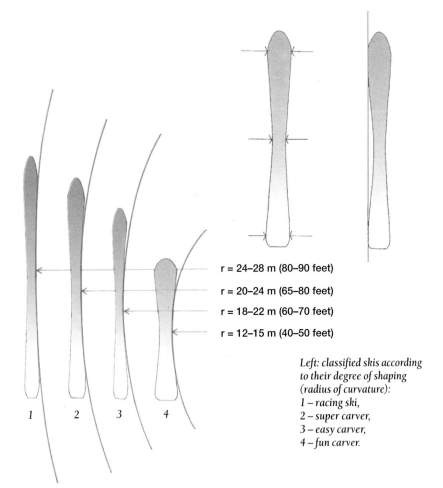

r = 24–28 m (80–90 feet)

r = 20–24 m (65–80 feet)

r = 18–22 m (60–70 feet)

r = 12–15 m (40–50 feet)

Left: classified skis according to their degree of shaping (radius of curvature):
1 – racing ski,
2 – super carver,
3 – easy carver,
4 – fun carver.

Competition skis (1: racing)

Competitions have always been a melting pot for technical innovations, and over the last few years there has been an enormous amount of research and experimentation on the concept of shaping. Shaping has become markedly increased, first in skis for giant slalom, and then also for ordinary slalom. The length of competition skis has gradually decreased as shaping has increased. The length of a giant slalom ski has gone from 208 cm.(82 inches) ten years ago to 190–198 cm (75–78 inches) today, while their curvature radius has gone from 36 to 24–26 m (118 to 80–85 feet).

Skis for advanced or expert skiers (2: super carvers)

These are high-performance, high-efficiency skis, built using the latest processes and the newest materials.

With these skis too the tendency in the last ten years has been a sharp decrease in length (average 10 cm [4 inches]) and a very conspicuous increase in shaping, which has taken their curvature radius from 36–40 m to 18–24 m today (120–130 to 60–80 feet).

Skis for beginners or intermediate skiers (3: easy carvers)

These skis are less rigid, so as to allow even less advanced skiers to perform any type of turn without too much difficulty. In any case, skiers in

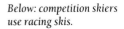

Below: competition skiers use racing skis.

this category usually perform their turns at lower speed and often on less uneven ground. The length of these easy carving skis has notably decreased, while shaping has increased, but the very noticeable flex of their tips and tails means that these skis are less responsive and precise in their movements compared to super carving skis. This is to the advantage of less expert skiers who need more time to recover their balance and correct their trajectory if they have made a mistake in the turn itself.

Skis for the fun carver (4: fun carving skis)

These skis are very short (150–170 cm [60–65 inches]) and very shaped (curvature radius 11–15 m [36–50 feet]), and are used by skiers who have a very good grasp of

Below: "easy carver" skis are for beginners or for those with only minimal experience. Bottom: "super carver" skis are for skiers who have a good level of skill.

technique, and are thus capable of an innovative and imaginative style of skiing. Fun carvers are the skis most far removed from traditional ones, and have given rise to a branch of skiing that is now well established. This is "fun carving," which involves very tight turns, usually executed at lower speeds, in which the skiers lean sideways in an extreme manner, pushing their balance to the very limit.

So a peculiarity of carving skis is that they allow extreme body leaning even at low speed, which means that it is a much less risky action than if it is done at higher speeds. The only risk presented by these skis lies in the surprising and novel course that they describe: fun-carving skiers with their very tight turns risk colliding with other skiers. So it is easy to see that to get maximum benefit from these skis, you need a wide run, or at least one that is clear of other skiers.

Above, "fun carving" skis are for expert skiers who are looking for new experiences.

Telemark skis

Increased shaping has brought revolutionary techniques to Telemark as well, so much so that a new phrase has been coined, "telecarving." More and more Telemarkers can be seen using skis for downhill skiing (even fun carving skis), the only difference being that they ski in the Telemark manner. Often, however, the heaviness of downhill skis is the factor that underlines the value of skis designed and built solely for Telemark. In Telemark the skis are in fact put under much less strain than in downhill skiing, so they do really need to be lighter and more flexible, especially if you are planning to do a lot of skiing in fresh snow off trail (off piste). You can also do Telemark with cross-country skis, but turning is difficult, and you have very little hold on the snow given the lack of cutting edge.

Telemark skis for trail skiing (telecarving) are quite shaped. Typical measurements for their tip, center, and tail are 100, 68, 90 mm (4, 2.7, 3.5 inches); the tail and tip are sometimes even wider. Each skis weighs around 1600 g (3.5 lbs).

Traditional Telemark skis are considered better for off-trail skiing. They are less shaped, more flexible, and lighter than telecarving skis. Typical measurements for their tip, center, and tail are 90, 65, 80 mm (3.5, 2.5, 3.1 inches); the tail and tip are sometimes even narrower. Each ski weighs around 1400 g (3 lbs). The use of even lighter and less shaped skis is confined to "back-country" Telemark.

Mountaineering skis

Ski mountaineering requires specialized equipment, even though from a technical point of view downhill skis are basically the same in structure. The main difference is that mountaineering skis have holes in the tip and the tail, which are needed for building a stretcher in the event of an accident.

classic ski
This is the
traditional ski,
not very long,
barely shaped,
and light,
suitable for long
hikes in the
mountains.

carving skis
These are shorter and
more shaped,
recommended for
skiing on compacted,
uniform surfaces.
However, excessive
shaping can lead to
problems on steep
slopes, in narrow
areas, and on ice.

free-riding ski
Free-riding skis
are particularly
recommended
for situations
where the snow
surface is very
changeable; they
are wider at the
center which
makes them
ideal for soft
powder snow.

touring skis
These occupy a
midway position
between
mountaineering and
cross-country skis.
The shaping is hardly
noticeable and they
are fairly narrow all
the way down. They
are very light and
maneuverable.

The mechanics of a ski and its components

Downhill skis are principally designed to satisfy two objectives: easy turning and guaranteed stability. These two ideas would seem to be technically opposed to one another: skis are in fact easy to turn when they are flexible, while sufficient rigidity makes them stable. So the decision to make a ski flexible or rigid determines what it will be used for right from the start:

– short flexible skis are better suited to beginners skiing on easy slopes at reduced speeds – longer hard skis are better suited to intermediate or expert skiers skiing on more difficult slopes at higher speeds.

Taking all this into account you can see how difficult it is to create a multi-purpose ski, suitable for beginners as well as for experts. Good skiers can ski perfectly well with skis suitable for beginners, so long as they do not go too fast, but beginners do not stand much of a chance with skis designed for experts.

Flexibility is one of the features that distinguishes skis, based on the skill of the skier: very flexible for skiers at a basic level (below right), and hard for skiers at an advanced level (below left).

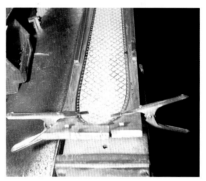

Edges

Another very important component of downhill skis is the edge. This is a thin strip of steel, placed on the bottom layer of the ski, and inserted into its multi-layered structure, the aim of which is to cut into the snow or ice to make a sort of mini step to lean on during turns and traverses. It is usually separated from the other materials by a 3 mm (0.112 inches) layer of rubber, which reduces the vibrations that the edge, because of its rigidity, transmits to the ski. The edge makes an angle of 90°, but in competition skis this angle is often more acute (88–86°) to make them cut into the snow more effectively. To guarantee their effectiveness they need to be sharpened before use, either by hand, using files and abrasive stones, or by specialized machines.

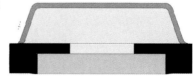

Top-level skis, especially if destined for competition, are still finished by hand. Above: three stages in the production process.

Right: transverse section of a ski with edges at an angle of 90° (above), and with edges at an angle of 86° (below).

The core of the ski

When skis were made of wood alone, it was the quality and the thickness of the wood that determined how effective or responsive the ski was. Wood still has its place in the construction of modern skis, but they are now assembled in a highly sophisticated manner, combining wood and other materials. Small wooden strips set vertically along the length of the ski are used in the construction of the ski's interior, called the "core" or the nucleus. The woods most commonly used are fir, ash, beech, okume, and maple. The wooden strips are coupled with a variety of other materials (glass fiber, carbon fiber, aluminum, Kevlar), so as to make the core less likely to become distorted.

In the lowest priced skis the core, instead of being made of wooden strips, is injected with a filling of polyurethane foam.

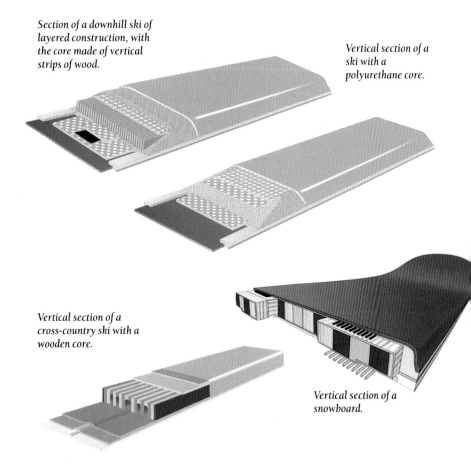

Section of a downhill ski of layered construction, with the core made of vertical strips of wood.

Vertical section of a ski with a polyurethane core.

Vertical section of a cross-country ski with a wooden core.

Vertical section of a snowboard.

The base

Another component of the ski is the base, which is the so-called running surface (the surface that has contact with the snow). All bases are made of polyethylene; in less expensive skis they are made by a process of extrusion, while those of the leading brands of skis are made by a process of sintering. Besides this, the soles of the latter are often improved by the addition of graphite powder, which makes them faster. This means that if you look at a competi- tion ski you will see that the sole is black (the base of the upturned tip will often be paler, without graphite), while if you look at a less expensive ski you will see that the sole is transparent, decorated with colorful and alluring designs. So, the soles of the latter are cheaper, not quite as fast as graphite soles, but also much less delicate, which can often be a great advantage.

Left, a ski seen from the tip, showing its curvature and base. Below, examples of various different bases.

Traditional (classic) cross-country skis

Cross-country skis for traditional cross-country skiing, unlike downhill skis, are not shaped. In fact, the tip and the tail are narrower than the central section. The tip of a cross-country ski also turns up a lot more than that of a downhill ski. Overall, compared to the latter, cross-country skis are much lighter, and are also extremely robust, thanks to the thickness of their central section (the part under the foot).

Traditional-style (classic) cross-country skis.

Skating (skate skiing, freestyle) cross-country skis

Skating cross-country skis are very slightly shaped (narrowed) at the sections just in front of and just behind the foot, and are also a little more rigid. This makes it much easier to push off when skating.

Skating-style cross-country skis.

Hardness of a cross-country ski

More important than length in a cross-country ski is how hard it is. If you look at it from the side when it is laid flat, you can see that its central part forms a sort of raised bridge. The tip of the ski needs to be fairly flexible to be able to adapt well to irregularities in the snow, while the tail is more rigid to make steering easier, especially in turns. Lastly, the central section is the part that determines how well it runs and how stable it is; a ski that is too hard will not give the right hold on the snow when pushing in traditional cross-country style, and will be ineffective in building up energy again in skating-style cross-country. This is why you should seek the advice of experts when you are about to buy.

As a general rule, you should bear in mind that you must be able to flatten the ski with your weight: if the skis do not give enough they will not provide you with enough grip at the central section, while if they give too much it will create too much friction and you will not build up all the elastic energy that is normally accumulated when your weight is on the ski. Many manufacturers label the skis that they produce with one of three levels of hardness: soft, medium, and stiff. Apart from this you can also find brands that differentiate even further, between skis for use on hard snow and those for use on soft or powder snow.

Cross-country skis have a central section (known as the camber or bridge) that is highly arched compared to downhill skis, and also much thicker than the tip and the tail.

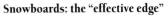

Snowboards: the "effective edge"

Assuming that a snowboarder knows whether he will be tackling the runs with a hard or a soft board, there are still certain things to look out for, common to both "families." The overall length of a board only has a relative value as a rough guideline. What has much more effect on how the board will perform is the actual length of the edge, i.e. the distance between the widest part of the tip and the widest part of the tail. An example: take two boards, both 160 cm (63 inches) long in total, but differently shaped. The first has a tip that is 20 cm (8 inches) long and a tail of 16 cm (6 inches). Its effective edge will be about: 160 – (20 + 16) = 124 cm (49 inches). The second has instead a tip of 16 cm (6 inches) and a tail of 13 cm (5 inches): its blade will be about 131 cm (52 inches). These 5–6 cm (2–2.5 inches) of difference, with the same rider, represent a marked difference in the how the board will perform. The longer the effective edge is, the better its grip and stability will be, especially at high speeds. A reduced edge length gives more maneuverability at medium speeds and the board will also be more temperamental. If you consider the two boards in the previous example, a rider weighing 75–80 kg (165–175 lbs; about 12 stone) could tackle powder snow with the first board, as it has a long tail and is therefore sweet on the turn, and also retain reasonable stability in turns on a trail; with the second board he would tend to go for compacted snow, hard pipes, and boarder cross: in other words he would be aiming for speed.

You should also take into account the weight factor; you should never buy a board intended for a rider of a weight different to yours. If you prefer a shorter board, then it will have to be a bit more rigid, and vice versa.

Shaping

Another factor that you should not underestimate is the shaping radius.

While there are very minimal differences in the type of shape in freestyle or free-riding, it is in Alpine snowboarding that problems can arise. This sector can be divided into two, free-carving and racing, and you should not leave out the most important factor to be taken into consideration when choosing a board: your own style. Free carving requires a medium-length board, up to 170 cm (65 inches), which means one with an effective edge of up to 150 cm (60 inches). Shaping radii

A, B Beginning and end of the edge

EFFECTIVE LENGTH OF EDGE

Left: the length of the board does not determine the length of the edge, which depends instead on the shape of the board. Above: two boards of equal overall length but with different edge lengths.

can go from 8 m (26 feet) at the shortest end of the range, up to 10 or 11 m (33–36 feet) at the top end. These boards are designed for medium speeds, for Alpiners, who make frequent and sudden changes of direction during the descent. Their primary objective is the carved turn. Someone who loves speed, on the other hand, should go for boards designed for giant or super-giant slalom, the length of which, for anyone really crazy enough, can exceed 200 cm (80 inches), with an effective edge of more than 185 cm (70 inches). These veritable torpedoes have a shaping radius of between 12 m at the shortest and 20 m (40–65 feet) at the longest, the latter being strictly for competition riders.

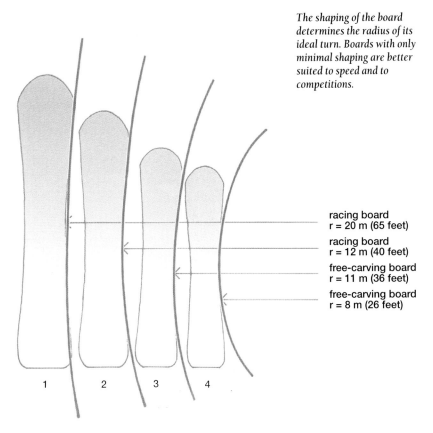

The shaping of the board determines the radius of its ideal turn. Boards with only minimal shaping are better suited to speed and to competitions.

racing board
r = 20 m (65 feet)

racing board
r = 12 m (40 feet)

free-carving board
r = 11 m (36 feet)

free-carving board
r = 8 m (26 feet)

1   2   3   4

Board width

The last factor to take into consideration is the width of the board in relation to the length of your feet and the style of snowboarding that you favor. If you prefer your basic stance to be very sideways facing, as favored by many freestylers, then you will have to position yourself on the board with feet almost at right angles to the length of the board. With US size 9 (UK size 8; European size 42) feet this is not a problem, but with US size 12 (UK size 11; European size 45) you will have to choose a board that is very wide at the center, 25 cm (10 inches) or more. If you ignore this and buy a smaller board, your blade will lose contact with the snow every time that you edge the board. This is because your feet will stick out and lift the edge off the snow, so that it

will no longer have adequate contact. For the same reason Alpiners who don't like a very forward facing position, and who have long feet, are obliged to go for a wider board. Modern super-giant boards can even be as wide as 20 cm (8 inches) at the center, allowing riders to have their rear foot at an angle of 50° or less.

What angle you choose to have your bindings attached to the board is a subjective matter, though as a general rule it can be said that less angled bindings favor stability and maneuverability, at the cost of speed in changing direction. In any case, when buying a new board you should make these technical aspects your prime consideration and other aspects, such as having graphics in the sole or not, should be secondary.

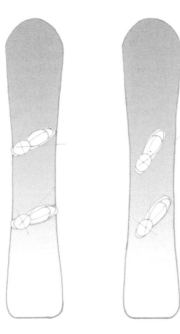

The width of a board depends largely on the length of the foot and on how the foot is angled in relation to the direction of travel.

BINDINGS
Downhill

The only link between the ski and the boot is the binding. This system of attachment has become technically extremely sophisticated, so as to almost always guarantee maximum safety in the event of a fall. Modern bindings are in fact designed primarily to prevent injury. When skis were made of wood and the system for attaching the boot to the ski consisted of rudimentary metal brackets and leather straps, skiers were frequently injured in falls, because the skis did not detach themselves from the boots. Today's safety bindings mean that the boot detaches itself from the ski when it is subjected to a pre-determined amount of sudden pressure, such as the toe of the boot pushing sideways, which typically happens when a leg is twisted in a dangerous and excessive manner. In this situation the boot comes loose thanks to the calibration of the spring inside the binding.

Bindings consist of two parts:
– the toe-piece–this is the front part of the binding, into which the boot is inserted in the first part of the procedure of attaching the skis

– the heel-piece–this is the rear part of the binding, into which the boot is inserted secondly in the procedure of attaching the skis. The heel-piece has a lever which is lifted when the boot is attached, and which

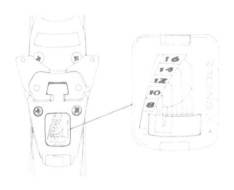

Above: the dial showing the level of resistance offered before the toe-piece releases the boot. Below: a collection of the different types of binding available. From left: downhill ski bindings, hard snowboard bindings, soft snowboard bindings, mountaineering ski bindings, and cross-country bindings.

must be pressed down if you want to free the boot.

Besides providing safety, the binding must also be able to instantly transfer the foot's movements to the ski. In other words, the movements that the skier wants to transmit to the skis should not be dispersed because the bindings are too elastic. This is a particularly important requirement for expert skiers and competition-level skiers.

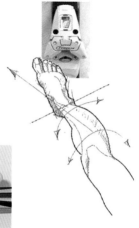

The drawings show the type of leg movements that will cause the binding to release the boot. Left: a selection of safety bindings complete with brakes for downhill skis.

Snowboard bindings

The majority of snowboarders underestimate the importance of using really good bindings. It is essential to understand which system and which model is best suited to each person's individual characteristics. The choices on offer can be divided into two groups or systems: soft or hard. Then there is a third system, which is becoming increasingly popular: step-in bindings, which deserve a separate discussion.

Soft bindings

Soft bindings are the most common and are used in freestyle, free-riding, powder snow, and snowboard parks. They are made up of a basis of plastic or aluminum, to which are attached two straps and a spoiler which are used to anchor the foot. Over the years this system has finally evolved to have a shape and materials that guarantee optimum comfort and a high level of movement transmission. To get an idea of what is involved and to find a good brand, you should check first of all how rigid the base is. If it is made of aluminum, this instantly guarantees a high level of rigidity, while if it is made of plastic its rigidity depends on how the various bands within it are set out and the mix of plastic used. A rigid base allows the rider's movements to be transmitted to the board more quickly and more effectively. In a toe-side turn, for instance, the body is hunched up and leans over towards the inside of the turn; the weight is concentrated at ankle height, which means on the band that encircles it. This band transmits the pressure to the base of the binding. If the base happens to be soft, the majority of the rider's energy is absorbed by the distortion of the plastic, and the movement is thus less effective. If you tend more towards free-riding, you are advised to use bindings that have fairly high and rigid spoilers.

Hard bindings

Hard bindings are continually evolving. At the moment there are two schools of thought: those who prefer a totally rigid binding and those who are more open-minded. Hard bindings generally consist of a plate fixed to the board, of two blocks with the lever on the toe section, and of a little restraining arch on the heel section. The materials used are aluminum, Ergal, plastic, and composite materials. The higher the speed, as in giant or super-giant slalom, the more the binding needs to be rigid; in free carving it works better to use a system that gives more, as this allows you to make up for mistakes and not to be overly affected by unevenness in the snow surface. Non-competitive snowboarders should choose bindings that are not too rigid but if you love carving at top speed with a 180 cm (70 inches) board, then you really should get a binding made of Ergal.

Step-in bindings

The step-in binding system is a halfway house between the other two types: it has a base, a rigid mechanism which is used with soft boots. There are various different models on the market, and almost all of them are aimed at free-riding and free-carving. A few people do use them for freestyle, but they are generally considered to have certain limitations in this field. Their great advantage is that they are ultra-easy to get in and out of, so much so that you do not even need to look, after you have had a bit of practice. They are comfortable and convenient, overall an excellent solution for free-riders. Don't be in a hurry to make up your mind as to which of the three systems of binding you will buy. It is better to try out some different models and get advice from experts. The whole world of snowboarding is continually evolving so do some research first.

"Free heel" bindings

This is the name used to describe all bindings for ski mountaineering, Telemark and cross-country, i.e. all bindings that allow the heel to be raised in order to perform the basic movements of ski mountaineering and cross-country skiing, or the knee-bend movement of Telemark.

Cross-country bindings

From being a simple strap to tie on the shoe, cross-country bindings have evolved so far that the shoe is now an integral part of them. In the latest models there is a slight distinction between bindings for traditional cross-country skiing and skating-style cross-country. The main difference is that the latter bind the boot more to the ski, even attaching to the ski the part of the boot under the heel whenever the foot is pressed down.

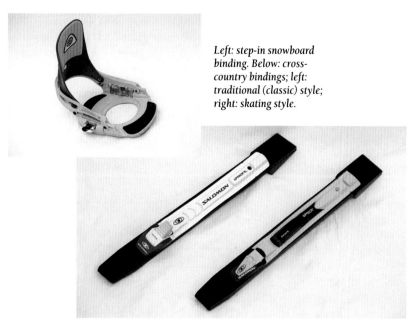

Left: step-in snowboard binding. Below: cross-country bindings; left: traditional (classic) style; right: skating style.

Telemark bindings

There are two types of Telemark bindings, reflecting the two styles currently practiced. The traditional-style Telemark binding is a cable binding, whereas the binding for modern-style Telemark is a rigid-transmission design. These differences have an obvious effect on performance, in that the rigid binding makes it possible to transmit steering movements to the ski with much greater precision, but Telemark purists claim that the cable binding better reflects the philosophy and tradition of this historical sport.

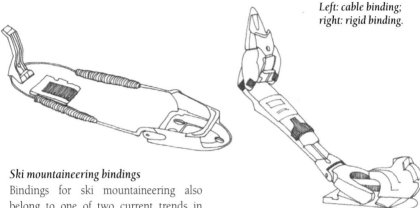

Left: cable binding; right: rigid binding.

Ski mountaineering bindings

Bindings for ski mountaineering also belong to one of two current trends in thinking. "German" bindings are seen as traditional, and are made of steel. "Swiss" bindings are seen as a development and an adaptation of downhill skis for the requirements of ski mountaineering.

Below, left: "German" binding; right: "Swiss" binding.

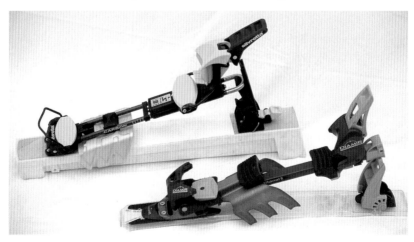

BOOTS AND SHOES

Of all the equipment used in skiing, boots are the part that come into direct contact with your body, and so are the part that most needs to be individualized. Many of the makers do in fact produce boots that are partly adjustable to fit the buyer's foot.

Below: the full range of different boot types. From left: downhill, mountaineering, traditional (classic) cross-country, skating-style cross-country, hard snowboarding, and soft snowboarding.

Downhill skiing boots

Up until the 1950s ski boots were made of leather with reinforcements of varying thickness on the sole and at the front and sides of the boot, which provided greater rigidity and thus better performance. Water resistance was provided by treating the leather with animal fats.

Towards the middle of the 1960s plastic appeared, and this material ensured two major principles: first, greater rigidity at

the sides and in the flex; and second, better water resistance. Since then all ski boots have been composed of two elements: an exterior casing of plastic, and an interior "sock" of soft material. Today the idea of a

Below: two types of downhill boot. Notice how much more the leg leans in the competition boot (right).

ski boot has not changed at all, although obviously performance has improved and production methods have moved on.

Below: a downhill ski boot must guarantee rigidity at the side and when flexed.

Boots for ski-mountaineering

A ski mountaineering boot is a bit more complex in its design than a downhill ski boot, with only minor differences between touring and mountaineering boots. Besides the essential and shared qualities of robustness and rigidity, it must:
• Be as light as possible, to make long climbs less tiring (c. 1600 g [.5 lbs]).
• Have a compact, streamlined outline so as to create as little unnecessary friction as possible in fresh snow.

• Use soft materials designed to fit the anatomy of the foot.
• Allow the ankle enough freedom of movement to make walking and climbing easy.
• Hold the foot solid enough to provide perfect control of the skis in difficult descents or (should the case arise) on groomed trails.
• Have good grip on the sole so as to be able to get a secure hold when advancing over hard snow or rocks without the skis.

Left: two different types of boot for ski mountaineering.

OUTER SHELL AND INNER SOCK

The shell is the outer part of the boot and is made of plastic. The different strength of the plastic used determines which sort of user it is targeted at: harder plastics are for competition skiers, softer plastics for beginners and intermediate level skiers. The sock, or liner, is the inner part of the boot and is made of different types of foam, often thermoform (which changes shape when it gets warm to fit the foot). With all types of boot it is possible to extract the sock from the outer shell, which becomes essential when you need to dry out the interior, soaked by all the condensation accumulated from a normal day's skiing.

Telemark boots

There are two types: one similar in style to a downhill boot, with an outer shell and an inner sock; the other made of leather which mirrors the traditional shoe and is used by Telemark purists.

Types of Telemark boot for different techniques and performance.

Cross-country boots

There are two types and, once again, they are related to the type of style that the skier intends to follow; for the skating technique the boot is higher so as to contain the ankle better during sideways movements and to thus protect the ligaments at the side of the leg. An important characteristic of the boot for classic cross-country is its great flexibility in a longitudinal direction, which is needed in order to prolong the important stage when the foot is weighted, and to thus ensure long "strides." In both types the shoe must be waterproof and fit tightly, while still providing comfort, to guarantee sensitivity and precision in controlling the skis.

Above left: a traditional (classic) style boot; right: a boot for skating-style cross-country.

Snowboard boots

As you will have seen, the world of snowboarding is divided into two categories: hard and soft. The boot for the hard style is very similar to a downhill ski boot: an external plastic shell and an inner sock in a soft material. The difference can be found in the bottom part of the casing, which is of a different thickness in order to be able to be attached to snowboard bindings. The hard boot has three or four clips for fastening and often also for adjusting the angle that the ankle is bent at. The soft boot looks like a slightly more solid après-ski boot. It is made of an internal sock in a soft, usually breathable material, and an outer layer of leather, corduroy, or plastic.

Above left: a hard snowboard boot; right: a soft snowboard boot.

PLATES AND RISERS

The plate is an object that is fixed between the ski and the binding and was the idea of a Swiss engineer, Luciano Bettosini, who had desperately been trying to find a way of limiting the vibrations of skis. His patent, called "Derbyflex," was at first not taken seriously by the competitive world (1980), but in the years that followed it became so successful that no competitor skied without one any more. Today there are many companies producing anti-vibratory plates, but they are all based on Bettosini's original idea. It is worth pointing out that not all plates are very efficient in performing their function of deadening vibrations, but this can only be checked by sophisticated measuring instruments.

Another important effect of the plate, but only for competition skiers, is that it increases both the rigidity and the elastic response of the ski-plate combination, which means that the competitor can get better results out of the energy employed in turns. However, this stiffening effect is not recommended for all skiers, who should think very carefully about how useful a plate will really be for them. A third function of the plate is the height clearance that it gives, which separates the boot some 15 cm (6 inches) from the ski. This makes it less likely that the boot will touch the snow during a turn. This height clearance is particularly popular with skiers who use fun-carving skis and are often forced to lean over in an extreme manner. But if a skier is

Risers and three different types of anti-vibratory plates mounted on skis (without bindings).

only after this last effect and is not interested in any of the other advantages peculiar to plates, then he can simply use risers that are placed between the ski and the binding. These risers are made of plastic and are much lighter than plates, and for this reason they are used in slalom competitions where swift edge changing requires an overall weight that is less than the ski-plate combination.

Right: two typical situations in which using a plate can be useful.
Below: the amount of vibration absorbed by a ski: left, without plate; right, with plate.

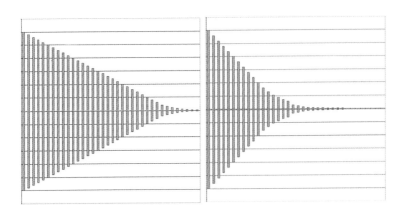

POLES

Poles are an important part of skiing equipment. In the early days of skiing poles carried out an important role in steering: the "Telemark" technique (end of the 19th century) and the "Lilienfeld" technique (early 20th century) entailed a single pole being used as a sort of rudder to make turning easier. Later on both poles were used for at least two main purposes: to push off and to aid balance during the descent. The first of these two purposes mainly evolved within the context of cross-country skiing, while the second belongs to downhill skiing. In fact, in downhill skiing poles are pretty well indispensable when skiing down very steep slopes, on unfamiliar territory, on fresh snow, and of course when performing a series of tight turns. In recent years some skiers using fun–carving skis (very short and shaped) have preferred not to uses poles at all: this gives the whole experience a greater sense of freedom but is only really possible on very even ground.

Poles are made up of three parts:
– the grip (with strap)
– the pole shaft
– the basket

The grip

This is shaped to fit the hand and made of plastic or rubber. The strap is indispensable, ensuring that you don't lose the pole when you plant it or if you fall. You should put the strap on by inserting your hand

Below: different types of grips for downhill skiing, ski-mountaineering, and cross-country skiing.

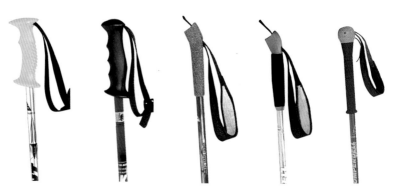

into it from underneath and then gripping it next to the handle itself. The strap can usually be adjusted to fit your hand.

The pole shaft

This can be made either of aluminum alloy or carbon fiber. The former is heavier, and "plastic" (in the sense that it tends to distort if put under a lot of strain). The latter is lighter and more elastic, but can break if struck very sharply.

The basket

This is a piece of plastic, circular in shape, fixed about 5 cm (2 inches) from the tip of the pole shaft. Its aim is to prevent the pole sinking into the snow and to ensure that it is safely planted. Baskets for poles used on the groomed runs are smaller than those for off-trail skiing, where powder snow makes a larger basket necessary.

Above: different types of pole: the first two (from left) are for slalom, the next for ski-mountaineering with telescopic expanding mechanism, and the last for downhill freestyle.
Below: various types of baskets for use in different types of snow.

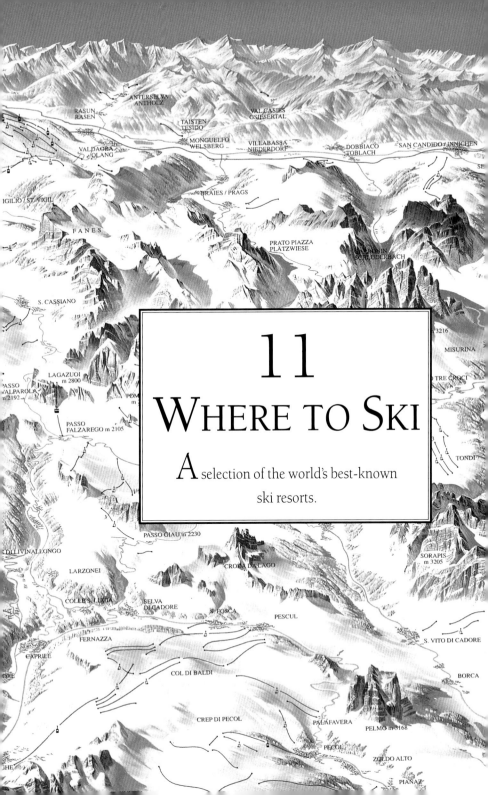

11
WHERE TO SKI

A selection of the world's best-known
ski resorts.

SIERRA NEVADA

This is the most southerly ski resort in Europe. From the summit of Mount Veleta you can see the coast of Africa. In 1996 it was host to the World Skiing Championships. It is only one hour's drive from Granada.

Web site: www.sierranevadaski.com	
Height: 2100–3300 m (6300–9900 feet)	
Downhill runs: 45; 60 km (40 miles)	
Number of ski lifts: 19	
Cross-country ski runs: 8 km (5 miles)	
Skating rinks: yes	
Snowboarding runs: yes	
Amusement parks: yes	
Artificial snow-making: 22 km (14 miles)	

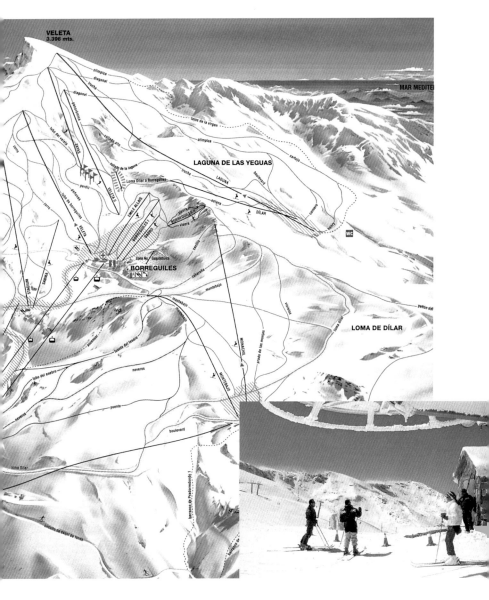

CHAMONIX

Chamonix is at the foot of Mont Blanc, the highest mountain in the Alps 4810 m (15,777 feet), on the border between Italy and France, 90 minutes' drive from Geneva airport. It is one of the most famous mountain resorts in Europe, for climbing Mont Blanc in the summer, and skiing on- and off-trail in the winter (the Vallée Blanche is a must for any good skier).

Web site: www.chamonix.com	
Height: 1035–3842 m (3395–12,602 feet)	
Downhill runs: 69; 170 km (105 miles)	
Number of ski lifts: 49	
Cross-country ski runs: 42 km (26 miles)	
Skating rinks: yes	
Snowboarding runs: yes	
Amusement parks: yes	
Artificial snow-making: 10 km (6 miles)	

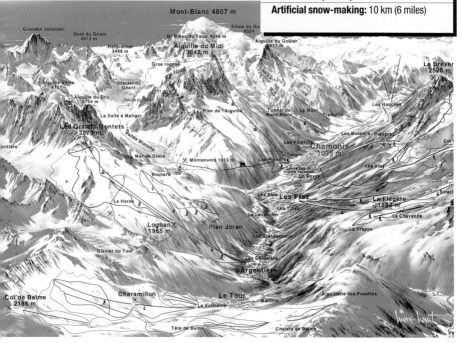

COURCHEVEL

Courchevel is part of a vast network in the Moûtiers Valley, in the heart of the French Alps, which also includes Méribel, La Tania, Les Menuires, and Val Thorens. It is located two hours' drive from Geneva airport and also has a small high-altitude airport.

Web site: www.courchevel.com	
Height: 1650–3560 m (5412–11,677 feet)	
Downhill runs: 70; 220 km (140 miles)	
Number of ski lifts: 67	
Cross-country ski runs: 27 km (17 miles)	
Skating rinks: yes	
Snowboarding runs: yes	
Amusement parks: yes	
Artificial snow-making: 24 ha (60 acres)	

FLAINE

One hour's drive south-west of Geneva, near to the small town of Cluses, in Haute Savoie. It is one of the most modern and best equipped ski resorts in France (opened in 1969).

Web site: www.flaine.com	
Height: 1600–2581 m (5248–8466 feet)	
Downhill runs: 49; 140 km (90 miles)	
Number of ski lifts: 29	
Cross-country ski runs: 10 km (6 miles)	
Skating rinks: yes	
Snowboarding runs: yes	
Amusement parks: yes	
Artificial snow-making: 80 cannons	

LA PLAGNE

This is one of the largest skiing areas in France, with six resorts at high altitude and four in the valley. It is two hours' drive from Geneva airport.

Web site: www.laplagne.com	
Height: 1250–3250 m (4100–10,660 feet)	
Downhill runs: 124; 212 km (132 miles)	
Number of ski lifts: 110	
Cross-country ski runs: 90 km (56 miles)	
Skating rinks: yes	
Snowboarding runs: yes	
Amusement parks: yes	
Artificial snow-making: 14 km (9 miles)	

LES ARCS

Just over two hours' drive from Geneva airport, in the Moûtiers Valley. Built in 1969, it is made up of many small centers linked by runs and ski lifts.

Web site: www.lesarcs.com	
Height: 1600–3226 m (5248–10,581 feet)	
Downhill runs: 121; 200 km (125 miles)	
Number of ski lifts: 76	
Cross-country ski runs: 15 km (9 miles)	
Skating rinks: yes	
Snowboarding runs: yes	
Amusement parks: yes	
Artificial snow-making: 20 ha (50 acres)	

LES DEUX ALPES

Les Deux Alpes is on the road from Lyon to Turin, 90 minutes' drive from Grenoble. It is one of the most prestigious resorts in the area, for summer as well as winter activities, and has a very pleasant atmosphere.

Web site: www.les2alpes.com	
Height: 1650–3560 m (5412–11,677 feet)	
Downhill runs: 70; 220 km (140 miles)	
Number of ski lifts: 58	
Cross-country ski runs: 27 km (17 miles)	
Skating rinks: yes	
Snowboarding runs: yes	
Amusement parks: yes	
Artificial snow-making: 24 ha (60 acres)	

MEGÈVE

Megève and its sister resort St. Gervais are one hour from Geneva airport. It is a resort with a long-standing tradition of tourism, and it also offers lively nightlife.

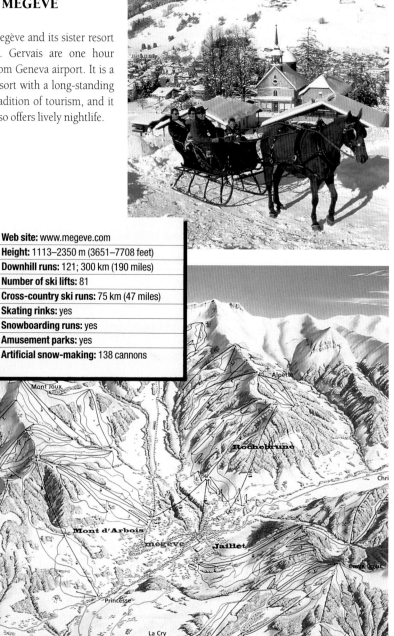

Web site: www.megeve.com
Height: 1113–2350 m (3651–7708 feet)
Downhill runs: 121; 300 km (190 miles)
Number of ski lifts: 81
Cross-country ski runs: 75 km (47 miles)
Skating rinks: yes
Snowboarding runs: yes
Amusement parks: yes
Artificial snow-making: 138 cannons

SERRE CHEVALIER

This resort consists of three villages in the Serre Valley. It is in the south of the French Alps, near the town of Briançon (railway station). The nearest airports are Lyon, Grenoble, and Turin.

Web site: www.serrechevalier.com

Height: 1200–2800 m (3936–9184 feet)

Downhill runs: 250 km (160 miles)

Number of ski lifts: 74

Cross-country ski runs: 45 km (28 miles)

Skating rinks: yes

Snowboarding runs: yes

Amusement parks: yes

Artificial snow-making: 15 km (9 miles)

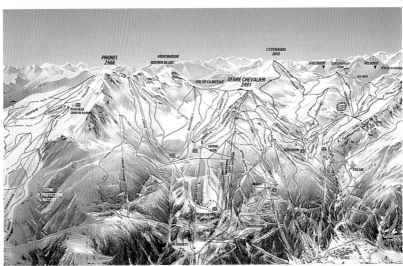

VAL D'ISÈRE

This resort has been going since the 1930s. The old center of the village is made up of stone houses grouped around the church. It is 35 km (20 miles) from Bourg St. Maurice (railway station) and 185 km (120 miles) from Geneva airport.

Web site: www.valdisere.com
Height: 1850–3450 m (6068–11,316 feet)
Downhill runs: 135; 300 km (190 miles)
Number of ski lifts: 100
Cross-country ski runs: 24 km (15 miles)
Skating rinks: yes
Snowboarding runs: yes
Amusement parks: yes
Artificial snow-making: 15 km (9 miles)

CRANS MONTANA

These are really two inter-linked resorts situated on a mountain plain at an altitude of 1500 m (4500 feet), looking out over the Rhône Valley. You can also ski here in summer on the Plaine Morte glacier (3000 m [9000 feet]). The railway station is at Serre (20 km [12 miles]), the nearest airport is at Sion, and the international airport at Geneva is two hours' drive away.

Web site: www.crans-montana.ch	
Height: 1500–3000 m (4920–9840 feet)	
Downhill runs: 59; 160 km (100 miles)	
Number of ski lifts: 39	
Cross-country ski runs: 70 km (45 miles)	
Skating rinks: yes	
Snowboarding runs: yes	
Amusement parks: yes	
Artificial snow-making: 10 km (6 miles)	

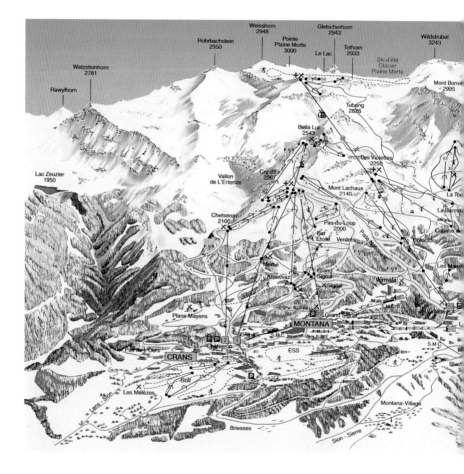

338

3102

Trubelnstock
2997

Les Faverges
2968

Petit Bonvin
2400

La Tièche

Varneralp

Aprili

Plumachit

La Cure

AMINONA

S.M.C.

Randogne

Mollens

© 1997
Pool des Remontées Mécaniques
Crans-Montana-Aminona
Commercialisation
Imprimerie Bachmann Montana
® Reproduction et duplication interdites

DAVOS

This is generally thought to be the highest town and the largest skiing area in Switzerland, with runs that are famous among skiing enthusiasts all over the world. The nearest airport is at Zurich.

Web site: www.davos.ch	
Height: 1560–2590 m (5117–8495 feet)	
Downhill runs: 80; 230 km (145 miles)	
Number of ski lifts: 44	
Cross-country ski runs: 75 km (47 miles)	
Skating rinks: yes	
Snowboarding runs: yes	
Amusement parks: yes	
Artificial snow-making: 8 km (5 miles)	

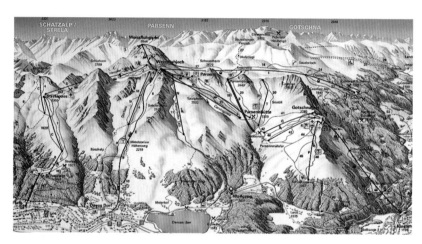

GSTAAD

A very select resort, closed to motorized traffic, set in a wide wooded valley near Lake Geneva with a narrow-gauge railway running through it. The nearest airport is at Bern.

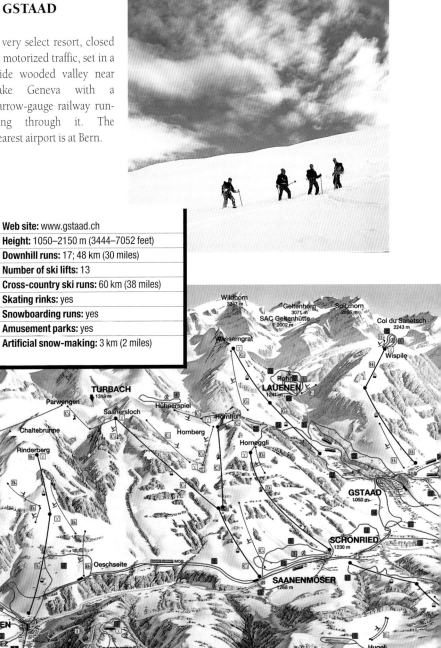

Web site: www.gstaad.ch
Height: 1050–2150 m (3444–7052 feet)
Downhill runs: 17; 48 km (30 miles)
Number of ski lifts: 13
Cross-country ski runs: 60 km (38 miles)
Skating rinks: yes
Snowboarding runs: yes
Amusement parks: yes
Artificial snow-making: 3 km (2 miles)

ST. MORITZ

This has been one of the
top ten resorts in the
world since the beginning
of the twentieth century. It
is situated in the south of
Switzerland and can be
reached by train from Italy
and from Chur; the nearest
airport is at Samedan.

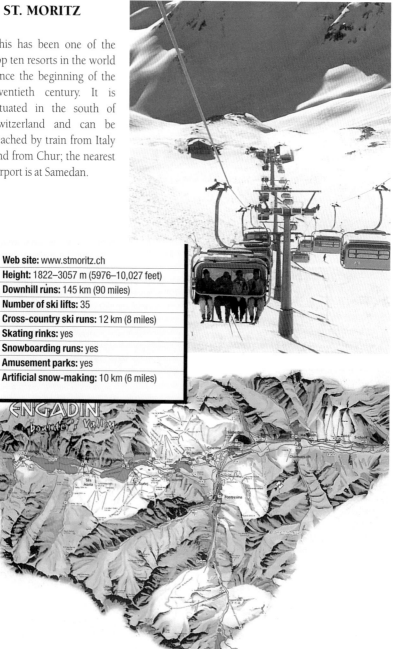

Web site: www.stmoritz.ch
Height: 1822–3057 m (5976–10,027 feet)
Downhill runs: 145 km (90 miles)
Number of ski lifts: 35
Cross-country ski runs: 12 km (8 miles)
Skating rinks: yes
Snowboarding runs: yes
Amusement parks: yes
Artificial snow-making: 10 km (6 miles)

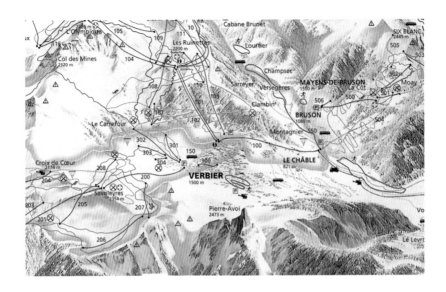

VERBIER

Web site: www.verbier.ch	
Height: 1500–3330 m (4920–10,922 feet)	
Downhill runs: 210 km (130 miles)	
Number of ski lifts: 43	
Cross-country ski runs: 9 km (6 miles)	
Skating rinks: yes	
Snowboarding runs: yes	
Amusement parks: yes	
Artificial snow-making: 13 km (8 miles)	

This is one of the best-organized resorts in the Alps. It can be reached by road or by rail from Martigny; the nearest airport is at Geneva (two hours).

WENGEN-GRINDELWALD

This resort is a must for anyone who loves
mountains. Wengen is situated on a small
plateau looking out over the Lauter-
brunnen Valley, and can only be reached by
means of a small mountain train. Grindelwald, at a slightly lower altitude, can be
reached by road or by rail. The nearest
airport is at Bern (one hour).

Web site: www.wengen.com	
Height: 1217–3454 m (3992–11,329 feet)	
Downhill runs: 180 km (110 miles)	
Number of ski lifts: 31	
Cross-country ski runs: 35 km (22 miles)	
Skating rinks: yes	
Snowboarding runs: yes	
Amusement parks: yes	
Artificial snow-making: 12 km (8 miles)	

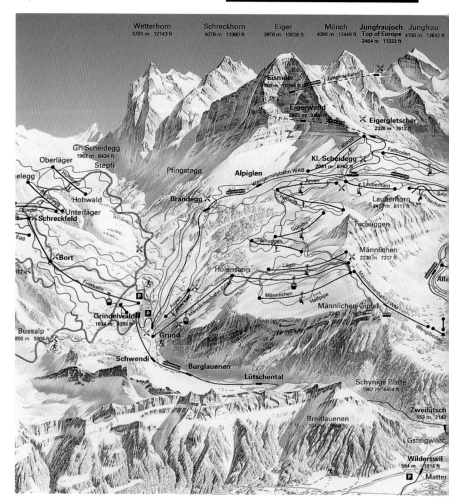

ZERMATT

Zermatt and the silhouette of the Matterhorn are the symbol of the Alps. A traditional destination for both skiers and climbers, it can only be reached by train. There is also summer skiing on the plateau of the Monte Rosa, 3400 m, (11,152 feet), which is linked to Cervinia (Italy).

Web site: www.zermatt.ch	
Height: 1620–3189 m (5314–10,460 feet)	
Downhill runs: 71; 175 km (110 miles)	
Number of ski lifts: 48	
Cross-country ski runs: 7 km (4 miles)	
Skating rinks: yes	
Snowboarding runs: yes	
Amusement parks: yes	
Artificial snow-making: 25 km (16 miles)	

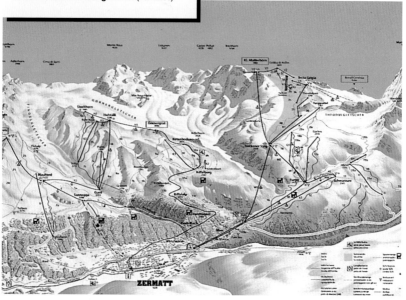

ALTA BADIA

This vast skiing area is part of the Dolomites Superski area (which comprises 12 prestigious centers in the eastern Alps). The nearest railway station is at Brunico; the nearest airport at Innsbruck (Austria).

Web site: www.dolomitisuperski.com/altabadia
Height: 1324–2600 m (4343–8528 feet)
Downhill runs: 91; 130 km (80 miles)
Number of ski lifts: 59
Cross-country ski runs: 40 km (25 miles)
Skating rinks: yes
Snowboarding runs: yes
Amusement parks: no
Artificial snow-making: 55 km (35 miles)

BORMIO

This is one of the first tourist resorts in Italy, famous for centuries for its thermal springs. It is situated in Alta Valtellina, below the Stelvio Pass, which is the highest in Europe (2758 m [8274 feet]), and a summer skiing destination. Milan airport is three hours' drive.

Web site: www.skifinals2000.com	
Height: 1225–3012 m (4018–9880 feet)	
Downhill runs: 11; 50 km (30 miles)	
Number of ski lifts: 19	
Cross-country ski runs: 13 km (8 miles)	
Skating rinks: yes	
Snowboarding runs: yes	
Amusement parks: no	
Artificial snow-making: 11 km (7 miles)	

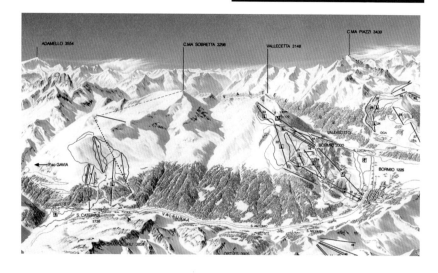

CERVINIA

This is one of the highest resorts in the western Alps, at the foot of Monte Cervino (the Matterhorn), where there is also summer skiing. The nearest airports are at Turin and Milan (90 minutes).

Web site: www.breuil-cervinia.com	
Height: 2066–3488 m (6776–11,441 feet)	
Downhill runs: 60; 241 km (150 miles)	
Number of ski lifts: 34	
Cross-country ski runs: 17 km (11 miles)	
Skating rinks: yes	
Snowboarding runs: yes	
Amusement parks: yes	
Artificial snow-making: 10 km (6 miles)	

CORTINA D'AMPEZZO

A popular tourist destination since the time of the Hapsburg emperors, in a wide valley in the heart of the Dolomites. The nearest airports are at Innsbruck (Austria), and Venice (two hours); the nearest railway stations are at Dobbiaco and Calalzo.

Web site: www.sunrise.it/dolomiti	
Height: 1224–3000 m (4015–9840 feet)	
Downhill runs: 76; 110 km (70 miles)	
Number of ski lifts: 39	
Cross-country ski runs: 58 km (36 miles)	
Skating rinks: yes	
Snowboarding runs: yes	
Amusement parks: yes	
Artificial snow-making: 60 km (38 miles)	

LIVIGNO

A duty-free town of the Alta Valtellina (Sondrio) near the Swiss border, famous mostly for snowboarding and Telemark. It is four to five hours from Milan by road, and is easily reachable from Davos via a private tunnel.

Web site: www.livnet.it	
Height: 1860–2795 m (6100–9168 feet)	
Downhill runs: 57; 110 km (70 miles)	
Number of ski lifts: 30	
Cross-country ski runs: 40 km (25 miles)	
Skating rinks: yes	
Snowboarding runs: yes	
Amusement parks: yes	
Artificial snow-making: 13 km (8 miles)	

MADONNA DI CAMPIGLIO

A secluded resort at the foot of the Dolomites at Brenta, but a popular destination since the time of the Austro-Hungarian empire. It is linked by runs and ski lifts to Marilleva. The nearest railway station is Malè; Verona airport is two hours' drive away.

Web site: www.campiglio.net	
Height: 1550–3016 m (5084–9892 feet)	
Downhill runs: 39; 90 km (56 miles)	
Number of ski lifts: 26	
Cross-country ski runs: 30 km (19 miles)	
Skating rinks: yes	
Snowboarding runs: yes	
Amusement parks: yes	
Artificial snow-making: 40 km (25 miles)	

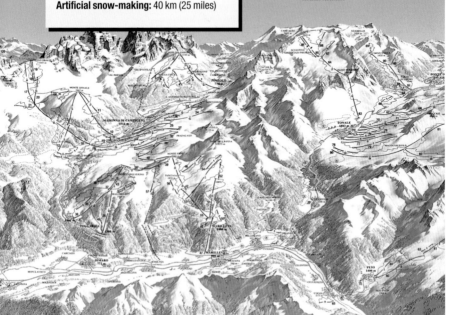

SESTRIERE

A famous tourist destination since the 1920s, this is part of the Milky Way, 300 km (190 miles) of runs. It is 90 minutes' drive from Turin airport; the nearest railway station is at Oulx (40 km [25 miles]).

Web site: TBA	
Height: 2035–2823 m (6675–9259 feet)	
Downhill runs: 145; 240 km (150 miles)	
Number of ski lifts: 90	
Cross-country ski runs: 3	
Skating rinks: yes	
Snowboarding runs: yes	
Amusement parks: yes	
Artificial snow-making: 75 km (50 miles)	

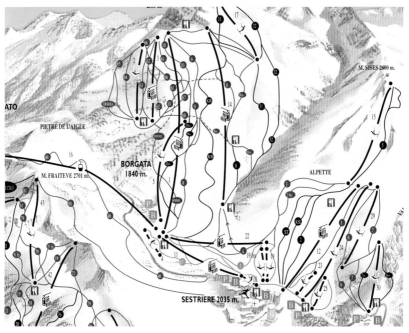

SKI CIVETTA

This is part of the Dolomites Superski area and it is the largest network in the Veneto, one of the few places in Italy to have runs illuminated for night-time skiing. The nearest railway stations are Longarone, 26 km (16 miles), and Belluno, 48 km (30 miles); Venice airport is 150 km (95 miles) away.

Web site: www.dolomitisuperski.com/civetta	
Height: 1000–2100 m (3280–6888 feet)	
Downhill runs: 30; 80 km (50 miles)	
Number of ski lifts: 28	
Cross-country ski runs: 12 km (8 miles)	
Skating rinks: yes	
Snowboarding runs: yes	
Amusement parks: yes	
Artificial snow-making: 70 km (45 miles)	

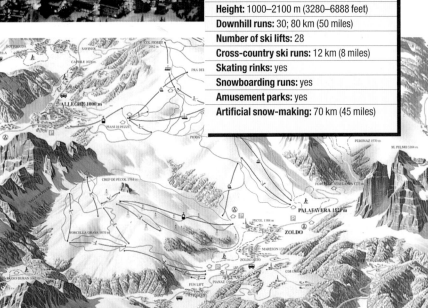

VAL GARDENA

Part of the Dolomites Superski area, known as a winter sports resort since the beginning of the 20th century. It is one hour's drive from the Brennero pass; the railway station is at Chiuso (Bolzano).

Web site: www.val-gardena.com	
Height: 1236–2680 m (4054–8790 feet)	
Downhill runs: 175 km (110 miles)	
Number of ski lifts: 76	
Cross-country ski runs: 98 km (61 miles)	
Skating rinks: yes	
Snowboarding runs: yes	
Amusement parks: yes	
Artificial snow-making: 35 km (22 miles)	

BERCHTESGADEN

Web site: www.berchtesgadenerland.com	
Height: 480–1874 m (1574–6147 feet)	
Downhill runs: 21; 58 km (36 miles)	
Number of ski lifts: 59	
Cross-country ski runs: 61 km (38 miles)	
Skating rinks: yes	
Snowboarding runs: yes	
Amusement parks: yes	
Artificial snow-making: 215 km (130 miles)	

An old mining town (rock salt) in southern Germany, now a summer and winter tourist resort two hours from Salzburg and Munich.

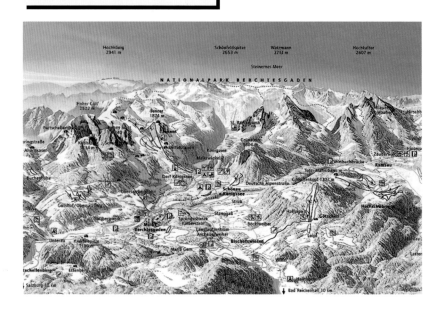

GARMISCH-PARTENKIRCHEN

This is Germany's most famous resort, and was the first place to host the Winter Olympic Games (1936). It is situated at the foot of the Zugspitze, less than 90 minutes' drive from Innsbruck and Munich.

Web site: www.garmischpartenkirchen.de
Height: 720–2830 m (2362–9282 feet)
Downhill runs: 40; 120 km (75 miles)
Number of ski lifts: 38
Cross-country ski runs: 39 km (24 miles)
Skating rinks: yes
Snowboarding runs: yes
Amusement parks: yes
Artificial snow-making: yes

BADGASTEIN

The Gastein Valley is two hours' drive south of Salzburg. It is an unforgettable place, not only for its impressive runs. Resplendent palaces recall the days of the old Austro-Hungarian empire, and for six centuries it has been famous for its thermal baths.

Web site: www.badgastein.at	
Height: 830–2682 m (2722–8797 feet)	
Downhill runs: 30 km (19 miles)	
Number of ski lifts: 53	
Cross-country ski runs: 63 km (40 miles)	
Skating rinks: yes	
Snowboarding runs: yes	
Amusement parks: no	
Artificial snow-making: 170 ha (425 acres)	

SAALBACH

Together with Hinterglemm and Leogang, Saalbach makes up a vast skiing network in the Kitzbühel Alps. It is about 100 km (60 miles) east of Innsbruck and just over 80 km (50 miles) from Salzburg.

Web site: www.saalbach.com	
Height: 1003–2100 m (3290–6888 feet)	
Downhill runs: 204 km (128 miles)	
Number of ski lifts: 61	
Cross-country ski runs: 45 km (28 miles)	
Skating rinks: yes	
Snowboarding runs: yes	
Amusement parks: yes	
Artificial snow-making: 47 km (29 miles)	

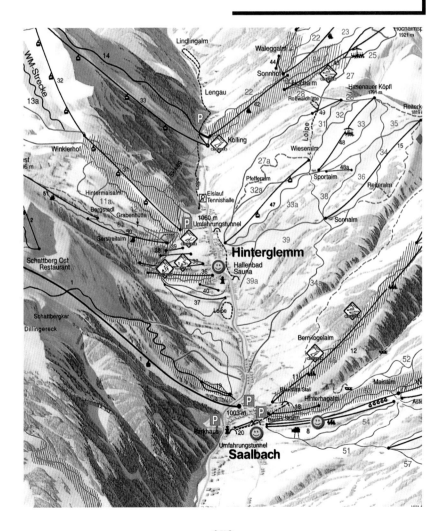

SCHLADMING

An historic town only one hour's drive from Salzburg airport, that can also be reached by train. It is right in the heart of a region rich in skiing possibilities, both downhill and cross-country, on the edge of the Sölktaler National Park.

Web site: www.schladming.com	
Height: 745–1900 m (2444–6232 feet)	
Downhill runs: 29; 54 km (34 miles)	
Number of ski lifts: 24	
Cross-country ski runs: 10 km (6 miles)	
Skating rinks: yes	
Snowboarding runs: yes	
Amusement parks: yes	
Artificial snow-making: 20 km (12 miles)	

ST. ANTON

This is part of a large Alpine network that includes Zurs, Lech, and other resorts. It is located in the secluded Vorarlberg Valley, two hours' drive from Zurich airport. There is also a railway station. It is a very popular high-quality resort.

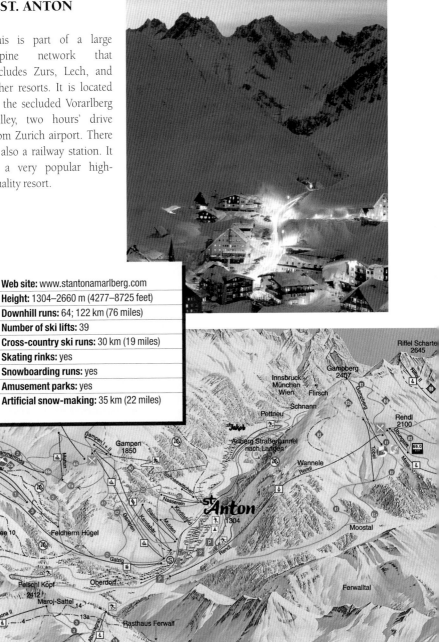

Web site: www.stantonamarlberg.com	
Height: 1304–2660 m (4277–8725 feet)	
Downhill runs: 64; 122 km (76 miles)	
Number of ski lifts: 39	
Cross-country ski runs: 30 km (19 miles)	
Skating rinks: yes	
Snowboarding runs: yes	
Amusement parks: yes	
Artificial snow-making: 35 km (22 miles)	

ZELL AM SEE

Zell Am See is also well known as the Europa Ski Region, which includes Kaprun and other resorts. It is 90 minutes' drive from Salzburg, on the shore of a charming lake, and can also be reached by train. Summer skiing takes place on the Kitzsteinhorn glacier.

Web site: www.zell.gold.at	
Height: 707–3028 m (2319–9932 feet)	
Downhill runs: 130 km (80 miles)	
Number of ski lifts: 61	
Cross-country ski runs: 58 km (36 miles)	
Skating rinks: yes	
Snowboarding runs: yes	
Amusement parks: yes	
Artificial snow-making: 20 km (12 miles)	

KRANJSKA GORA

This is the largest skiing area in Slovenia, located in the north-west of the country near the Austrian and Italian borders. The airports at Ljubljana and Graz (Austria) are one hour's drive away.

Web site: www.kranjska.gora.sl	
Height: 810–1620 m (2657–5314 feet)	
Downhill runs: 20; 30 km (19 miles)	
Number of ski lifts: 20	
Cross-country ski runs: 40 km (25 miles)	
Skating rinks: yes	
Snowboarding runs: yes	
Amusement parks: yes	
Artificial snow-making: 10 km (6 miles)	

ASPEN

An old mining city in the heart of the Rocky Mountains (Colorado), Aspen made its entry into the world of skiing after it was host to the World Championships in 1950. There are altogether four resorts in this area. Aspen is less than two hours' drive from Denver and also has an airport.

Web site: www.skiaspen.com	
Height: 2600–3700 m (8528–12,136 feet)	
Downhill runs: 76; 255 ha (631 acres)	
Number of ski lifts: 8	
Cross-country ski runs: 80 km (50 miles)	
Skating rinks: no	
Snowboarding runs: yes	
Amusement parks: yes	
Artificial snow-making: 85 ha (210 acres)	

HEAVENLY VALLEY

Stretched out around the southern shores of Lake Tahoe in the Sierra Nevada, Heavenly Valley is popular for its skiing but also for the nearby casinos of Nevada. It is three hours' drive from the airport at Reno and also has its own small airport.

Web site: www.skiheavenly.com	
Height: 2210–3300 m (7249–10,824 feet)	
Downhill runs: 82; 1940 ha (4800 acres)	
Number of ski lifts: 26	
Cross-country ski runs: 20 km (12 miles)	
Skating rinks: yes	
Snowboarding runs: yes	
Amusement parks: yes	
Artificial snow-making: 98 ha (242 acres)	

WHERE TO SKI - USA

MAMMOTH MOUNTAINS

This is one of the largest skiing areas in the world, with lifts capable of transporting 50,000 people an hour. It is in California and the nearest airport is Reno (four hours' drive).

Web site: www.mammoth-mtn.com	
Height: 2610–3600 m (8561–11,808 feet)	
Downhill runs: 150; 1415 ha (3500 acres)	
Number of ski lifts: 28	
Cross-country ski runs: 15 km (10 miles)	
Skating rinks: no	
Snowboarding runs: yes	
Amusement parks: yes	
Artificial snow-making: 38 runs	

SQUAW VALLEY

Also known as Olympic Valley (the Winter Olympics were hosted here in 1960), Squaw Valley lies on the southern shores of Lake Tahoe in the Sierra Nevada, three hours' drive from Reno airport.

Web site: www.squaw.com
Height: 2050–3000 m (6724–9840 feet)
Downhill runs: 100; 1620 ha (4000 acres)
Number of ski lifts: 30
Cross-country ski runs: 18 km (11 miles)
Skating rinks: yes
Snowboarding runs: yes
Amusement parks: yes
Artificial snow-making: 140 ha (350 acres)

STEAMBOAT SPRINGS

Web site: www.steamboat-ski.com	
Height: 2100–3800 m (6888–12,464 feet)	
Downhill runs: 141; 380 ha (940 acres)	
Number of ski lifts: 21	
Cross-country ski runs: 8 km (5 miles)	
Skating rinks: yes	
Snowboarding runs: yes	
Amusement parks: yes	
Artificial snow-making: 177 ha (438 acres)	

A modern skiing resort in Colorado, with runs spread over three mountains, where you breathe the air of the Far West. It is three hours' drive west of Denver, and also has its own airport.

Web site: www.sunvalley.com
Height: 1800–3100 m (5904–10,168 feet)
Downhill runs: 78; 831 ha (2054 acres)
Number of ski lifts: 18
Cross-country ski runs: 40 km (25 miles)
Skating rinks: yes
Snowboarding runs: yes
Amusement parks: yes
Artificial snow-making: 255 ha (630 acres)

SUN VALLEY

This is one of the oldest resorts in the United States, and one that has several times been voted the best in the world. It is situated in the Rocky Mountains (Idaho), 130 km (82 miles) from the airport at Boise.

VAIL

First opened in 1960, Vail expanded enormously in the 1980s as a resort "for everyone". The international airport at Denver is 190 km (120 miles) away, while Eagle County, 65 km (40 miles) away, serves flights from within America.

Web site: www.vail.com	
Height: 2600–3750 m (8528–12,300 feet)	
Downhill runs: 124; 1879 ha (4644 acres)	
Number of ski lifts: 26	
Cross-country ski runs: 15 km (10 miles)	
Skating rinks: yes	
Snowboarding runs: yes	
Amusement parks: yes	
Artificial snow-making: 140 ha (347 acres)	

WHISTLER/MT. BLACKCOMB

This is one of the vastest skiing areas in North America and perhaps in the world, with more than 200 runs for skiers of all levels. It is two hours' drive from Vancouver.

Web site: www.b.c.whistler-blackcomb.com	
Height: 675–2285 m (2214–7795 feet)	
Downhill runs: 200; 2896 ha (7157 acres)	
Number of ski lifts: 36	
Cross-country ski runs: 41 km (26 miles)	
Skating rinks: yes	
Snowboarding runs: yes	
Amusement parks: yes	
Artificial snow-making: no	

NOZAWA ONSEN

This resort lies at the foot of Mount Kenashi, which is famous for its thermal springs. It is a very popular skiing resort in Japan, and in 1998, together with Nagano, it hosted the Olympic Games. In Nozawa Hannes Schneider introduced the Arlberg technique in 1930. It is approximately a six-hour bus ride from Tokyo's Narita airport.

Height: 565m–1650 m (1853–5412 feet)
Downhill runs: 32 km (20 miles)
Number of ski lifts: 30
Cross-country ski runs: 5 km (3 miles)
Skating rinks: yes
Snowboarding runs: yes
Amusement parks: yes
Artificial snow-making: no

l'espace killy

le plus bel espace de ski du monde   TIGNES

12
SIGNS AND REGULATIONS

Information signs, danger signs, and compulsory instruction signs. Rules for skiers' behavior.

SIGNS

Downhill and cross-country runs often have danger signs or signs giving a particular instruction. Ski resorts are usually well organized when it comes to everything being clearly signed, not just on the runs (pistes) but as soon as you enter the resort. Signs are obviously of great importance, when you consider that skiing is a sport with quite a bit of risk involved, which can be greatly reduced if you pay careful attention to the signs.

Below you will find details of the various categories of signs:

– run (piste) classification signs
– danger signs
– prohibition signs
– compulsory instruction signs
– information signs
– vital information signs

It should be pointed out, however, that the following signs are only the most important, and may vary slightly from ski resort to ski resort, and from country to country.

Run (piste) classification signs

Runs are classified according to their difficulty, and you will find this shown on circular signs of different colors.

- **Blue run:** this is the easiest type of run, within everyone's capabilities, even those skiing for the first time.

- **Red run:** this is a medium-difficulty run, possible for anyone who has already learnt the snowplow (wedge), and is capable of keeping good control of parallel skis during turns.

- **Black run:** this is a difficult run, which might not have been mechanically groomed, and should only be tackled by expert skiers.

Danger signs

Potential dangers are indicated by triangular signs that are usually yellow.

- General hazard

- Caution—run / track / path narrows ahead

- Caution—trail maintenance machines

- Caution—snow buggies (skidoos)

- Caution—snow cannons

- Caution—concealed rocks

- Caution—drag lift (surface lift) with steep gradient

- Caution—crevasses

- Caution—precipice

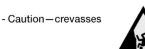

Prohibition signs

Prohibition signs are circular with a white background and a red edge and diagonal bar.

- Skiing forbidden

- Cross-country skiing forbidden

- Tobogganing forbidden

- Snow buggies (skidoos) forbidden

- Pedestrians forbidden

- Do not ski outside the drag lift (surface lift) track

- Do not let go of the drag lift (surface lift) hook

- Do not swing the seat lift (chair lift)

Compulsory instruction signs

Compulsory instruction signs are circular with a blue background and white symbols.

- Turn right

- Leave the chair lift

- Turn left

- Let go of the T-bar / hook / button and turn left

- Go straight ahead

- Let go of the T-bar / hook / button and turn right

- Queue (make a line) two abreast (at the ski lifts)

- Hold poles in one hand in order to take hold of the lift with the other

- Queue three abreast (at the ski lifts)

- Move off the track immediately to the right if you fall

- Queue four abreast (at the ski lifts)

- Move off the track immediately to the left if you fall

- Lower the security bar

- A child must be accompanied by an adult (on chair lifts [seat lifts])

- Raise the security bar

- Two children must be accompanied by two adults (on chair lifts)

- Lift your ski tips

Information signs

The purpose of these is to inform you of the facilities available in the skiing area. They are square with a blue background and white symbols.

- Gondola

- Cable car

- Funicular railway

- Cross-country run

- Skating-style run

- 1-person chair lift (seat lift)

- 2-person chair lift

- 3-person chair lift

- 4-person chair lift

- Drag lift (surface lift)

- First aid station

- Emergency telephone

Vital information signs

Some signs are there to prevent you running into serious danger. This type of sign is rectangular with a symbol in red.

- STOP: risk of avalanche

- STOP: leave lift 50 m (150 feet) ahead

- STOP: leave lift now!

- Run closed

Directional arrows

Some signs point out the way to a particular area (a run, a restaurant, a ski lift, etc). These signs usually show the name of the run and its difficulty rating.

- Turn right for the "Vallone" run.

- Turn left for the "Cima Alta" funicular railway.

CORRECT BEHAVIOR ON THE SLOPES

There are no laws governing how you should behave on the slopes. However, the International Ski Federation (FIS) produced, in Beirut in 1967, a set of guidelines as to how to behave. These ten rules, known as the "ten commandments of skiing," are the only standard code that can be cited, when necessary, to find out who is the guilty party in the event of an accident. Over the years these rules have become very important, and every skier should know them, so as to minimize the risk of an accident involving two or more skiers.

The number of collisions between two skiers has increased in recent years, owing among other reasons to the many different types of skiers on the slopes. Nowadays the runs are used by skiers with traditional skis or with fun–carving skis, snowboarders, Telemarkers, and people skiing on snow blades (very short skis). Each of these styles of descent involves different movements, different turn angles, different speeds, and requires different amounts of space to stop. It is particularly noticeable that the runs are being used more and more in a widthways rather than a lengthways manner: i.e. skiers are using much wider turns than in the past and moving from left to right, and vice versa, at great speed. This has meant that all skiers need to take much more care.

On cross-country runs the risk of two skiers colliding is much lower, but once again, the different styles in this sport (traditional cross-country and skating style) mean that more caution is needed. So starting with the FIS rules, you will find below a framework for behavior that holds good for all types of skiers, including students of ski schools and even competition skiers.

Below, the skiers' code of conduct refers to behaviour on the piste. However, it is most of all in the queues at the ski lifts that skiers need to behave in a courteous manner.

DOWNHILL SKIERS' CODE OF CONDUCT

1 - Consideration for others. All skiers must behave in a way that will not endanger or cause injury to others.

2 - Control of speed and manner of skiing. Every skier must adapt his speed and method of skiing to his own ability, as well as to the terrain and prevailing weather conditions. All skiers, both experts and beginners, must slow down in crowded areas, especially at the bottom of the runs and near the ski lifts.

3 - Choice of course. It is the responsibility of the skier on the uphill side, who is in a position to be able to choose his course, to avoid a collision course with skiers below him.

4 - Overtaking. A skier can overtake either on the right or on the left, but he must always allow the skier being overtaken plenty of room for movement. As a general rule, skiers should not ski right at the edge of the run, so as to leave adequate space for others to overtake. The skier being overtaken should never be put in a difficult position by the overtaker.

5 - Joining or crossing a run. The skier who is joining a run or crossing a skiing area should first look both up and down the slope to ensure that he can do so without endangering himself or others. The same rule applies every time a skier wants to start off again after stopping. Particular care is needed when entering a run and when crossing a nursery slope.

6 - Stopping. A skier should avoid stopping on narrow sections of the run or where he is not easily visible to those descending, unless it is absolutely necessary. A skier who falls should move off the run and out of the way as quickly as possible. Stopping on a run obstructs the flow of other skiers. A skier should therefore only stop at the edge of a run.

7 - Climbing. A skier who is climbing back up a slope should be aware that this can obstruct the run. He should therefore climb at the very edge of the run, and should leave the run altogether if the visibility is poor. A skier descending a run on foot should follow the same rule.

8 - Attention to signs. All skiers must obey the signs on the runs.

9 - Accidents. In the event of an accident, every skier is obliged to stop and offer assistance.

10 - Identification. Anyone who is involved in or witness to an accident is obliged to give details of his identity to the personnel in charge of rescue.

CROSS-COUNTRY SKIERS' CODE OF CONDUCT

These rules are derived not from the FIS rules, but from the code of the Italian Association of Ski Instructors and Ski Schools (AMSI). They are nonetheless applicable to any place in the world where cross-country skiing is practiced.

1 - Consideration for others. All cross-country skiers must behave in a way that will not endanger others, especially those who are less experienced.

2 - Attention to signs. A cross-country skier must stay on the marked runs and obey all signs. He must stay on the side of the track indicated.

3 - Track conduct. If the run has more than one set of tracks, the skier should use the one on the right. Groups of skiers should always proceed in single file in the right-hand track.

4 - Overtaking. Cross-country skiers are not obliged to give way to skiers coming behind them. They should, however, let faster skiers get past whenever they are able to do so without risk. Overtaking can be done, so long as no risks are involved, either on the right or on the left, on a free track, or at the side of the run, after first warning the skier who is ahead, but never endangering themselves or other skiers.

5 - Encounters with other skiers. If one skier meets another going the opposite way on a single track, both skiers should clear the way, moving off the track to their own right. If the encounter takes place on a slope, the skier who is coming downhill takes precedence. Skiers should always hold their poles close to their sides to avoid problems at the moment of passing.

6 - Control of speed and manner of skiing. Every cross-country skier, especially when going downhill, should adapt his speed and his skiing style to suit his own abilities, and the condition of the snow, the weather, the visibility, and the number of other users on the run. Skiers should always keep a safe distance from the skier in front.

7 - Stopping and falling. Skiers should stop only outside the tracks and beside the run. In the event of a fall, skiers should move themselves off the track to leave the run clear for others as quickly as possible.

8 - Accidents. In the event of an accident, skiers should always be ready to proffer assistance to another skier in trouble.

9 - Identification. Anyone who is involved in or witness to an accident is obliged to give details of his identity to the personnel in charge of rescue.

10 - Respect for the natural environment and for the runs. Well-behaved skiers never leave rubbish on the runs or damage the natural environment in any way. The track should not be spoilt by walking on it without skis, or by using it with downhill skis, toboggans, or in any other way.

©2001 Colophon srl,
San Polo 1978, 30125 Venice, Italy

Concept: Andrea Grandese
Project Management: Paolo Lazzarin
Design and Layout: Graphotek/Bruno Quattro
Text: Sandro Del Pulp, Mario Fabretto, Max Galtarossa, Patrik Lang
Illustrations: Maria Borghi, Gabriele Frione
Photography:
C. Burton, M. Cupat/Kranjska Gora, D. Ferrer, S. Del Pulp, M. Maccioni,
A. Martinuzzi/Ski Civetta , G. Pagnoncelli, F. Panunzio, P. Perrotti
Acknowledgements:
Centro Valanghe Arabba, Marco Garbin, Amedeo Gasparin, Francesco Mazzadi,
Marco Molteni/IFL, Vittorio Nava, Germana Sperotto, Studio G.M./Montebianco, Alfredo Trad
Special thanks to the Tourist information offices in:
Alta Badia, Alta Valtellina, Arlberg, Aspen, Badgastein, Berchtesgaden, Bormio,
Cervinia, Chamonix, Cortina D'Ampezzo, Crans Montana, Courchevel, Davos,
Dolomiti Superski, Flaine, Garmisch Partenkirchen, Gstaad, Heavenly Valley,
Kitzbühel, Kranjska Gora, La Plagne , Lech, le 3 Vallée, Les 2 Alpes, Les Arcs, Livigno,
Madonna di Campiglio, Mammoth Mount, Megève, Nozawa/Onsen, Schladming,
Serre Chevalier, Sestrière, Sierra Nevada, Ski Civetta, Squaw Valley, St. Anton-Arlberg,
St. Moritz, Steamboat Spring, Sun Valley, Tirolo, Trentino, Vail, Val d'Isère,
Val Gardena, Verbier, Via Lattea, Wengen Grindelwald, Whistler-Blackcomb,
Zell am See-Kaprun, Zermatt
and to the companies:
Blizzard, Fischer, Garmont, Head, Komperdell, Lange, Leki, Liski,
Morotto, Rossignol, Salomon, Scott, Tua, Tyrolia

Original Title: Sci

©2001 for this English edition:
Könemann Verlagsgesellschaft mbH
Bonner Str. 126, D-50968 Cologne

Translation from Italian: Liz Clegg, Harriet de Blanco, Sue Delaney in association with
Cambridge Publishing Management
Editing: Virginia Catmur in association with Cambridge Publishing Management
Consultant for the English edition: Jim Wood
Typesetting: Cambridge Publishing Management
Project Management: Jackie Dobbyne for Cambridge Publishing Management, UK
Project Coordination: Nadja Bremse-Koob
Production: Petra Grimm
Printing and Binding Societa Torinese,Industrie Grafiche,Ediroriale S.p.A., San Mauro, Italy
Printed in Italy

ISBN 3-8290-5750-4

10 9 8 7 6 5 4 3 2 1